In the Wake

of the *Wake*

Some writers in the wake of the *Wake*

David Hayman

Joyce schooled himself in the basics, learning the tradition, spelling out the letters of style and form, intuiting slowly and in stages the contours of his personal vision. Like Flaubert, he never dealt with the frozen, selective, and secondhand "reality" of camera or journalism, but with experience as handmaid to perception, or directly with the materials of perception. His real preoccupation was with systems of presentation. His development was toward the amplification of the verbal, the creation of autonomous forms in motion; toward the vitalized word in *Finnegans Wake*, the "collideorscape." To arrive there he was obliged to alter and recombine, but not to destroy, existing expressive codes. This purposeful alteration is one source of our discomfort (and joy) when we are faced with that ultimate text. It is, perhaps, Joyce's major contribution to literature.

"Yes, of course, we all know Anna Livia"; yet *Finnegans Wake* has for years been an acknowledged but unread master-piece, the least dog-eared book on every English graduate student's shelf, a cult item conned by footnote hounds and cita-tion grubbers. When, after a decade and a half of teasing prepublication in little mags, Joyce finally published his "Work in Progress" in 1939, the *Wake* fell seemingly into a black hole. The date itself was symbolic of future function; the end of an era (as was 1914, when he published the *Portrait*[1]) marked the beginning of a new one. And the *Wake*'s form, which readers through the years have gradually mastered, calls upon other writers to reshape the very tools of their craft, to say nothing of their means of perception. Not too many writers have answered the call, though a great many have responded and continue to respond to the less extreme challenge of *Ulysses*. Still, something else is now clear. The *Wake* belongs to a class (not a genre) of works which invite the reader to perpetuate creation. It is an extreme example of what Umberto Eco calls the "*opera aperta*" (open work) and Roland Barthes, thinking perhaps of Mallarmé, has called the "scriptible" (writable) text. Mallarmé's *Un coup de dés,* Pound's *Cantos,* Joyce's *Ulysses* and *Finnegans Wake* are among the archetypes of today's *texte scriptible.* All of them are so closely related in tendency and execution as to constitute virtually a single model of the sort of work now in process, the invitation to perpetuate creation. For a growing number of writers of "experimental" fiction, however, Joyce's *Wake* must be the primary exemplar.

In the following discussion, those who have or will have assimilated aspects of the methods of the *Wake*, or of the *Wake* as method, will be dubbed "writers in the wake" or "post-*Wake* writers." Like Joyce, who for nearly two decades sinned with the word and knowingly made words his wares, these writers in the wake have begun to discover the meaning of language as a medium within a universe of signs, to write with varying degrees of success their own essential letter to be "unfilthed" from an "orangeflavoured mudmound" (111)[2] by "the hen in the storyaboot" (336).

We can point to many writers who would not be writing quite as they do were it not for at least a minimal exposure to the *Wake*. But in most cases it is hard to follow the trace, to say where the influence or impact of the early Joyce shades off into that of the later, to spot what derives directly from Joyce rather than from a secondary source, from one of his sources, or even from the current vogue in farce-saturae and media magic. Even if we should think of the post-*Wake* novel as growing out of

4

tendencies central to the *Wake* rather than directly out of the *Wake* itself, our case for both influence and impact is still strongest when limited to writers who have actually read and studied Joyce as the "connundrurumchuff" (352).

To date, most of the work in this "tradition" has been done by writers in languages other than English. Neither the English, since Lewis Carroll and apart from a few like Anthony Burgess and Christine Brooke-Rose, nor the Irish, apart from Flan O'Brien, have begun to see prose as a medium for reader-writer collaboration, to recognize the creative-play functions of reading, or to apprehend and exploit the explosion-implosion of the word. Few writers in either nation read *Finnegans Wake*. In America, we are just now getting beyond *Ulysses*, but at least we have been there. Only a chosen few—like those publishing in the kabbalistic magazine *Tree* and in experiment-welcoming periodicals like *Tri-Quarterly*, certain of our critics (McLuhan, Hassan, Norman O. Brown, and in a sense Northrop Frye) and avant-garde figures like Stan Brakhage, John Cage, and perhaps Robert Wilson[3]—are branching out from the *Wake*. Though a cult object in English and American academe, and increasingly a source book for writers of verse and fiction, *Finnegans Wake* is not yet the model and integrated source it could and may become.

In Europe and Latin America, though fewer have a firm grasp of English, and though the majority, even among the avant-garde, look to other models, we find writers whose awareness of the *Wake* profoundly affects their writing. (Among Latin Americans, Leopoldo Marechal and G. Cabrera Infante come to mind.) The declared Joycean bias of Arno Schmidt, Philippe Sollers, Maurice Roche, and the Brazilian concrete poets is something more than a straw in the wind—if something less than a tradition. For these are major writers and trend setters with radically different gifts. In this connection, other factors may be crucial: the pull of revolutions in the other arts and in technology, the support received from currently fashionable philosophical and psychoanalytic thought (especially from Jacques Derrida and Jacques Lacan in France), the continuing interest in linguistic theory, political theory, semiology, and eccentric literary predecessors like Mallarmé, Lautréamont, Artaud, and Bataille. All these combine to throw Joyce's pro-

5

cedures into high relief, illuminating the *Wake* as a phenomenon and model as the fringe slips into focus.

The *Wake* as a *texte scriptible* provides its readers with objective counters in unstillable encounter, conceals its vestigial plot, and refuses the artist's sensibility as an immediately accessible component of the text—only to communicate it through a flux of rhythms and attitudes, seemingly implying a deeper, more universal awareness. That is, we as readers are privy to aspects of the creative psyche at the point where they may intersect with aspects of our own creating nature. Incorporating references to myriad aspects of the reader's experience, as well as to what we might call the private sector of the artist's own experience, the *Wake* uses words to challenge the willing accomplice/reader. It constitutes a medium which does not pretend to present any sort of "reality" or, rather, which announces its roots in a purely verbal universe. At the same time, it attempts, through violations of conventions, to break loose from the restraints and preconceptions which trammel that universe. Forcing readers to drive through an engrossing web of language toward ever-retreating but tantalizing points of reference, it purports to tell a story but refuses to reveal its ultimate nature. It conveys a sense of character while reducing characterization to a bundle of generalities. Yet the reader apprehends both storiness and character, both actions and reflections upon actions. He processes the language, encoding his experience of it, becoming the text without losing himself as he reads.

We all know, of course, that there's "lots of fun" at *Finnegans Wake*. The plays on words, words as self-destroying but resilient objects; the texture of clowning which imitates but does not create chaos, suggests but does not enforce order; the unending variation of verbal surfaces, the pleasure of sounds, the manipulation of techniques and conventions, the exploitation of the boundaries of knowledge and reason—all these sleights occur in the *Wake* and eventually condition the reader's mind, thinning that veil and letting in lights. Ultimately, the *Wake* is a system of tantalizing disclosures based on an awareness of the ludicrous, undercut or underscored by pathos, and laced with beauty. These constant stirrings in a verbal universe which is by no means infinite, these permutations and combinations of delight within a medium that at first seems uniform if not opaque and then seems impossibly heterogeneous, are what characterize the *Wake* and some of the books in its wake.

But we may also point to the deliberate inversion of perception and convention. Joyce's "narrative," for example, only pretends to (or flatly refuses to) tell tales. Tales reveal their analogical freight before they spill their "action." Visual and verbal effects vie for our attention. Language suggests before it says, and then often refuses to make even the simplest statement, drawing tangents to experience, leaving the reader to create and fill the substantial center or to weight the central void. The *Wake* is in the best sense a mystery novel in solution, and the reader-as-dreamer is the ultimate mystery. Perhaps this, more than anything else, is the source of its glamor today in the light of our growing awareness of the nature and psychological and social roots of both language and experience. Joyce's novel reflects and projects the insecurity of a post-Flaubertian baroque age—an age which appropriately and insistently remembers what it has been trained to reject.

Critics seem to agree that we have left behind the well-crafted novel of the Flaubertian tradition and are entering a "postmodern" phase. Let's say, rather, that certain "experimental" writers have abandoned the readily accessible mimetic tendencies of that tradition, retaining the underlying structures and even the discipline. Authors, like other artists, are refusing the superficial classical finish, the "elitist" polish of certain masterpieces, to indulge in postclassical exuberance, elaborately controlled "free" invention. Thus, according to Ihab Hassan, "*Finnegans Wake* carries the tendencies of high art and of popular culture to their outer limits, there where all tendencies of mind may meet, there where the epiphany and the dirty joke become one."[4] The parallels with other uneasy ages—with the Hellenistic period, the late Roman, the Baroque, the late Romantic movement in Germany, and the *fin de siècle*—are worth noting. Perhaps we are in what Northrop Frye calls the ironic period. Certainly we have entered a period characterized by positive and negative invention, a period that may produce, given its amplitude and energy, any number of great works but that, given its lack of focus, may also dissipate itself in many and varied minor efforts. The *Wake* has a place in this, being at once inimitable and inevitable, eliciting a contemporary mode and participating in and perverting a continuous tradition of intensely personal but hardly dead-end masterworks.

This said, we may heed a double-edged caveat in the comments of Anthony Burgess during a *Paris Review* interview:[5]

> Burgess: *Joyce opened doors only to his own narrow world; his experiments were for himself only. But all novels are experimental . . .* [Finnegans Wake] *looks spectacular because of the language . . .*
>
> Interviewer: *Isn't Joyce's attempt to devote virtually an entire novel to the unconscious more than a purely linguistic experiment?*
>
> Burgess: *Yes, of course, the wakeworld is only narrow in that it's asleep, fixed on one set of impulses only, has too few characters.*
>
> Interviewer: *Can't contemporary writers use some of Joyce's techniques without being mere imitators?*
>
> Burgess: *You can't use Joyce's techniques without being Joyce. Techniques and material are one.*

Note the easy outs taken by Burgess, whose understanding of his subject is as limited as his gab is facile, though he has produced three books on Joyce. The line is orthodox Flaubert, but twisted to fit the individual talent of the speaker. Besides, the writers treated below and many others not mentioned have already disproved Burgess by showing that without being in Joyce's skin they can capitalize on his advances and discoveries. Joyce was clearly writing more of a book than Burgess has read, a different book as well. "Impulses" and "characters" are beside the point, while "techniques" and "vision" are crucial here. These writers have illustrated what can be done with the *Wake* as an example: a point of departure or support. Each of them is interpreting his own Joyce and therefore producing afresh, despite the precedent.

Among the most alert and self-conscious post-*Wake* writers is a group of poets who quite early turned Joyce's achievement to their ends: the Brazilian Noigandres group of concrete poets. Concrete Poetry, to crib from Joyce, is a very *spatial* poetic form or *ob*-verse. Like the French, the Brazilians are manifesto-minded. The Noigandres leaders (Augusto de Campos, Haroldo de Campos, and Décio Pignatari) published in 1965 under the title *Teoria da Poesia Concreta a* collection of critical texts and manifestos written between 1950 and 1960.[6] That volume contains as clear and rational an account of sources and impact as we could wish for—one which roots a revolutionary movement in the recent revolutionary past and doesn't pretend that something has come unstuck, that we need a whole new set of perceptions to see what is going on around us. Ignoring or rejecting the "mythic center" of "modernist" prose and poetry and playing down the more obvious traits of the Flaubertian line, these Brazilian apologists, whose base is determinedly international, derive their movement primarily from Stéphane Mallarmé. Their interest is naturally in formal, presentational innovation, in style as statement. They focus on the pervasive quest for more direct means of saying (conveying), on the exploitation of the vehicle (or as McLuhan would have it, the medium). In this they are attuned to modern artists' tendency to inspect their means in an attempt to discover new and frequently popular sources of power, a tendency dating back at least to the Romantics but certainly to Flaubert and the Symbolists.

The Noigandres group seeks ways to incorporate the visual component of print in their poetic "message," to weld the two together. They belong to an energetic and growing number of writers, among whom are numbered some of those collected in Eugene Wildman's *Experiments in Prose*, Maurice Roche, Arno Schmidt, Hélène Cixous, Christine Brooke-Rose, and to a degree Michel Butor, Raymond Queneau, and Raymond Federman. All of these and many others use the page and the book in startlingly new ways. Our interest, however, is in the rationale of the Noigandres group and the lineage they claim for a formal tendency which they correctly see proliferating in the poetry-resistant mass media and hence rapidly becoming a part of our daily experience.

The sources of Noigandres are among the most arcane. First, there is Mallarmé's *Un coup de dés*, a cosmic poetic statement printed in a variety of typefaces (many of which can be read consecutively for meaning), with the type distributed in such a way as to suggest images on the page. It is a particularly dense poem, a palimpsest designed to convey a complex of cognate actions—from the writing of a poem to the conception of a child, to the creation of the universe; from a toss of the dice to a shipwreck, to a drowning, to a sunset, to the poet's

failure to say what he means, to the meaning of failure. It is
also a dramatic and narrative poem of great but hidden intensity,
a poem which resists translation but perhaps for that very reason
invites imitation and stimulates emulation. The second major
source is Pound's *Cantos*, with its typographical extravagance,
polyglotism, breadth of reference, and rhythmical variation.[7]
Both of these prime sources refer us "to music, painting and
cinema" and thus to the wider possibilities of print. *Finnegans
Wake* is the third major precursor.

Writing polemically but with great precision and insight,
Augusto de Campos traces the lineage of the poem-as-ideogram
from Mallarmé through the Futurists (especially Marinetti)
and Apollinaire's *Calligrammes* to Pound's publication of Ernest
Fenollosa's theories in "The Chinese Written Character as a
Medium for Poetry," a source also tapped by Joyce for *Finnegans Wake*. What strikes de Campos is the ability of the
ideogram to allude to two or more objects in order to convey a
third, while still suggesting a relationship between the original
elements. Also from Pound he derives the application of musical
counterpoint to language, thus "establishing the circuit Pound-
Mallarmé," and the fact that *Un coup de dés* and the *Cantos*
belong "structurally to the same genre."

This may seem far from our own concern with the putative
followers of *Finnegans Wake*, but a case can be made for the
multimedia and polygeneric aspects of the *Wake* and of its
impact. Passing by way of e. e. cummings, who uses "ideogram
and counterpoint in miniature," de Campos arrives at *Finnegans
Wake* as the summit of the development he has been describing.
According to this argument, Joyce has managed to create
ideograms by way of the superimposition of words and, like
Mallarmé, has written a circular poem in prose. De Campos
could not have known this, but a continuing interest in the
gestural potential of language caused Joyce to set as his goal the
ideal of Concrete Poetry (and of Mallarmé's great poem):
complete and simultaneous aesthetic communication. In addition,
Joyce shared with the Symbolists, of whom Mallarmé was the
first and greatest, the perennial dream of uniting the arts in
one glowing context, a dream expressed in de Campos'
concluding polemic:

The truth is that the "prismatic subdivisions of the idea" in Mallarmé,
Pound's ideogrammatic method, the "verbivocovisual" presentation of Joyce
and the verbal mimicry of cummings converge as a new compositional
concept, a new theory of form—an organiform— . . . traditional notions
like beginning-middle-end, syllogism, verse tend to disappear to be sup-
planted by a poetico-gestaltian, poetico-musical, poetico-ideogrammatic
structural organization: CONCRETE POETRY.[8]

This is strong language, but it has a prophetic ring to it when
we look around us at what is happening in all the arts and see
the explosion of mixed forms, of intertextuality, of spatial texts,
of simultaneity and crosscutting.

In the fifties and sixties, the Noigandres group made repeated
references to the *Wake* as a model or at least as an example.[9]
Thus Concrete Poetry is the "tension of words-things with
space-time"[10] and poetry must be brought to the level of contemporary painting and music. Though hardly exhausting the
theoretical bases for the movement, such statements suggest the
parameters of the Joycean impact—the impact of his "space-time,"
his revision of Bergsonian *durée:*

No longer is it a question of denying time a spacial structure but rather
of a spacial-time: placing "all space in a notshell." By means of this organic
interpenetration, each "verbivocovisual" unit is, simultaneously,
container-content of the entire work, a "myriadminded" instant.[11]

While Pound, with Fenollosa, contributed the "ideogrammatic
method" and a "lexicon of essences and precisions," cummings
the "method of phonetic pulverization," Mallarmé the "method
of prismatification," Joyce contributed in the *Wake* the
"palimpsest method atomization of the language (word-metaphor)."

In practice we cannot separate out the various sources, nor
need we try. But certainly, as a meaning-filled particle presenting
itself in a two-dimensional typographic space, attempting to
destroy linear perception while conveying a complex idea, and
milking the syllable, "etym," phoneme, and even letter of their
possible significance, the concrete poem reflects the influence of
the *Wake*. From this quality of the concrete verbal object, we
can project the indirect (and sometimes direct) influence of the
Wake on concrete fiction, the ful-fill-ment (however unevenly
successful) of the printed word, its gesturalization (immediacy
and motion). Our prime examples of this formal tendency will be
the work of Arno Schmidt and Maurice Roche.

Though among the most inventive, the concrete poets were not the first to register the *Wake*'s impact. One thinks tentatively of Eugene Jolas' *transition* and the cult reactions to "Work in Progress" in the thirties, or of Thornton Wilder and Samuel Beckett, on each of whom the impact was radically and instructively different.

Wilder's play *The Skin of Our Teeth* is apparently a reworking of the *Wake*an temporal vision, the first such comic allegory on the human condition to appear after World War II. A gently ironic play, devoid of unpleasant reference, it picks up directly from Joyce's Earwicker clan the vision of the single universal family living throughout history and prehistory.[12] The source is neither overtly stated nor carefully concealed. Such thematic and situational borrowing resulted in a rather mild and quite popular piece of "experimental" theater, experimental in its treatment of plot and in its staging. But then Wilder had already produced *Our Town* with technical effects borrowed from Pirandello. Both of these plays indicate a profound interest in the avant-garde; both are aesthetically viable popularizations rather than genuine contributions to evolving traditions—this despite Wilder's undeniable gifts. But *The Skin of Our Teeth,* by virtue of its marriage of vaudeville and farce conventions, points up Joyce's reworking of the popular Christmas pantomime format in the *Wake* in a manner not equaled by any of the more explicit attempts to stage or film that book. If nothing else, Wilder was attuned to the spirit, the comic vigor, and concomitant gravity of his prime source.

Beckett raises a completely different set of problems, bringing us closer to the heart of our subject. We need hardly repeat the oft-told tale of Beckett's artistic genesis, his early contact with and friendship for Joyce, the splendid essay he contributed to *Our Exagmination Round His Factification for Incamination of Work in Progress* in 1929, the translation of passages from the ALP chapter which he and Alfred Péron started and Joyce and several others completed in 1931. Few writers have been so thoroughly immersed in Joyce so early; few could be more readily suspected of discipleship.

But the early works, with their numerous Joycean references, suggest a progressive break with, rather than a continuing commitment to, the Joycean manner. Beckett—as a friend of Joyce, a neophyte writer pledged to the *transition* brotherhood, and an Irishman in Paris—had a great deal to go through and live down. Significantly, he refused until recently to permit the reissue of the most obviously Joyce-inspired of his books, the disturbingly hilarious episodic near-novel *More Pricks Than Kicks,* and he has not reprinted his early short fiction and poems.[13] On the face of it, the remainder of his fiction and drama is both brilliantly original and unmarked by Joyce's influence. It is also on the leading edge of the modern, far in advance of its new novelistic followers, moving toward an ideal stasis of distressful comic-cosmic silence.

Still, to my mind, his later work is more emphatically post-*Wake*, though far less derivative, than are the works of apprenticeship. The early indoctrination (the word may be too strong), direct or indirect, by an author who was in every sense more meticulous than even Flaubert—though not than Mallarmé— has led to a Beckettian oeuvre which has been teaspooned out in increasingly small doses over the years. The omnipresent but humane paradox and irony in the *Wake* is reflected in every line written by Beckett after World War II. Like the *Wake*, Beckett's later narratives and plays deal exclusively with lowest-common-denominator human situations, emblems for the human condition in, through, and beyond history. But here he has gone Joyce several better, refusing to imagine fertile (in any sense) relationships, moving toward the Flaubertian ideal of the "book about nothing," though the universe of human experience participates in that nothingness.

The *Wake* deals with the stereotypical family, blowing it into a universe metaphor of infinite complexity and scope. Beckett simply and effectively reverses that metaphor. Joyce's pater-familias ("patter of so familiars," 333.15), "hoar father Nakedbucker" (139.06), becomes Our Father without half trying. Beckett's homeless or static questers are not assured of becoming anything, even human. All are subsumed by the help-less, nameless creator who speaks the *Unnamable*. The *Wake* is a dream with an indeterminate dreamer (who may be the reader or the creator/Creator) and an expandable/contractible setting; Beckett's setting is an enclosed universe which guarantees

either existence or its opposite. Chaos in Joyce prefigures at
least an order of random repetition; but Beckett's orderly
presentations convey, better than Joyce's apparent disorder, the
nightmare essential to both men's visions. Paradoxically, both
the *Wake* and Beckett's postwar fiction are written, if not from
the perspective of god/God, at least in the mode of revealed
truth/uncertainty (see, by analogy, the mode of Dante in the
Commedia, a book favored by both writers). In both we hear
repeatedly the divine laughter of God at his creation, that
primal bad joke.

Beckett's first essay, "Dante . . . Bruno. Vico . . Joyce," written when he was twenty-three, has a programmatic ring. In it he
attempts with some considerable success to apply the practice
and theory of three thinkers to Joyce's conception of the *Wake*.
Two of Beckett's views interest us. The first is that Joyce is
everywhere following Giordano Bruno in equating opposites,
which, in Bruno's definition, may be seen as generating each other:

> There is no difference, says Bruno, between the smallest possible chord and
> the smallest possible arc, no difference between the infinite circle and the
> straight line. The maxima and minima of particular contraries are one and
> indifferent. Minimal heat equals minimal cold. Consequently transmutations
> are circular. . . . Maximal speed is a state of rest. The maximum of
> corruption and the minimum of generation are identical: in principle,
> corruption is generation. And all things are ultimately identified with God,
> the universal monad, Monad of monads.[14]

(This principle applies, incidentally, to our methods here in
describing Joyce as, if not a source, at least an important
personal influence and an inescapable exemplar.)

In *Finnegans Wake*, the meeting and identification of extremes
is a thematic constant. Thus we have "the meeting of morning
and evening"; the repeated identification and reversal of the
twin identities of Shem-the-pen and Shaun-the-post, the transcriber
and the deliverer (purveyor-perverter) of the word; the renewal
of life through the funeral banquet; and so on. More important,
the language itself is rich in such *verbiversals*. Statements,
words, and expressions often contain or conceal self-annulling
counterstatements. An assertion of light will carry with it an
awareness of the dark; joy is a form of sorrow. Even nursery
rhymes turn sour in a night or dream world where "order is
othered" and "Reeve Gootch was right and Reeve Drughad was

sinistrous" (197.01)—left bank was right and right was left. By discovering this principle in Joyce, perhaps at Joyce's prompting, Beckett unwittingly disclosed one of the central and recurring themes of his own gestating work. The theme of the identity of opposites is almost everywhere. Murphy, for example, is in search of the ultimate or cosmic chaos which for him is order. He finds sanity among the insane, virtue in a whore named Celia (heavenly). Like Joyce, Beckett reproduces the universal in the trivial, though with important differences. Where Joyce finds glimmers of hope in small things, discloses a microcosm for universal order, and nourishes us on a revivifying humor, Beckett seems unremittingly faced with comic-cosmic despair which he sees mirrored both in the human condition and in the systems we have created to mask that condition, to paper over the flaws. Where Joyce chooses the little man, the norm, as his paradigm of grandeur, elevating and debasing him at will and often in the same phrase, Beckett chooses the out-cast, the clown, the marginal man, the repressed impulse, life's refuse and refused, turning him (or it) into a quester after meaningless goals, magnifying squalor. A similar strategy leads him to identify the fool with the writer and God with confused humanity, turning creation into inadvertence, disclosing (in *Imagination Dead Imagine, Play,* and *Not I*) life glimmering phosphorescent in the grave.

As in Joyce, the subject matter dictates the rhetoric. There are few puns, but many possibilities of contradictory interpreta-tions. The situations serve as embodiments or projections of the Brunoesque vision, the rhetoric disallows (surpasses) logic and coherence. Beckett, like Joyce, posits an impossible confusion as his context, creating a kaleidoscopic vision. Thus, in the impossible world of the *pen*-ultimate we have an "Unnamable" (compare the idea that God's name is unutterable) giving reluctant voice interminably to unverifiable and constantly under-cut assertions, a perpetual motion machine in an imperfect void. What is more, like the know-nothing Molloy and the insane Watt, Beckett liberally sprinkles his words with references to learning and an awareness of everyday reality which such a persona could not or should not possess. Like the others, he is given to thinly disguised philosophical musings, but then his situation is strikingly similar to the one which Descartes posited as his starting point.

This brings us to a second post-*Wake*an attribute, the purgatorial vision, which applies as well to Beckett's quest heroes as it does to each aspect of the *Wake*an vision. According to Beckett, Joyce creates a perpetual motion purgatory from which we neither rise nor fall:

> There is a continuous purgatorial process at work in the sense that the vicious circle of humanity is being achieved. . . . Then the dominant crust of the Vicious and the Virtuous sets, resistance is provided, the explosion duly takes place and the machine proceeds. And no more than this; neither prize nor penalty; simply a series of stimulants to enable the kitten to catch the tail.[15]

In the *Wake* there is hope in motion—false hope: for every action has its counteraction, every rise its fall. Man thinks vertical but never leaves the horizontal. Life is a (bad) dream. HCE may be the hero, but he is also the "puny"; he may be God, but he is also the great sinner; and ultimately he is the most normal of men and a sort of clown. Shem is identified with the moon and with Satan, while Shaun is the rising or setting sun and the archangel Michael; but both are acting in a pantomime, and their identities tend to blend when they become quarreling twins like those on the beach in "Nausicaa" (*Ulysses*). Shem's habitat is his "house of thoughtsome" or brain, Shaun's a slowly filling Guinness barrel or home of spirits. Both are prisoners. In Beckett, the metaphors for the universal dream, because they are less openly stated but more completely realized, touch deeper nerves. His fiction goes underground, into a cerebral if not oneiric universe with *Watt*. The fiction and most of the plays locate their action within the no-exit contest of the skull, if not within the universal dream. The interior voyage or quest or development is repeated and amplified, and the intercranial locus of all the action, inescapable in *The Unnamable, Imagination Dead Imagine*, and *Endgame* (set in a room with two eyehole windows), can be posited for all the other works. Significantly, Beckett's work is always cyclical and generally autodestructive.

I would suggest that Beckett, at first influenced by the formal tactics of the *Wake* of which he was more intimately aware than any contemporary writer, was later and ultimately engaged by Joyce's project—the self-annulling, self-perpetuating, self-propelling creation through language of the complete non-statement—the wor(l)d and the human condition as unstillable flux. Needless to say, this was also the project of Flaubert and Mallarmé (if not Kafka); but Joyce's mark, like God's thumb-print, is as inescapable as the question where-to after the *Wake*. Beckett's progress toward the minimal evocation, the minimal and most open situation, the rhythmical statement of absence is a development which mirrors and reverses Joyce's creative evolution from the generalizing realistic minimum to the oneiric universal which can be reduced by the reader to the specific norm.

Wilder and Beckett, like the concrete poets, have understood Joyce. What of Anthony Burgess? Author of three books on Joyce, two dealing with the *Wake*, Burgess disclaims influence, all but the slightest. He tends to write witty, imaginative, beginning-middle-ending narratives, complete with the usual trappings of character and setting. This does not rule out allusion, however, and even an occasional adaptation. In what may be his best book, the future-fantasy *A Clockwork Orange*, delinquents speak "Natsat," an international jargon composed of gypsy cant, Russian, French, scraps of German, and the occasional polyglot pun. (Burgess' "horrorshow" for *kharashò*—Russian for good, fine, O.K.—echoes "Horrasure," 346, in *Finnegans Wake*.) Like the reader of the *Wake* lost in dream jargon, Burgess' reader must gradually find his way about in this juvenile language as he might in a futuristic London. In *Honey for Bears* and *The Doctor Is Sick* there are direct and oblique references to Joyce, among which we find a version of Bloom's litanied adventures ("Circe").

Most significant is my own favorite, *Enderby*, with its Bloom-like poet, its focus on scatological preoccupations, and the generally seamy physical and psychological aspects of a cuckold and failure. However, the Brobdingnagian opening sequence is not from *Ulysses* but from *Finnegans Wake*. We are introduced to a repugnant sleeping Enderby by the voice of a schoolmaster-guide located in future time, conducting his unruly pupils on a dream tour of the still-living monument. Burgess' idea of pre-senting a major persona through the medium of what appears to

17

be his own dreaming psyche comes more or less directly from the fourth chapter of Book III of the *Wake*, where HCE and ALP are presented from four camera-eye perspectives after being awakened by the noise of Shem crying. Joyce's unflattering portrait is presented in the sardonically objective and at times mawkish voice of the four masters and complemented by a tour of the couple's genital regions, a mocking map of love. The schoolmaster's attack on the poet's person also suggests Shaun's attack on Shem in Ivi. Finally, there is a hint of the incomprehensible sleep noises which startle the four questioners bent over the sleeping form of the giant Shaun-Yawn in IIIiii.

None of these clever adaptations should stand as examples of what to do after the *Wake*, though they do obviously reflect one rather common sort of impact. Burgess is a gifted, facile, witty novelist in the relatively unadventurous British vein. His love of Joyce has reaffirmed the basic moralistic bent reflected in his view that the *Wake* is "about guilt." It is natural that he should be unaware that the *Wake* presents "everything" in the person and concerns of HCE ("Here Comes Everybody") but is not *about* anything. As Beckett was the first to note, the *Wake is* something, an enactment of the human condition through and despite time and space, presented in the guise of a dream. Above all, it *is* the flux of language through which myriad images and concepts pass flittingly. The best sense of its nature is given in the "professor's" description of ALP's letter of history:

> *Well, almost any photoist worth his chemicots will tip anyone asking him the teaser that if a negative of a horse happens to melt enough while drying, well, what you do get is, well, a positively grotesquely distorted macromass of all sorts of horsehappy values and masses of meltwhile horse. Tip. Well, this freely is what must have occurred to our missive. . . . Heated residence in the heart of the orangeflavoured mudmound had partly obliterated the negative to start with, causing some features palpably nearer your pecker to be swollen up most grossly while the farther back we manage to wiggle the more we need the loan of a lens. . . . (111–112)*

The reader aware of the ultimate and original horse has gained no sense of the aesthetic document unless he has first been aware of the image in dissolution which is the text and its language, the process of reading and apprehending *through* words in action.

Maurice Roche, speaking of his own fine post-*Wake* ideo-

grammatic novel, *Compact*, supplies an image which might
serve to describe another central aspect of the *Wake*'s impact.
Here superimposed street maps are a palimpsest of our condition:

> *As a matter of fact, the plan of* Compact *was not a true outline or précis.
> It was more like a spatial plan, a superposition of city maps . . . reducing or
> enlarging where necessary. After all, New York is much larger than Papeete.
> We get them all in the same format. There is an itinerary within these
> cities which constitutes the real plan/structure of* Compact. *These travels
> take place, of course, inside, since everything takes place within a series
> of ghostly sequences, in the city-skull.*

It is this effect which Christine Brooke-Rose, the only significantly
post-*Wake* English novelist, has inadvertently achieved in
Between, the third of her novels, written in a style suggestive of
the *Wake* with its polyglot puns ironed out—in short, of
post-*Wake* fiction. On the other hand, her *Thru*, which is even
more post-*Wake* and which purports to be a "texterminator,"
owes much to current linguistic theory but in places looks and
reads like the *Wake* viewed through Lewis Carroll's gamey optics.
This aspect is clear in the fragment of *Thru* printed in this
issue of *TriQuarterly*, but I might also point to the reader/text
functions—games for which the reader, in finding the rules,
finds himself as player, engages with the text as phenomenon
and tradition. The following passage illustrates how a text which
includes all the textuality of a culture ceaselessly expands its
field and contracts its audience, and vice versa:

> blue lacuna of learning
> and unlearning a text within a text passed on from generation to generation
> of an increasing vastness that nevertheless dwindles to an elite initiated
> to a text no one else will read[16]

There are, of course, more overtly imitative writers than
Christine Brooke-Rose—writers of talent, fortunately. Take
Arno Schmidt, whose limited-edition, grand-format *Zettels Traum*
is an attempt to write a German *Finnegans Wake*. Patrick
O'Neill gives a suggestive account of that book:

> *The text on each page is positioned according to its nature in a fluid
> arrangement of three columns. A large centre column usually contains the
> narrative, that on the left usually references to Poe's works and often
> extensive extracts from it in English, while the right-hand column contains
> a variety of marginal reflections from the narrator. The main body of text
> can be in any column or in all at once. It is written in eccentric German,*

highly eccentrically spelled and punctuated, and frequently breaking into
English, French, or otherwise. The typescript is McLuhanesque in impact,
and incorporates very numerous blacked-out excisions and handwritten
additions and corrections.

    Not only is traditional orthography abandoned in favour of an attempt
to reproduce the sounds and rhythms of colloquial German, words are
further tortured to reveal their inherent Etyms, *as Schmidt calls them:*
EDDY-POE'S COMPLEX, *or pussynäss ist pussynäss. In his essays on the* Wake
he has developed his theory of Etyms, Freudian "pre-words," embryonic
wordforms embedded by the conscious expression.[17]

Most striking in *Zettels Traum*, apart from its enormous
format and bulk, are the adaptations (rather than direct borrowings), the sort of tricks played by an author fully aware of
Joyce's contribution but intent on doing something radically
different. Schmidt's opus can best be described as a running
transcript of an extended seminar, with marginal notes. The
purpose of this seminar is to explore Poe's work in terms of the
Etym theory. Much of the first section is devoted in large
measure to Pagensticher's exposition of the term and its implications and the countering and encountering of objections, a
playful testing rich in allusive byplay (or should we say
"foreplay," since so much of the Etym-sense is polymorphously
sexual if not perverse?). The operation of the Etym is often a
function of homonymy as well as of etymological roots. Indeed,
the problem in this first part is to decide how the Etym
principle functions across linguistic traditions as well as within
them. The effect of all this is distinctly Germanic as opposed to
Irish-English. But *Zettels Traum* is also a spoof on Germanic
pedantry, falling frequently into irreverence, resorting to a sort
of dramatic discourse quite different in tone and feeling from
the traditional philosophical discourse on which it is otherwise
patterned.

    Unlike the *Wake*, there is a clearly developed argument but
no visible story line. There are five recognizable characters
whose five speech patterns are continuously juxtaposed. In the
Wake we seldom, if ever, find more than two characterized
voices in any passage. Further, where the *Wake* generates a
commonplace reality out of the dream texture, in *Zettels Traum*
the oneiric erotic texture is generated out of a commonplace
reality. The pun texture and the style shifts of the *Wake* constitute prime obstacles to scanning, and constant sources of

reader participation and delight. In Schmidt's text, which resembles nothing so much as an MS draft of passages from *Finnegans Wake,* the notation functions both as clarification and as obfuscation. We are overwhelmed by an array of punctuation, of whimsical spacing and spelling, of allusive devices: in short of editorial gesticulation. It is this notation which enables the text to record words and gestures of participants along with the asides of an implied editor. But paradoxically these words and gestures, replete with in-jokes and allusions, are an obstacle to full understanding and a challenge to the reader. Further, since the whole text is presented as though told by an outside observer, we are obliged to fill in blanks in the thought processes as we might in real conversation.

Like the *Wake,* the reading/text becomes an extraordinary lived experience, an encounter with language. Unlike the *Wake,* however, *Zettels Traum* insists upon explaining and examining its premises. Written in dialogue, it has its dramatic component, but the drama, so far as I can judge, is not expressive in the aesthetic sense of conveying an organically coherent emotional circumstance or development. The reader is asked to participate in an enormously attenuated human situation, which despite its psychological content, and because of its length and complexity, resembles the flat surface rediscovered earlier in this century by artists like Fernand Léger. Schmidt's book insists upon itself as a work-in-progress, a concept enforced by the mode of presentation of the "traumscript" (see the term Joyce coined to describe ALP's famous letter). By contrast, *Finnegans Wake* presents itself as a finished text and only gradually reveals to the reader how much of the making is still to be accomplished. Again, *Zettels Traum* alludes to many texts but draws its substance from texts by Poe and Schmidt himself, divagates upon them. Although *Finnegans Wake* alludes to many other texts, it proposes as its focus the emblematic and absent letter, whose manufacture and delivery constitute the tale of the text which is also the text of the tale—the letter being finally identical with the uttered *Wake.*

Then there is the emphasis on synchrony, at the expense of diachronic or linear development. The page is only one aspect of this. Its three columns function, as do effects in novels by

Maurice Roche and in Brooke-Rose's *Thru*, to provide an interchange of elements, a yo-yo of parallels, a tension or flux of signifiers or blocks of signification that virtually destroys linearity or at least impedes movement through, as opposed to across and within, the text. (As a parallel, in the *Wake* we find the schoolbook format of the lessons in chapter IIii, with its irreverent marginalia and footnotes.) On another level we have the calculated redundancy in both works, the continual cross-referencing or crosscutting of materials. In the *Wake*, at any given moment all the components of a development are present; only the order and emphasis are subject to change. But their constant presence serves to complicate the game texture, placing the emphasis on the delights of a shifting linguistic field within an otherwise stable frame.

Another attribute is a quality I call nodality, also found in Brooke-Rose, Sollers, and Roche. The nodes I refer to are nodes or knots of allusion or signification, clusters which constitute topics and serve as means of structuring the text rather than as integral parts of the argument. We may see, for example, a scattering of references to Ezra Pound or Oscar Wilde or Irish history on a page or two of the *Wake* without assuming that the passage in question is primarily about such matters. Such nodes occur nearer the surface of the post-*Wake* texts. In *Zettels Traum* we have what we might call digressive nodes which, without sacrificing the essentially "palimpcestuous" nature of the multilayered text, *occupy* the conversation, serve as a topic, a focus for our interest not unlike that provided by action in narrative. In general, these elements require decoding, as in a passage which toys with the syllable or Etym "pen" in order to labor the concept penis.[18] The passage turns on a Freudian joke which identifies the pen as a procreative instrument (see Joyce's expression "penisolate war," 3). Schmidt's joke is dressed out in a quantity of philological and pseudoscientific and even dramatic rags, but it retains its crucial nodal quality. Anyone with the patience to read will recognize the nodes and react to them within the welter of stylistic typographical effects. By contrast, the nodal elements in *Finnegans Wake* have a way of vanishing or of hanging on the reader's awareness and knowledge. Anyone who knows Irish history, or the Kabbala, or the life of Oscar

Wilde, or Irish literature may be able to pick out (sooner or later) the nodal underpinnings of passages where such details coalesce. But to do so one must pick one's way through a welter of allusive effects.

Schmidt's jokes are less numerous and more pointed than Joyce's, but his dramatic effects, the shifts in voice and tone, the shock of attitudes, the text's fluid format, and the typography all contribute to a textual richness which makes the nodal structure analogous to that of the *Wake*. Thus, in the dialogue rebutting Wilma's view of the Etym "pen," we find the sentence:

Auch in umwallten Etyms, à la 'indePENdent'; oder Seinen Lei(ie)bWort 'perPENdicular'.: 'the PEN phalls powerless from shivering hand' —(wenn De noch 10 Minutn aus HEL+SD, wirrSDe einsehn, daB hier dem NachMaler wahrlich der Pe(e)ni(i)sl aus der zitternd'n Hand sinkn kann).[19]

Here we note such devices as the misplaced capital letter, dialectical German mixed with funnier English ("phalls"), immured Etyms, syllabic doubling, split words ("De noch"), all leading up to the usual play on penis-pen-drooping phall-writerly impotence. What is perhaps more important, since this is a reported conversation, is that many of the gestures are visible only to the reader, and could not have taken place in the dialogue. Thus, as in Joyce, we have the double text, visible vs./plus audible. (Also note the use of German vs./plus English.) In Schmidt, however, there is an added tension derived from the explicit and even realistic base. The pages may dream, the characters do not. The passage points up another difference between Schmidt's enterprise and Joyce's, the relatively loose texture of his language. We may compare this with the dense but focused texts by Roche and the rich allusive patterns in Sollers' texts, with their emphasis on tonal variation.

Finally, Joyce's text conceals high seriousness beneath a comic surface and an irreverent play of textures. Schmidt uses the theory of the Etym to turn Poe's high seriousness into scatological farce. As such, it constitutes a parasite text unveiling its host. It refuses to take itself seriously and is generated largely out of the skeptical responses of the auditor-participants. An exegetical session, an event about which one should not expect to read, is deliberately inverted when, with the aid of the Etyms and Freud,

23

Poe's writings are the occasion for a text which frequently rivals the *Wake* in subtlety and humor.

The two writers I have saved for the last are thoroughly aware of Joyce's work and capable of understanding and interpreting the achievement of *Finnegans Wake*, yet have found very different but cognate ways of writing post-*Wake* novels. Neither Philippe Sollers nor Maurice Roche is more than a name in this country, though Sollers' first book, *A Curious Solitude*, written at the age of twenty-one in a mode he now disavows, has been published here.[20] Sollers edits the controversial left-wing journal *Tel Quel*, which was publishing essays on, and translations from, the *Wake* as early as 1967. *Tel Quel* recently printed, along with a sensitive translation of parts of Book IV, three essays on the *Wake* by the English critic Stephen Heath.[21] Sollers' own mature novels (*Nombres, Lois, Drame, H*) are among the most innovative to appear recently in France. His forte is a plotless development partitioned like music, or according to mathematical principles, or divided into uncharacterized voices in a sort of anti-dialogue. The project outlined for his novel *Nombres* is manifestly post-*Wake*, though it may owe less to Joyce than to Sollers' theory of the *oeuvre limite* (Dante, Sade, Lautréamont, Mallarmé, Artaud, Bataille). But Sollers' theory has no trouble accommodating Joyce's last book, which stubbornly resists the conventions and convenient categories and hence is often excluded from the "library." According to Sollers, this "library" excludes the extremes, imposing a set of neutral values on the aesthetic universe.

In the latest of his books, the unpunctuated but intensely and dramatically rhythmical *H*, Sollers registers a personal awareness of the *Wake*, discovering in Joyce a true subversion of language and a profound historical vision. *H* also focuses on Ezra Pound's accomplishment, the epic thrust through time and across space. It is the first of Sollers' books to have frequent glimmers of humor (though there is fairly extensive wordplay in *Lois*), and the first to come to its public, as did the *Wake*, without an explicit "key," a preliminary road map. The reader must chart his own *H* space and time, carve out chunks of *H* meaning, and supply punctuation and emphases.

We find in Sollers an already formed talent receptive to

Joyce's innovations in terms of a particular critico-creative vision. *H* is not a passing phase in Sollers' development. His current work-in-progress, *Paradis,* points toward more radical departures in post-*Wake* fiction—that is, toward important modifications in the method of his novels. Significantly, he has suggested that the movement generated by *Tel Quel,* and now called the "new-new novel," should be called the "Wake" in a punning allusion to the book of puns: see the celebration of the funeral of a social order, the patterns which follow the passing of a ship, the organization of molecules of liquid in motion, and the reshaping of expressive form in the wake of radical changes in aesthetic, scientific, and cultural perception.

In an interview taped in June 1973,[22] Sollers outlines his view of the *Wake* as a "dangerous" book which subverts basic modes of communication, breaking through the taboos of nineteenth-century realism, preparing the way for experiments in fiction which would approximate those in other arts. Three aspects of the *Wake* concern him: its tendency to dissolve linguistic barriers through multilingual puns, the rhythmic qualities through which subjectivity is projected, and the manner in which it telescopes history to create the effect of a unified historical (or "epic") dimension. This rhythmic quality in prose is to be equated with the lyrical impulse which he is trying to regenerate as a means of balancing the "epic" thrust of his own frequently polemic novels. For Sollers, the epic is something both between and beyond Pound's and Joyce's historical visions, something approaching his own Maoist view of history. The *Wake* serves, then, to provide not so much a model as a pointer toward the realization of a very un-Joycean goal.

It should be noted that *H* is an integrated system of nodal divagations on various sociohistorical and personal-psychological as well as literary-aesthetic themes. Joyce's book is also nodal (focusing by means of discrete allusions), but it is above all a polysemous supermyth of human paradigms. Only in the most abstract sense is it political. While the *Wake* has strong, if hidden, elements of plot and character, and a coherent and systematic development, there is no plot line in *H* or *Paradis.* If there are personalities, there are no personae. Instead we have the overarching person (*sujet*) of the writer imposing itself discreetly through its rhythms upon a vision of history as process, or rather of historical flux.

Sollers' own readings from the texts of *H* and *Paradis* point up dramatic qualities which might otherwise pass undetected: a complex verbal surface, crowded with semantic and rhythmic events, a quality of wit belied by the seemingly uniform surface, and an engrossing dramatic development. The oral component of the *Wake*, the need to perform as well as perceive its words, is one of Joyce's best known and most significant legacies. The *Wake* notebooks and MSS testify to the fact that Joyce started with the oral tradition, basing the earliest of his sketches on told tales and oral renderings. His famous recording from the ALP chapter illustrates the textural richness of the *Wake*. Similarly Schmidt, Sollers, Roche, and other writers in the tradition—like G. Cabrera Infante (*Très Tristes Tigres*, translated as *Three Trapped Tigers*) and Leopoldo Marechal (*Adán Buenosayres*)—privilege rhythm and sound and bring about a fuller utilization of the printed word. Such writers are recapturing magical properties lost to the mechanical verbosity of the printing press: the signaling or gestural nature of print as sign and the letter-word-sentences as instances and clusters of signifying sound. They are struggling to reestablish the glyph and the gesture as basic components of recorded expression.

One may doubt that Sollers has read and understood all of the *Wake*, or that he has fully understood Joyce. Why should he? He has read enough of and about Joyce to be able to create his own paradigm, which would include madness in the picture, confirming in his imagination Joyce's own cautious fears. (See the disturbing references to madness in *A Portrait*, *Ulysses*, and *Finnegans Wake*.) But then, not only is madness, especially schizophrenia, a fetish for the neo-Freudian followers of Lacan, but Antonin Artaud and Lautréamont are among Sollers' sainted order-disturbing forebears. As one would expect, it is in terms of a developed system of belief that Sollers has found himself in Joyce. He has self-consciously turned Joyce's genuine fringe status as a writer self-immolated by integrity into that of the subversive who is reversing expressive canons. There is absolutely nothing wrong with this procedure, since it can encourage creation, at least by Sollers, and since Sollers is close to being a genius with words.

Joyce capitalized on his Irish heritage of *sounding* language to produce a book which is itself a complex action. Sollers' reaction is in some measure to translate Joyce's action in terms of the grand French rhetorical traditions, a heritage jettisoned by the post-Romantics of the last century. Both men engage in literary archaeology, though Joyce's book, viewed in the context of his slowly evolving work, may seem more obviously organic than Sollers' sometimes forced intellectual and political utterance (speedily produced with all the savage seriousness such acts often imply).[23] Still, there is in the *Wake,* and in none of the other *oeuvres limites* to which Sollers refers, a viable model that displays a concern for modulated verbal surfaces, for textures and rhythms, for structures of permutations linked to a historical vision which does indeed approximate the epic. *Finnegans Wake*, the way-out English cult book by an apolitical Irishman, a book seldom seen integrally and seen more as a process than as a product, has been transmogrified by the Frenchman's doubly exoticizing perspective. But even the distortions are instructive, constituting genuine post-*Wake* novelistic documents, controlled by principles of permutation and combination but bigger and more human than their rules.

Maurice Roche, whose novels are published in Sollers' prestigious *Tel Quel* series, writes, or rather composes, a very different sort of book out of an aesthetic consciousness which may be closer to that of Joyce himself. Like Joyce, Maurice Roche creates *oeuvres limites* in the truest sense. He too is sui generis, a writer's writer creating novels for tomorrow out of a profound awareness of yesterday's art. He claims to be among the first French readers of the *Wake* and displays a wide range of linguistic and literary experience. What is more, though accepted by the *Tel Quel* group and for a long time adhering to the *Change* splinter group (French literary politics is notoriously *cénacle* oriented), he is stubbornly independent.

Journalist, composer, musicologist,[24] actor, novelist, draftsman, a man who combines in his person all the arts and who has been a fixture on the French art scene for two generations,

Maurice Roche defies easy categories. All the more strange, then, that this essay has come full circle. Maurice Roche's typographical extravaganzas, like the still/vibrating type-poems of the Brazilian Noigandres group, can point to Mallarmé, Pound, Joyce, and new music for precedents while producing something refreshingly different from Concrete Poetry. Not surprisingly, Haroldo de Campos has contributed an informed essay on Maurice Roche's use of person and tense in *Compact* to a special issue of *Encres Vives*,[25] but one suspects de Campos would list Roche among the predecessors (metaphorical) rather than the followers of Concrete Poetry.

How to describe the novels of Maurice Roche? Deconstructed narratives, typographical music, extended puns, encyclocitations, systematic disfigurations of the white page, *tatouages,* machines dissolved in mechanical fluid? Distilled and enriched, these books contain most of Arno Schmidt's devices while seeming far less monomaniacal and retaining an almost classical lightness and control. They are *saturae* rather than satires, discontinuous mélanges of forms and styles joined by the strategy of constant surprise. They are farces regulated by the presenting clown who wears all the masks and bears the text in his person, but for whom language is a bag of tricks, a barrier to "sense," a clown whose statements tend to become cosmic probes and whose gestures are subject to endless inconclusive readings. Like Joyce in *Finnegans Wake,* like Beckett in the trilogy, like Mallarmé in *Un coup de dés,* and like Laurence Sterne in *Tristram Shandy*, and, yes, like Rabelais, Roche writes brightly of death and the night. His favorite image is the skull with its terrible grin, the clown's totem, on which he rings innumerable changes, inevitably turning it into an anagram for his own name:

His books are all about his books, about pages, about words, about the rich culture in which he swims, on which he feeds. They are also, like Mallarmé's poem, about the attempt to fill the void with creative actions, which are, once committed, dead —until the reader reanimates them by the act or gesture of reading. Thus in the beginning of his latest novel, *Codex,* we read:

Anguish enabling avoidance of
worse, I try to make myself
(beside myself) a big machine,
infernal and co(s)mic
        mechanical silent
(out of sketches of words
reproduced (of solids) encased
one inside the other having
no longer any tonal relief,
flattened so that they enter
into the thickness of the
imagined page whose opacity
affords as it happens but a
diaphanous impression)
        slyly
replaced by the odor of the
room: a gentle insinuating
aroma—which makes me turn
to turning the alcohol I have
in my stomach.[26]

Roche's protagonist or persona, sick and afraid of death, failing to lose himself in his machine made of words on paper, is creating both the process we call creative and the product we read. By introducing alternative readings with the aid of parentheses, puns, blank spaces, pictographs and ambiguities, he produces the dizziness of cosmic drunkenness in us, shares both physical and metaphysical impulses, doubles the machine back on itself. For alcohol, like the

text, is a mechanism for self-destruction and in*spir* $\begin{cases} \text{ation} \\ \text{iting} \end{cases}$. Relying

on extended puns, exhibiting a mordant wit but little of the clownish spirit available elsewhere, this passage does not suggest the full relevance of the *Wake*. But then this is but one voice in Roche's polyphonic fiction, a fact which points up the first of many similarities. The interplay and sudden interjection of voices, the deliberate disorientation of the reader, style shifts which accord with shifts in voice and perspective—all this is part of a single strategy.

Unlike the superserious and hypersensitive Mallarmé (from whom some of his typographical techniques derive directly enough), but like Joyce and especially like Sterne, Roche uses type and the word on the page to elicit delight and shock. In fact, Roche's playful use of type, space, and image is one form of punning, a means by which the reader is obliged to break his pace, to reconsider, to reorganize, to multiply meaning, to uncover serious as well as comic intent, to play and reject play. Roche, unlike the concrete poets, is not primarily interested in the aesthetic presentation of the page, in its pure impact on the eye. He uses special effects to intrude upon and enforce the pace of a narrative which defies the rules of narration while relying on our awareness of these rules. It is finally the continuous but erratic development of a vaguely defined argument that draws us through a text whose development is perceived, as in the *Wake*, through a screen of comic asides which fill out, but refuse to animate, the context.

Like the *Wake*, Roche's text is cosmic, encyclopedic. That is, it depends on the reader's ability to perceive gradually a universal vision more than it does on any true or conventional narrative sequence. It is also a polytext which changes with each reading, yielding different views of itself, the universe, the reader. The effect is what Joyce describes as kaleidoscopic. Roche's books, each in its own way, are collections, arrangements, or compendiums, just as the *Wake* is finally a subtly organized body of interrelated, superimposed, and juxtaposed patterns. The story told is the tale of the text as total history. Here is Roche's own jacket blurb for *Codex*:

> *A collection designed to collect everything, from prehistory to history's end. Text whose gaps whose tears and scrapes lacerate the object: thanks to them all efforts to reconstruct are foiled, all memory becomes unremembered. . . . After* Compact *(or the insighted-blindman-seeing) and* Circus *(or the incorporated-outcast-madman), here is . . .* Codex, *book of the full and the empty, at once molecular and molar, work treating of the masses' bulk and its interstices. Text on the burying of the text and the bringing forth (exposure) of the book—the latter being never the same, each reading changing it.*

That this description of *Codex* is readily applicable to *Finnegans Wake* points up both similarities and differences.

Where Joyce packs meaning into the word and includes an impossible number of oblique and direct allusions to "molecular" details, Roche depends more on the technical shaping, the sentence as polyseme, the text as variable image or gesture, and the naked theme carried (as in Mallarmé's great elegy to creativity and failure) to macrocosmic extremes but grounded in the mundane. Roche's own remarks are instructive in this context. After illustrating his lavish use of allusion, he reverses his field, pointing to an evacuative tendency:

I don't want to suggest that there is a deliberate attempt in my work to exploit polysemy. In Circus *I exploit* asemy, *that is, as a result of forcing all the senses of a word, I finish by emptying it completely of meaning.*[27]

Such a statement may suggest why Roche's books, for all their verbivocovisual pyrotechnics, remain spare and elegant. By contrast, the *Wake* is cornucopious. Where Joyce chooses to *present* (however obliquely) the least dramatic of life situations, the purest of social and cultural paradigms, Roche approaches Beckett by treating the dying—in this case, the sick-of-life-unto-death—and intercranial space, undercutting or rejecting narrative development and all but the most rudimentary and ambiguous narrative situations.

We have the Japanese collector of tattoos in *Compact*, whose presence adds color and a hint of character and plot to the disjunct musings of a moribund blindman. In *Circus* we have only the labyrinth of the brain filled with noxious and voided commonplaces, a novel made up of the detritus of novels. *Codex* is a schematic apocalypse in which a dying man meditates upon the last things of a civilization which he gradually comes to represent. To the degree that we have a story, it is the story of man's accumulation of self-destructive impulses, impulses reflected in language's capacity to equivocate:[28]

$$\text{EN}^{\text{vers}}_{\text{droit}} \quad \begin{array}{l}\text{et contre tout}\\ \text{Protégé Défendu}\end{array}$$

This technique, quite different from the evacuation process described above by Roche, is a Brunoesque staple of the *Wake*. Like Joyce in this too, Roche uses language to counterfeit a baring of teeth in the primal grin of menacing fear. His exuberant verbal play insists upon the signification of words and images, only to undermine it: "*Que Ma Chine arrière soit à l'avant*"[29] ("So that reverse gear [*machine arrière*] is forward / So that my backward China is in the forefront in the Orient [levant]"). In the *Wake* we read, "The playgue will soon be over, rats!" (378) Examples proliferate, culminating in the spectacular typographical skull, raining peace and death, with which *Codex* concludes:[30]

31

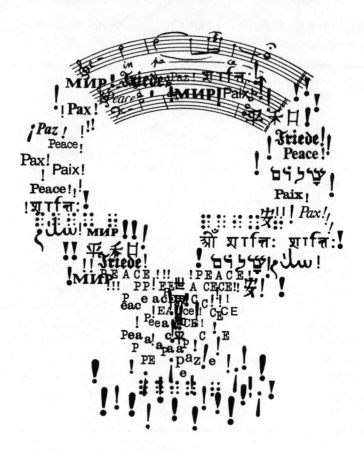

Joyce himself is occasionally cited in Roche's books (as he is in those of Schmidt and Sollers). Thus we find the following reference to Molly Bloom's final affirmation buried in the sado-religious context of the bitterly comic funeral "CANTATE" of *Codex*:[31]

LA, CRIME Ô SADE — DIS : « YES —
« I said yes I will yes »

                                                    I.R.A. (ça   ça)

                                              point
                                          ↗   ↘
Le jour (celui de l'arme au pied) point.   **.**

L'aube.
          On vous réveille   mieux
vous endormir, à la fin !

Here the large caps contain a pun on the Latin "Lacrimas a
Dies Irae," signaled as it might be in the *Wake* by certain
ungrammaticalities. The page continues, playing upon Joycean
and Irish themes, followed by an equally Joycean play upon the
theme of morning and awakening toward a pointlessly pointed
"*fin.*" The themes of Roche and Joyce overlap conspicuously here,
just as the end-beginnings of Joyce's last two books coincide as
evocations of accumulated mornings leading to the night of the
tomb:[32]

                    Exécution!   Repos !

          Point de jour pour chialer maintenant et à jamais

          ┌──┐
          │ **MORT POUR AVOIR REGARDÉ LA VIE EN FACE** │
          └──┘

There is no need to posit influence in the sense of borrowings.
Rather I would suggest that, consciously or not, Roche has
digested many of the techniques of the *Wake* as part of his
enormous culture—exploiting, adapting, or reinventing them with
vigor and originality unmatched by other writers in the wake.
It follows that, like the Noigandres poets, Roche freely admits
a debt to Mallarmé, whose *Un coup de dés* is alluded to in[33]

$$\left[\text{un}_e \ \text{coup}_e\right]$$

$$C^a_l\text{va} \qquad \text{(d'os)}$$

where the throw (*coup*) of the bones (*os*) elicits a skull (Latin, *calvarium*) in type and a shot (*coupe*) of apple brandy, or calvados. We may also point to Pound's use of ideograms, political outrage, associational cacophony, and a polyphony of interlinguistic reference—all found in Roche's fiction.

But specific Joycean techniques are sprinkled throughout Roche's pages: multilingual puns and pun effects achieved either by homophony or visual tricks; playfully serious absurdities, either specific as in "*senescence—c'est naissance*"[34] or combinations of sounds as in "*à en crier*";[35] portmanteau words like *utoptique* and *miraginer*;[36] suggestive use of the wrong word;[37]

$$la \diagup poliss^{onne}_{euse} \ de \diagup$$

unexpected additions or substitutions or wordplays upon the title of the book (or upon the author's name):[38]

$$\times \ \text{Code contenant l'essentiel des ouvrages } ^o_p\text{ubliés}$$

It is in terms of this last citation that *Codex* qualifies as a *cri de coeur*—the exposition of all that is left over after civilization destroys itself. Here we are close to Joyce's traum-antic book which has been found buried in a midden after the catastrophic fall of night-life-Finn-civilization. Unlike the *Wake*, however, which builds toward a reawakening from the thunderous fall, Roche's latest book builds toward a spine-chilling conclusion full of political overtones. In the final double hieroglyph of *Codex*, a radar screen (posing as a TV screen) alongside which is written *VIDE PARTOUT!* is followed on the next page by a skull made of words for peace in many languages, punctuated by bomb-shaped exclamation points (see above). The paradox is worthy of Joyce; the pessimism is of a different order. Still, both books pass for, and claim to be, palimpsests (see ALP's "letter," which is simultaneously the *Wake* itself and any number of sacred texts)—a term used along with "ideogram" by the Noigandres poets to describe Joyce's contribution. Both achieve their effects by expanding upon the ordinary—totalizing their visions, drawing their myths out of the debris of civilization in the manner of artists working with found objects, animating clichés, and recreating a language with the immediacy of gesture. The gestural quality of Roche's pages is immediately evident, prolonged as it is by visual effects. But the recovery of the gestural potential of language was also Joyce's stated goal for "In the beginning was the gest . . ." (469), and the beginning was where "it was at" for Joyce.

The potential of the *Wake* has yet to be fully realized in this country and England, if not in Brazil, France, and Germany; but on the partial and tentative evidence already advanced, it seems clear that the *Wake* has had its impact, already has had consequences. First, there is the use of language as a medium, the preoccupation with the process of saying as doing. In Joyce's wake we see this tendency extended by the Noigandres group as well as by Schmidt, Sollers, and Roche. Deprived of a set significance, the word becomes an actor on the page, arrangements of words become actions. In his new role as arranger of verbal effects, as animator of dead or moribund language, the writer becomes a demiurge, or at least a prestidigitator.

Second, with the failure of realism and the rejection of fiction as statement, the refusal of plot, even in the face of a return to didactic fiction (of the left, mainly), we see a revival of the baroque mentality. Post-*Wake* fiction tends to approximate a portable infinity; meanings proliferate amid a welter of effects. Sollers' curious backward development toward traditionally French rhetorical embellishment and, following Pound, toward referential enrichment parallels Roche's reliance on allusions, verbal play, visual games, and references—all to create a texture of endless delight, a sparkling dress for existential despair. Perhaps this is a form of exoticism, perhaps it is an honest acceptance of the surrounding or impending chaos, perhaps a means of controlling disorder and the lack of values, a modern version of Frazer's "sympathetic magic." Certainly in the case of Joyce, Schmidt, Roche, and Sollers, and to a degree Beckett (whose current spareness is a surrogate for the ornament of the earlier work), the artist brings to his texture unusual if not unprecedented knowledge, an almost perverse joy in encyclopedic display. Paradoxically, we must recall the baroquery of Flaubert, more focused and in a sense tamer but a factor in his fabled researches and in the texture of *L'Education sentimentale, Salammbô,* and *La Tentation de Saint Antoine,* and in the content of the unfinished, perhaps unfinishable *Bouvard et Pecuchet.* Flaubert is the father of both moderns and postmoderns in more than one sense. Roche claims *Bouvard* as a precedent; Pound insisted upon its influence on *Ulysses.* But, as Northrop Frye points out, there are other precedents for the "encyclopedic" genre. After all, the *Wake* borrows heavily from the later chapters of *Ulysses,* and writers unaffected by the *Wake* directly yet influenced by Joyce (e.g. John Barth) may exhibit parallel tendencies. But the question of impact inevitably mingles with that of fashions, and one may ask, Would the same thing not have occurred without Joyce?

Third, as a corollary to the second development, we see the increased attention to universals, the generalizing or (to use Sollers' term) "epic" tendency. This may have as its consequence the removal of masks, the stripping away of appearances, even the exposure of the artist as writer—not through message (which, like the "letter" of the *Wake,* never gets delivered, never gets said because it has neither destination nor sender) but by reestablishing the total context for essential experiences. The result is a yo-yo of tease and disguise, referring us back to the first of our consequences: the play of debasement and sophistication which seems to be a characteristic of our age. Thus in Joyce and Roche and others like them we find a reaching for the commonplace and a refusal of the accepted, a mining and undermining of pretense.

Fourth, as a consequence of all this, there is a tendency to sublimate (not destroy) structure, harmony, and radiance in order to avoid the appearance, if not the fact, of aesthetic control. These works are all, and many post-*Wake* works will continue to be, elaborately and rationally structured. Indeed, post-*Wake* fiction is, if anything, more highly articulated than any preceding fiction, more conscious of its parts and particles, more theme- and phrase-bound. Its innovative nature lies in a regrouping of structures, their nodalization. The closer we move to the irrational, which is perhaps the ultimate in universals, the more carefully we must balance our accounts. Writers in the post-*Wake* tradition tend to be meticulously lavish, selectively joyous, consciously destructive, circumspectly exuberant. The end result may not be pretty, but more often than not it will be elegant, occasionally de-light-full, and always play-filled and decor-ative. And there will be more of it.

Notes

1. Periodical publication began before the book was completed in 1915.
2. *Finnegans Wake* (New York, Viking Press, 1958). Unless otherwise noted, all page numbers in the text will refer to this edition.
3. See Brakhage's letters in *Tree,* No. 1, and Cage's *M.*
4. From "*Finnegans Wake* and the Post-modern Imagination" in *Paracriticism* (Urbana, University of Illinois Press, 1975).
5. Spring 1973, No. 56, pp. 142–143.
6. Ediçôes Invençáo, Sâo Paulo, 1965 (republished by Libraria Duas Cidades in 1975). For a further sample of their work and thought, see *Concrete Poetry: A World View,* ed. Mary Ellen Solt (Bloomington, Indiana University Press, 1971).
7. The Noigandres movement takes its name from the Provençal mystery word Pound puzzles over in Canto XX.
8. *Teoria da Poesia Concreta,* p. 23.
9. In 1962 the brothers de Campos collaborated on the translation of eleven short but significant passages from the *Wake* into Portuguese, *Panaroma do Finnegans Wake* (Conselho Estadual de Cultura, Coleçâo Ensaio, Sâo Paulo; augmented and reissued in 1971 by Editôra Perspectiva). The significance of the translations from the *Wake* lies less in the early date of this volume than in the fact that the translators are practicing poets, a pattern which has repeated itself in other literary contexts.
10. *Teoria da Poesia Concreta,* p. 43.
11. *Ibid.,* p. 100. The writer credits Adelhaid Obradovic's early book concerning space in Joyce's work.
12. See also Italo Calvino's *Cosmicomics* and *t zero,* both of which toy with space-time, contemplating in human terms the implications of moments in the development of the universe. In many ways Calvino's vision is the more vital and innovative.
13. The latter are available in Lawrence Harvey's thorough and useful *Samuel Beckett: Poet and Critic* (Princeton, Princeton University Press, 1970).
14. *Our Exagmination Round His Factification for Incamination of Work in Progress* (London, 1929), p. 6.
15. *Ibid.*
16. *Thru* (London, Hamish Hamilton, Ltd., 1975), p. 7.
17. Patrick O'Neill in *A Wake Newsletter,* XI, 3 (June 1974), 52–54.
18. See the facsimile edition of Arno Schmidt's *Zettels Traum* (Karlsruhe, Stahlberg, 1970).
19. *Ibid.*
20. Translations of extracts from Roche's work can be found in *The Paris*

Review, Nos. 44, 66, and a translation of part of Sollers' *H* in *The Iowa Review* No. 5/4.

21. Of late there has been considerable French interest in Joyce and especially in his last book. The French periodical *Change* has done a complete issue on the *Wake* under the direction of Jean Paris. *Poétique* has published two essays and an entire issue on *Finnegans Wake.* An anniversary volume, *Ulysses: cinquante ans après,* has appeared in the series Etudes Anglaises, published by Didier.

22. See *The Iowa Review,* No. 5/4 (Fall 1974), pp. 91–101.

23. Sollers insists, however, on the meticulous care exercised in the composition of his texts. Care, skill, and control are surely his hallmarks.

24. His first book was a study of Monteverdi (1961).

25. "La Peau de l'écriture," in *Special Maurice Roche, Encres Vives,* Spring 1973, pp. 22–33.

26. *Codex* (Paris, Seuil, 1974), p. 12.

27. This is most true of *Compact* and *Codex. Circus* is another sort of machine, more musical and perhaps polyphonic.

28. *Codex,* p. 157.

29. *Ibid.,* p. 158.

30. *Ibid.,* p. 61. See *Finnegans Wake,* pp. 470–471, for Joyce's play on words for "peace."

31. *Ibid.,* p. 111.

32. *Ibid.*

33. *Codex,* p. 113.

34. "senescence—it is birth," *ibid.,* p. 82.

35. "à l'encrier," *ibid.,* p. 58.

36. *Ibid.,* p. 91.

37. *Ibid.,* p. 61.

38. "X Code is the code containing the essence of published/forgotten works," *ibid.,* p. 81.

Eugene Jolas, *transition,* and the Revolution of the Word

Michael Finney

Just about the time some of Joyce's most faithful friends and supporters began to express skepticism about his new work, Eugene Jolas founded in 1927 *transition*, a little magazine of experimental literature, and asked Joyce to publish "Work in Progress" serially. In spite of some difficulties and delays, the first installment of "Work in Progress" appeared as the first piece in the first number of *transition*. Over the next eleven years, Jolas published in *transition* all, or nearly all, of "Work in Progress" and more than a hundred articles in which Joyce's work was discussed and defended.

If Jolas could be set down in literary history simply as an enlightened editor who took a certain risk to make available to the reading public the work of a true genius, the story would be simply told. But Jolas was also the founder and the chief supporter and proponent of the Revolution of the Word. That might be irrelevant if Joyce were not also one of Jolas' causes and if "Work in Progress" were not, as Richard Ellmann puts it in his bography, *James Joyce,* "the principal text of his revolution of the word."

More to the point, any reader, critic or amateur, who read

"Work in Progress" before its publication as *Finnegans Wake* in 1939 had to have read all of it, except for fragments published by small presses, in *transition*. There it was often used to support, and was frequently defended in terms of, a naive philosophy of linguistic nihilism. Since that philosophy affected both the immediate and long-range critical response to the *Wake*, it seems worthwhile to discuss it in some detail.

Although Jolas does not officially proclaim the Revolution of the Word until *transition* 16–17 (June 1929), the movement had been building almost since the birth of *transition*. In an editorial in *transition* 3 (June 1927), "Suggestions for a New Magic," Jolas calls for the disintegration of old language and the creation of new words:

We believe there is no hope for poetry unless there be disintegration first. We need new words, new abstractions, new hieroglyphs, new symbols, new myths. By reestablishing the simplicity of the word, we may find again its old magnificence. (179)[1]

Later in the same issue, in "K.O.R.A.A.," Jolas defends *transition*'s publishing the works of Joyce and Gertrude Stein by assuring the reader that the editor's only compunction was that Joyce and Stein might be too old-fashioned. In *transition* 5 (August 1927), Elliot Paul, then Jolas' co-editor, advocates linguistic and intellectual anarchy: "If logic is to crash for such trivial reasons as innovations in grammar, spelling and syntax . . . I say, 'Let it crash.'" (157) In *transition* 7 (October 1927), Jolas equates poetry and revolution:

Poetry to us is a philosophy of life. Poetry is the revolt of the heart, the refuge of the wounded by the terrifying brutality and stupidity of men, the escape into the beyond. (158)

Though as yet unsupported by arguments or evidence, the revolutionary rhetoric and the antiauthoritarian destructive impulse behind the movement are clearly manifest.

By the time he publishes *transition* 9 (December 1927), Jolas seems to feel the need to defend *transition* against charges of dogmatism:

The misconceptions with which the experiments of transition *are being received in many quarters necessitates once more a clarification of the general ideas underlying our venture. We have no intention of indulging in dogmatic pronunciamentoes. . . . (191)*

But he goes on to do just that:

> *Realism, as it is still preached in America, is a movement with which we have no sympathy. We believe that the police reporter's mentality has nothing to do with poetry. We are against all methods that believe that the photographic representation of life is the aim of art. (194)*

> *We have no patience with the idea that the spirit of revolt can be expressed through political means. Poetry in itself is a revolt. (196)*

And he goes on to repeat his claim that "Poetry can be renewed through the recreation of the word." (196)

In "The Revolution of Language and James Joyce," in *transition* 11 (February 1928), Jolas expands his conception of the revolution and implicates Joyce in it:

> *. . . the disintegration of words and their subsequent reconstruction on other planes constitute some of the most important phenomena of our age. The traditional meaning of words is being subverted and a panic seizes the upholders of the norm as they contemplate the process of destruction that opens up heretofore undreamed of possibilities of expression. (109)*

> *Words in modern literature are being set side by side in the same banal fashion as in preceding decades, and the inadequacy of wornout verbal patterns for our more sensitized nervous systems seems to have struck only a small minority. The discoveries of the subconscious . . . should have made it apparent that the instrument of language in its archaic condition could no longer be used. (109–110)*

> *It is in the new work of James Joyce, the first book of which has been published serially in* transition, *that this revolutionary tendency is developed to its ultimate degree, thus confounding those timid minds who regard the English language as a static thing, sacrosanct in its position, and dogmatically defended by a crumbling hierarchy of philologists and pedagogues. Words have undergone organic changes through the centuries. It is usually people, who, impelled by their economic or political lives, create the new vocabularies. The* vates, *or poetic seer, frequently minted current expressions into a linguistic whole. Mr. Joyce, whose love of words and whose mastery of them has been demonstrated in huge creations, should not be denied the same privilege as the people themselves hold. (110)*

It is not altogether clear just what Jolas is rebelling against: language itself, the formal and stodgy use of language, linguistic conservatives and purists, or all three. Nor is it easy to extract the substance from the revolutionary rhetoric and, although I am not sure Jolas does not intend it literally, the revolutionary metaphor. Jolas may be making a quasi-legitimate point about the "philologists and pedagogues," a version of the structural linguists' argument that grammar should be descriptive, not, as they suppose traditional grammars are, prescriptive. But the structural linguists' objections are to a theory of language, not to language itself.

Jolas' assertion that words change is, of course, true. And it is true that individuals have intentionally created words which have become a part of the vocabulary of the language, although not so often as Jolas suggests. But Jolas perverts this general truth and this half-truth so that they appear to support the democratic conclusion that Joyce and all people have the right to create words. Of course, the whole argument is senseless, because the right to create words is not really at issue. Obviously, anyone can create as many new words as he pleases, but at the risk of having no one understand him.

Jolas is no better when he discusses, specifically, the language of "Work in Progress":

> The texture of his neologies is based on a huge synthesis and there is an artistic logic back of every verbal innovation. The English language, because of its universality, seems particularly fitted for a rebirth along the lines Mr. Joyce envisaged. (112)

> In his supertemporal and multispatial composition, language is reborn anew before our eyes. (113)

> His word formations and deformations spring from more than a dozen languages. . . . Mr. Joyce has created a language of new richness and power to express the new sense of time and space he wishes to give. . . . Even modern American, so fertile in anarchic properties, has been used by him. The spontaneous flux of his style is aided by his idea to disregard the norms of orthodox syntax. His construction of sentences follows a psychological logic rather than a mathematical one. (113–114)

> Whirling together the various languages, Mr. Joyce, whose universal knowledge includes that of many foreign tongues, creates a verbal dreamland of abstraction that may well be the language of the future. (115)

Jolas obviously uses terms like *universal* and *universality*, and distinctions like the one between *mathematical* and *psychological logic*, evaluatively rather than descriptively. His elevation of modern American to the status of a separate language and his attribution to it of anarchic properties (presumably because America successfully rebelled against England) are, of course, absurd. His remarks contain no real information about the language of "Work in Progress," but they do create a kind of messianic vision of Joyce as the redeemer of fallen language.

In "A Review" in *transition* 12 (March 1928), Jolas reviews *transition*'s goals and achievements at the end of its first year of publication and recommits the magazine to the disintegration of language:

> transition *in the coming year will continue to reflect the chaos born of our age. . . . We will try to hasten the disintegration of "spine-intrenched parloritis," as Gillespie puts it. (146–147)*

A. Lincoln Gillespie, Jr., was, incidentally, the first of *transition*'s contributors to attempt to write criticism in the new language. In *transition* 12 he has an essay called "Textighter Eveploy or Hothouse Bromidick," and here is part of what he has to say about Joyce's work:

> *anent B.—demfew Logogriphs being cut. For an exception here, v. Joyce's recentwork,* (transition) *Punpassing* IMPORT-*Neo's, combining museMindBespeak with fetirhapsic* SONE-*Tumble-display. (173)*

Gillespie's criticism bears about the same relationship to Joyce's text as most literary criticism bears to a text: the text makes more sense.

After a two-issue lull, Jolas returns to action in *transition* 15 (February 1929). In "Super-Occident" (he apparently does not intend the pun), he deplores the generally bad state of the world and proposes the universal word as the solution to its problems:

> *The reality of the universal word is still being neglected. Never has a revolution been more imperative. We need the twentieth-century word. . . . With this must go the attempt to weaken the rigidity of the old syntactic arrangements. The new vocabulary and the new syntax must help destroy the ideology of a rotting civilization. (15)*

Aside from the hint at the idea that language determines ideology and culture, there is nothing new in the essay. In "Notes," however, Jolas issues an invitation to join his cause:

> *We are tired of the word that does not express the kinetic and the subconscious.* transition, *which has encouraged the breaking up of traditional language from the very beginning, will continue to aid the process of subversion along this line as long as we go on. I invite those interested in this campaign to express themselves in these pages. (187)*

He must have had some response. *transition* 16–17 (June 1929) opens with a new section, the title in bold capitals on an otherwise blank page: THE REVOLUTION OF THE WORD. The first item in the section is a proclamation:

PROCLAMATION

Tired of the spectacle of short stories, novels, poems and plays still under the hegemony of the banal word, monotonous syntax, static phonology, descriptive naturalism, and desirous of crystallizing a viewpoint . . .

We declare that:

(1) *The revolution of the English language is an accomplished fact.*

(2) *The imagination in search of a fabulous world is autonomous and intact. . . .*

(3) *Pure poetry is a lyrical absolute that seeks an a priori reality within ourselves alone. . . .*

(4) *Narrative is not a mere anecdote, but the projection of a metamorphosis of reality. . . .*

(5) *The expression of these concepts can be achieved only through the rhythmic "hallucination of the word" (Rimbaud).*

(6) *The literary creator has the right to disintegrate primal matter of words imposed on him by text-books and dictionaries. . . .*

(7) *He has the right to use words of his own fashioning and to disregard existing grammatical and syntactic laws. . . .*

(8) *The "Litany of Words" is admitted as an independent unit.*

(9) *We are not concerned with the propagation of sociological ideas, except to emancipate the creative elements from the present ideology.*

(10) *Time is a tyranny to be abolished.*

(11) *The writer expresses. He does not communicate.*

(12) *The plain reader be damned. (13)*

Although Joyce himself did not sign the proclamation, many of his supporters did, including some of the authors of *Our Exagmination*. (It may not be particularly significant that Joyce did not sign the proclamation, since he did not sign petitions on principle.)

The proclamation is, of course, a statement of beliefs, not a justification of those beliefs, so, although the rebelliousness is transparently sophomoric, it would hardly be fair to criticize the statements in detail. However, in "Logos," in the same issue, Jolas presents his most articulate, least rhetorical defense of the Revolution of the Word. It is relatively easy to see both the substance and the fallacy of his arguments. He states a more or less explicit hypothesis about the creation of new words, that the poet as "composer of words . . . is merely using certain automatic laws that have governed the development of language since time immemorial." (27) That is, the creator of neologisms creates them according to natural, historical processes. Jolas' expansion and defense of this hypothesis is relatively subtle and contains several commonly accepted linguistic "facts":

The idea that a loosening of linguistic material is either a divine prerogative or happens as a sudden phenomenon of common impulses has, of course, been exploded long ago. Changes in the organism of language are made as the result of instinctive individual activity and the history of philology shows conclusively, through a vast deductive process, that the linguistic evolution from early days was one of constant metamorphosism, synthetism, deformation, adjustments. . . . The history of Indo-European speech gives us an illustration of the fact that there was a constant growth and mutation through phonetic changes, combinations, duplication of meanings, changes in grammatical canons, sound transmutations, assimilations, abbreviations. Phonetic experimentation played an important role in this. The sound evocations often had the result of completely changing the meaning of the mutilated word. (28)

It is interesting, or at least amusing, that Jolas should fall back on evidence provided by his enemies, the philologists, but then he misrepresents it. Although he accepts that language change is the result of neither *divine prerogative* nor *sudden common impulse*, the alternative he proposes, that language change is the result of *instinctive individual activity* is, at best, only a half-truth. Later in the essay, Jolas clarifies what he means by *instinctive individual activity* and defends the concept:

The powerful tendency of children to create words of their own is an embryonic impulse which the poet duplicates. It is also a scientific fact which our observation may bear out that we form strange and exotic words in the state of sleep—words that are often without the slightest reference to those we have known in our waking condition. We cannot doubt that there is a deep-rooted instinct in humanity to make changes in speech. The poet by deforming the traditional words or by creating word combinations is only following an organic law of linguistic psychology. (29)

It is true that children play with language, and it is possible that such language play is instinctive, but although there is still much to be learned about children's language behavior, the evidence indicates that language play is a part of the process by which the child acquires the conventions of the language of the community in which he lives, not a process for altering those conventions. I assume the source for Jolas' *scientific fact* about dream neologisms is Freud's *Interpretation of Dreams*, but Freud never claimed that dream neologisms do not have any reference to waking words. On the contrary, for Freud the form of dream words is always derived from waking words, and, strictly speaking, words in dreams—whether or not they are neologisms—have no meaning. Their *significance* lies in their association with the repressed nonverbal content of the subconscious. So Jolas' particular scientific law of linguistic psychology appears to have no basis in fact.

To return to the main line of argument, it is obviously true that some individual speaker had to be the first person to pronounce a word in a new way, and in that sense it is always an individual who initiates language change. But that single utterance does not, in itself, constitute a language change. Language change, however it is initiated, is the result of a long process which involves the whole linguistic community, and sound change generally affects the whole phonological system, so that not one word, but every word which contains the sound, will change. And such sound change does not, as Jolas suggests, change the meaning of the word, although it may ultimately be a factor in a change of meaning. Consequently, Jolas' long catalogue of types and processes of linguistic change is irrelevant to his point, and he is left with little more than his assertion that poets create words according to natural historical processes. It is, of course, possible for a writer to create neologisms by consciously modifying existing words through processes which are imitations of historical processes, although that does not appear to be exactly what Jolas means by his claim. If it is, however, a reader would be able to interpret or decode the transformed words only if he knew exactly the processes by which the creator made them.

transition 16–17 introduces another new section, "COMBAT" —a sign of the increased, if still metaphoric, militancy of the movement. In "Observation Post," Robert Sage joins the battle to defend Joyce against Max Eastman's charge that "Joyce speaks a private language whose meaning cannot be conveyed to the reader" and which has "its parallel in the madhouse":

> *The fact that a Stuart Gilbert, a Rodker, a MacLeish, a Jolas can follow*
> *with intense pleasure the footprints of Joyce's mind along the elliptic . . .*
> *is sufficient justification, if justification is needed, of this work and*
> *its sanity. (202)*

And Sage goes on to ask, I assume rhetorically, "Are there as
many men who can follow Einstein?" (202). Sage modestly omits
his own name from the list of those who understand Joyce, but later
in the essay he attempts to explain some of Joyce's neologisms:

> *He invents the word auriscenting (to catch the smell of something on the*
> *breeze); he coins the new word "cropulence," a combination of corpulence*
> *and crapulence . . . he removes the letter "g" from the word strength when he*
> *wishes to show the dying out of desire like the dying out of the colors*
> *of the rainbow; he refers . . . to Benjamin Franklin as Benjermine Funkling*
> *because "funkel" in German means electric spark and Franklin is the*
> *American Prometheus. . . . (203)*

However silly Max Eastman's charges, Sage's defense hardly
constitutes a refutation. Although *cropulence* and *Benjermine
Funkling* are part pun and part portmanteau and might be interpreted in a similar way by anyone with the appropriate vocabulary and knowledge, I have my doubts that even a Jolas could
get "dying out of desire like the dying out of the colors of the
rainbow" out of *strenth* without being told.

It is Sage again, in "Word Lore," *transition* 18 (November
1929), who defends Jolas' arguments in "Logos" and launches a
counterattack against "the defenders of the language":

> *The defenders of language in its accepted form appear to rely on principally*
> *two arguments: 1. The language is already sufficiently large and embracive*
> *to express any idea or describe any object. 2. Change in language comes*
> *about gradually in the vernacular and when a new word has proved its*
> *worth it will be absorbed in the accepted literary vocabulary.*
>
> *Respectively, these views may be roughly categorized as the classical*
> *view, or that which accepts a changedefying absolute (stasis of perfection),*
> *and the liberal view, which theoretically admits cautious elasticity but which,*
> *like liberal attitudes, is a specious facade of broadmindedness covering an*
> *ashamed faith in the status quo ("evolution not revolution"). (199)*

Sage takes on the classicists first:

> *But what do the classicists say? Our language is already ample to express*
> *anything we want to express. Just a moment. "Our language," as these*
> *gentlemen understand it, is not the popularly employed language of today,*
> *but a medium which is very little different from that of the eighteenth*
> *century. . . . (200)*

Sage goes on to suggest that the classicists would have difficulty describing certain phenomena in the twentieth century if they had recourse only to eighteenth-century vocabulary, and he rejects an imagined rebuttal that those who require a technical vocabulary could develop one without "molesting the written or 'correctly spoken' language," because it is necessary "to include the technical and scientific in our ordinary range of experience." (200) Sage admits that the "liberal attitude comes nearer the truth" (200) and that language has changed slowly, by which he appears to mean that language has acquired new words slowly. But he argues that, since things change faster in modern times, it is impossible to wait for the slow process of language change to produce words necessary to express contemporary life.

It is almost pathetic that Sage cannot even knock down his own straw men. Even his concession that language normally changes slowly misfires. The general truth that the process of language change is gradual does not apply to the acquisition of new vocabulary. Borrowed words, new words formed on existing morphological patterns, technical terminology, and even fairly inventive neologisms are often assimilated into the language quite rapidly. And any student of the Renaissance will know that that is not true, as Sage's arguments imply, only of recent times.

Also in *transition* 18, and sounding very much like one of Sage's liberals, Stuart Gilbert comes to the defense of the Revolution of the Word. It is both interesting and surprising that he does so—interesting because, of all Joyce's supporters, Gilbert comes closest to being his spokesman; surprising because previously, in his essay in *Our Exagmination . . .* , he attempts to disassociate "Work in Progress" from at least the destructive aspects of the movement:

> . . . it would be wrong to see in Work in Progress *the promise of a systematic destruction of language. . . . Indeed, disciples of the New Word would defeat their own ends. The word-building of* Work in Progress *is founded on the rock of petrified language, of sounds with solid associations; were this groundwork to be undermined by a general decomposition of words, the edifice would in time be submerged in the shifting sands of incoherence.*[2]

In "Function of Words," however, in *transition* 18, Gilbert attempts to conciliate the reader who might be put off by the revolutionary rhetoric of the movement:

> For some of us, and with reason, the word "revolution" has an ominous

resonance. And, if the "revolutionaries of the word" were mere iconoclasts,
out to damage and destroy for the sheer delight of destruction, the chorus
of communion which greeted our announcement in the last number of
transition *would have been amply justified. (203)*

Gilbert then goes on, ostensibly to discuss the constructive
aspects of the revolution. First, he distinguishes between the
emotive and symbolic functions of language:

For language has two uses, two distinct functions. Words, as Mr. C. K.
Ogden points out in his Meaning of Meaning, are both symbolic (of a
"reality": i.e. communicative) and emotive signs. "The logical element and
the affective element," another writer on language has said, "mingle
constantly in language." (203)

Each word has, in fact, its "aura," or, as Vendryes puts it in Le Langage,
"a light vapour which floats above the expression of the thought." (204)

Then he points out that the "evocative, implicit function of
words is apt to be overlooked in our scientific age" (204), and
claims that that function is the legitimate provenance of the Revolution of the Word:

The "Revolution of the Word" is a movement to explore this secondary
non-utilitarian function of language. . . .[I]n so far as he [the revolutionary]
has apprehended and can express the racial affective values of the signs
he employs, he will enable the reader of the work to share his emotions.
Every word of the language has its own nuances; the "revolutionary in
words" mixes those nuances as he will. . . . [H]e creates his own "syntax"
(in the exact meaning of the word: the setting together of things), composing
new word forms whenever these are necessary to render the nuance at
which he aims. (204)

Gilbert may have thought himself a mediator between the purists and the revolutionaries, a voice of reason, but in reality his
remarks undermine and trivialize not only the Revolution of the
Word but any literary use of language. His token allusion to
the best semantic theory available to him is more than overpowered by the frivolity of his definition of "aura" and the pedantry
of his redefinition of syntax. The principal effect of his arguments is to assure the "enemy" that there is no danger to be
feared from the "revolutionaries." His claims amount to little
more than an announcement that the Revolution of the Word
is no threat to the practical use of language because it concerns
itself only with the aesthetic, nonfunctional use of language.
Irrelevance seems rather a high price to pay for respectability.

In *transition* 19–20 (June 1930), Jolas announces that he

will suspend the publication of *transition* indefinitely. In "The King's English Is Dying: Long Live the American Language," he declares, Nixon-like, that the revolution is suceeding:

> *The mechanical acceptance of language which pedantic philology and utilitarian literature continues to force upon the writer is drawing to a close. The struggle to give the poet unlimited liberty to recreate each word in his own image is still going on, but a new sense of the word which professors, newspapers and novelists have abused to the point of sterility is now developing and a modern mythos of language is being established.*

When Jolas revived *transition* two years later, he continued to serialize "Work in Progress," but Joyce was no longer so important a part of the magazine. In fact, there is one issue in which his name is not even mentioned. Jolas spreads himself thin. He gets involved with myths, paramyths, and anamyths, with orphic signs and chthonian grammar, with dreams, the collective unconscious, the night-mind and night language, to say nothing of meta-anthropological and other crises. He invents a new philosophy, Vertigralism, which incorporates all his concerns, including the Revolution of the Word.

Still, a couple of things in the post-lapsarian *transition* are worth noting. One is *The Revolution of the Word Dictionary*. In *transition* 21 (March 1932), Jolas began publishing "wanted" posters, one of which is:

WANTED: A NEW COMMUNICATIVE LANGUAGE

. . . The old words have reached the age of retirement. Let us pension them off! We need a twentieth century dictionary. (285)

Jolas published two installments of the new dictionary, the first in *transition* 22 (February 1933), the second in *transition* 23 (July 1935). In both installments, Joyce's *creations* head the list of entries:

constation	*. . . a statement of concrete fact*
couchmare	*. . . nightmare . . . cauchemar*
mielodorous	*. . . honeyed emphasis of odorous*
Dance McCaper	*. . . an Irish danse macabre*
returningties	*. . . eternities . . . cycles turning upon themselves . . . the serpent that bites its own tail (123)*
luft	*. . . air*
sojestiveness	*. . . picaresque suggestiveness*
gawk	*. . . to look sheepishly*
gnutsch	*. . . to smack one's lips (122)*

50

I don't know if Jolas had Joyce's authority for his definitions, but I doubt it. Joyce would almost certainly have resisted pinning single definitions on his neologisms. His purpose was to enrich the text, to add, not limit, meaning. At any rate, the list includes words which are neither neologisms nor original with Joyce. And some of the definitions are clearly arbitrary; most take inadequate consideration of the derivation of the word.

In *transition* 23 (July 1935), Jolas prints the results of an "Inquiry About the Malady of Language." He has asked several prominent people concerned with literature to answer two questions:

> *I. Do you believe that, in the present world-crisis, the Revolution of Language is necessary in order to hasten the reintegration of the human personality?*

> *II. Do you envisage this possibility through a readaptation of existing words, or do you favor a revolutionary creation of new words? (144)*

A few accepted Jolas' assumptions and answered the questions seriously. More refused to accept the assumptions and answered either critically or, like Malcolm Cowley, cynically:

> *I. In the present world crisis, a revolution of language would hasten the reintegration of human personality just about as much as a slug of applejack would help a corpse.*

> *II. . . . For a writer to sit in his study and talk about creating new words is about as useless as sitting in the Ritz bar talking about the equality of man. (148)*

I do not know if Malcolm Cowley intended the first part of his answer as an insulting allusion to the resurrection of Tim Finnegan, but it is clear that in the second part he was taking a significant cut at parlor revolutionaries like Eugene Jolas.

Before I attempt to determine the relationship between Jolas and Joyce—or, rather, between the Revolution of the Word and "Work in Progress"—I should point out that Jolas did publish several interesting works of experimental literature in *transition*, particularly during the early years of its publication. And he also published some critical essays about "Work in Progress" unrelated to the Revolution of the Word. He published, for instance, all the essays which are collected in *Our Exagmination . . .* , and whatever defects time has permitted us to find in those essays, they are a valuable contemporary contribution to *Wake* scholarship. But still, the relative sanity of those essays is overpowered in the pages of *transition* by the shriller voices of the revolutionaries.

It is fair, I think, to speculate about Joyce's opinion of the Revolution of the Word. We have Gilbert's attempts to disassociate Joyce from the destructive elements of the movement and, later, to point out the constructive elements of the movement as evidence that Joyce did not entirely approve of Jolas' linguistic philosophy. But I think it would be too simple to conclude, as David Hayman has suggested to me privately, that the revolutionaries were just plain silly at times and that Joyce went along with their silliness. Such a conclusion raises the question of Joyce's motives for tolerating the silliness. An obvious possibility, but one unpleasant to consider, is that Joyce put up with Jolas' nonsense because he, Joyce, needed a place in which to publish "Work in Progress." But it would be unfair to Jolas, I believe, to assume that he took undue advantage of his role as publisher to use "Work in Progress" to perpetuate his own philosophy. His honesty and sincerity are not in question. Besides, both Joyce's record of integrity with regard to the publication of his earlier works and his friendship with Jolas argue against such a conclusion.

I suspect the truth is something like this: Joyce agreed with some of the things Jolas had to say about reconstructing language, and he was indulgent of any philosophy or approach which would justify his linguistic and literary experiment. But whatever the truth, the fact remains that until its publication as *Finnegans Wake* in 1939, "Work in Progress" was intimately associated with the Revolution of the Word—physically and ideologically—in the pages of *transition*.

To attempt to establish guilt by association is admittedly a pernicious legal practice, and it is a suspect literary one; but it would be difficult to blame the contemporary reader or critic of "Work in Progress," who could have read it only in *transition*, if he were to assume that Jolas' nihilistic linguistic philosophy fairly represented Joyce's intentions in "Work in Progress." The close association of the Revolution of the Word and "Work in Progress" accounts, I think, for the rejection of Joyce's work by several intelligent contemporary critics. And it also accounts, in part, for naive and simplistic approaches to the text which were supported by some of the early fans and enthusiasts—approaches which in some form still persist among readers of the *Wake*, both common readers and professional critics.

Notes

1. For all references to *transition*, the title of the item and the number and date of the issue are included in the text. Page references are given in parentheses following quotations.

I would like to acknowledge the kind assistance of the staff of the John Hay Library at Brown University. The Harris Collection, housed in the Hay, includes a complete set of *transition* in very good condition, and, in spite of the rarity of some of the issues, the staff allowed me free access to them.

2. Stuart Gilbert, "Prolegomena to *Work in Progress*," in *Our Exagmination Round His Factification for Incamination of Work in Progress* (Norfolk, 1962), p. 57.

Sanscreed latinized:
the *Wake* in Brazil
and hispanic America

Haroldo de Campos

The diffusion of *Finnegans Wake* in Brazil was largely due to the movement of Concrete Poetry, launched in the early fifties by Décio Pignatari and the brothers Augusto and Haroldo de Campos. The latter, by a favorable coincidence—"by a commodius vicus of recirculation"—were great-grandsons of an Irishman, Theobald Butler Browne; he had emigrated from Galway to Salvador, which is the capital of baroque Bahia, northeast of Brazil, and is also called the "Land of All Saints."

Their first articles and manifestoes concerned Concrete Poetry. (See "Poetry: Structure" and "Poetry: Ideogram," 1955, by A. de Campos; "Poetry and Paradise Lost" and "The Open Work of Art," 1955, by H. de Campos; "Concrete Art: Object and Objective," 1956, by D. Pignatari.) Joyce's work—*Finnegans Wake* in particular—was a fundamental point of departure and an obligatory term of reference (along with Mallarmé's *Un coup de dés* and Ezra Pound's *The Cantos*, as well as the "gestural" poetry of e. e. cummings) for the developing project of a new poetry, corresponding to a new, "semiotic" textual conception and akin to new trends in music (serial and postserial) and in painting (post-Mondrian).

The "verbivocovisual" elements of Joyce's prose—the "montage word," regarded as a composite mosaic unit or a basic textural node ("silvamoonlake," for instance)—were emphasized from the very beginning of the Concrete Poetry movement:

> *The Joycean "micro-macrocosm," which reaches its pinnacle in* Finnegans Wake, *is another excellent example of the problem we are discussing. The implacable novel-poem of Joyce succeeds too, in its own manner, as a feat of structure. Here counterpoint is* moto perpetuo. *The ideogram is obtained by superimposing words, true lexical montages. Its general infrastructure is "a circular design, of which every part is beginning, middle, and end" (cf. J. Campbell and H. M. Robinson). The scheme of the vicious circle is the link which joins Joyce and Mallarmé by means of a "commodius vicus of recirculation." Mallarmé's cycle in* Un coup de dés *is very similar to that of Vico reinvented by Joyce for* Finnegans Wake. *The common denominator, according to Robert Greer Cohn, for whom Mallarmé's poem has more in common with* Finnegans Wake *than with any other literary creation, would be the formula: unity, dualism, multiplicity, and again, unity. The circular construction common to both works is evident at first glance: The first sentence of* Finnegans Wake *continues the last, and the last words of Mallarmé's poem are also the first—"Toute Pensée émet un Coup de Dés."*[1]

> *Joyce is led to the microscopic world by the macroscopic, emphasizing detail—*panorama/panaroma—*to the point where a whole metaphoric cosmos is contained in a single word. This is why it can be said of* Finnegans Wake *that it retains the properties of a circle, of the equidistance of all points on it from the center. The work is porous to the reader, accessible from any of the places one chooses to approach it.*[2]

Décio Pignatari, in his 1956 manifesto "New Poetry: Concrete," reshaped for programmatic purposes a Joycean leitmotif ("'Tis optophone which ontophanes," *Finnegans Wake*, p. 13), with the simultaneous invocation of Dante (". . . *esto visibile parlare, / novello a noi perchè qui non si trova*," *Purgatorio* X, 95):

> *O olhouvido ouvê*
> (The eareye seeshears).

It is important to accent here a most significant fact. While several American and European scholars and critics were still insisting on considering Joyce's work (in particular *Finnegans Wake*) as a kind of dead end or blind alley, the Brazilian founders of the Concrete Poetry movement (the members of the 1952 Noigandres group) were using the *Wake* to stimulate and focus their poetical experiments—looking at it not as an apocalyptical finale of Western literature, but rather as an open ground, full of manifold possibilities, seminal.

Quite apart from the theory, they made use of some Joycean devices in their poetry. The montage word is an operative function, for instance, both in D. Pignatari's 1955 "Stèles pour vivre" and in H. de Campos' poems, printed in white ink on black paper, "O â mago do ô mega" ("The core of the omega"; *mago* in Portuguese means also "magician"), subtitled "a phenomenology of composition" (1955–1956). The same is true of A. de Campos' 1953 "poeta menos" ("poetminus") series, which draws its principles of composition from Anton Webern's *"Klangfarbenmelodie"* ("tonecolormelody").

Another dimension of the concrete poets' concern with *Finnegans Wake* is illustrated by the fragments of *Finnegans Wake* translated by A. de Campos and H. de Campos (together or separately) which began to appear in the Brazilian press in 1957.[3] In 1962, both translators brought out the result of their work in book form, under the title *Panaroma do Finnegans Wake*. The 86-page volume consisted of the creative transposition ("transcreation") of eleven fragments (bilingual presentation), accompanied by interpretative comments. In its appendix, besides bibliography and a bio-bibliographic Joycean synthesis, was a companion translation, by A. de Campos, of Lewis Carroll's "Jabberwocky" (in Portuguese, "Jaguadarte")—the *cellulamater* of Joyce's scriptural art. The book also contained a Portuguese version of "Introduction to a Strange Subject" (from *A Skeleton Key to Finnegans Wake*) and a critical essay by A. de Campos, "O Lance de Dados do *Finnegans Wake*" ("The Throwing of Dice in *Finnegans Wake*"), dealing with David Hayman's 1956 *Joyce et Mallarmé*.[4] At the time, the Brazilian *Panaroma* and the French selections from *Finnegans Wake* edited by André du Bouchet (1962) were the largest anthologies of translated fragments from Joyce's most challenging work.

It is worth mentioning that *Finnegans Wake* was rebaptized by its Brazilian translators as FINNICIUS REVEM: FIM + INICIO =

END + BEGINNING, onomastically resounding with an echo of both FINN and VINICIUS. The latter is a latinized Portuguese proper name which carries a hint of *vinho / vinum* = wine; RE (AGAIN) + VEM (COMES).

In 1962, Pignatari wrote one of his most ambitious "*stèles*": No. 3, "Cuban stele." It is a "mural poem," a condensed epic pivoting about three typographically marked axes (phrases intermittently in Latin, English, and Portuguese), which reproduces bits of the fable "The Wolf and the Lamb" ("*Lupus et Agnus*"). The three "major syntagms" that semantically and visually govern the entire composition are the following:

LUP	US	STAB	AT SUPER
LUC	ROS	NA BA	SE DE AÇÚCAR
LAMB	USA	ÁGUA DE OUT	UBRO

In the first line: LUPUS STABAT SUPERIOR / US (U.S.) STAB AT SUPER; in the second line, in Portuguese: LUCROS NA BASE DE AÇÚCAR (profits derived from sugar, plus a hint of "nababo" / "nabob," a wealthy luxury-loving person); in the third line: LAMB (corresponding to LUPUS in the first line): USA OUT (in Portuguese: USA/LAMBUSA ÁGUA DE OUTUBRO/[Lamb] uses water of October to splash [lupus].) Differentiated by typographical characters, other subjacent levels of discourse spread over the page—from indistinct chattering rumor (gulping down speech, utilitarian, enervating admonitions from father to refractory son) to a clarifying final statement in which the admonished young man rebuffs the "paternalistic" ("colonialist") peroration and proclaims his struggle for new values. The poem unfolds in a double mood: subjective-existential and politico-satirical. This discussion is, of course, schematic and simplified with regard to the actual complexity and richness of the original text (published as a folder, a *dépliant*, in *Noigandres Anthology*, 1962).

Augusto de Campos, since his 1953 "poetminus" series, has written several works that are of interest from a Joycean perspective. A good example is the trilingual poem *cidade-city-cité* (1963)—one enormous polysyllabic word, consisting of enchained vocables ending with the suffix *-cidade* and conveying a

somewhat terrifying diorama of a modern "megalopolis" like
São Paulo (whose "omnivoracity" emerges in the process). The
"one-hundred-letter words," or "thunderclaps," of *Finnegans
Wake* are called up by association. Another more explicit instance is
the book-poem COLIDOUESCAPO (1971). Its title, a direct hom-
age to Joyce, derives from the phrase, "Answer: A collideorscape!" (*FW*, 143), taken as an epigraph. By combining its
unbound pages (each of which contains a different segment of a
word), the reader forms new, frequently "portmanteau," words.
On the other hand, the reader's expectation is frustrated by
words which could appear but in fact never do—words that
"collide" or "escape" in a Joycean card game. To give a single
combinatory example: EXISPERO (EXIS+PERO), hinting at EXISTO,
ESPERO, EXASPERO, or, in English, I EXISPAIR (EXIS+PAIR),
suggesting EXIST, DESPAIR, EXASPERATE, EXPIRE.

In 1963 I began to write my BOOK OF ESSAYS / GALAXIES. Its
first fragments were published in numbers 4 (1964) and 5
(1966–1967) of the magazine *Invention* (*Invenção*, S.
Paulo). The book was conceived as an experiment in doing
away with the limits between poetry and prose, and projecting
the larger and more suitable concept of *text* (as a *corpus* of
words with their atextual potentials). A short introduction,
"*Dois dedos de prosa sobre uma nova prosa*" ("Little chat on a
new way of writing")—brought out in *Invenção* 4 under a
Mallarmé epigraph, "*Tout au monde existe pour aboutir à un
livre*"—outlines the project of the book. The *text* is defined as a
"flux of signs," without punctuation marks or capital letters,
flowing uninterruptedly across the page, as a *galactic* expansion.
Each page, by itself, makes a "concretion," or autonomously
coalescing body, interchangeable with any other page for reading
purposes. There are "semantic vertebrae" which unify the whole,
a kind of leitmotiv such as the idea of a book being like travel
and travel like a book ("travel" here is taken in all its possible
meanings, from a transoceanic geographic voyage to daily peri-
pateia, to a psychedelic "trip"). It constitutes a search for "language in its materiality," without "beginningmiddleend."
"Exterior monologue" was the phrase I used to express this
"materiality" "without psychology," that is, language that auto-

enunciates itself. The expression is first found in my 1964 introductory essay, and was employed in deliberate contradistinction to Molly Bloom's "interior monologue," to emphasize an intensified concentration on language by itself, as a kind of locutorial outer space. In one of the first fragments, the book, as its own interlocutor, auto-states itself as *"uma álealenda"* ("an alealegend"), *"um milicoro em milicórdio"* ("a millichorus in millichord"), *"um caleidocamaleoscópio"* ("kaleidochameleonscope").[5] At the time, the more innovative books in French were Michel Butor's *Mobile* (1962) and Maurice Roche's *Compact* (1966), the latter more audacious in its handling of language.[6] Philippe Sollers' *Nombres* (1968) did not offer any noticeable innovation in terms of lexical texture. His first Joycean experiment was *Lois* (1972), parts of which began to appear in *Tel Quel* number 46 (Summer 1971).

In the larger context of Brazilian literature, one cannot help mentioning the work of Guimarães Rosa, especially *Grande Sertão*: *Veredas* (1956). (Its English translation, *The Devil to Pay in the Backlands*, 1963, didn't do justice to the original, missing almost completely its linguistic inventiveness.) Though some Brazilian critics refuse to admit this, the influence of various Joycean processes (from *Ulysses*, in particular) on Rosa's major novel is manifest. And his later work, as for instance the story "Meu Tio o Iauaretê (My Uncle the Jaguar," 1961) or the miscellaneous book *Tutaméia* (*Trifles*, 1967), derives some of its effects from *Finnegans Wake*, or at least from the 1962 Brazilian *Finnegans Wake* anthology.[7]

Recently Paulo Leminski, a young writer from Paraná (southern Brazil), brought out his first novel, *Catatau* (*Chitchat*, 1975). Influenced by Joyce's *Finnegans Wake* and its Brazilian translations, by Rosa's *Grande Sertão*, and by H. de Campos' *Book of Galaxies*, it is a wide-ranging monologue using Descartes (Renatus Cartesius) as soliloquist. The author pretends that Descartes was a member of the Dutch expedition commanded by the Prince of Nassau, who in 1636, with his army, invaded the northeastern coast of Brazil and settled down in Recife. While inspecting Brazilian flora and fauna through a glass, Cartesius smokes a miraculous herb (marijuana) and finds himself dissolving into a tropical delirium, conveyed through Joycean rhetoric.

Even in Brazilian popular music (in its sophisticated urban forms derived from the bossa nova), one finds the stimulating presence of *Finnegans Wake*. Having read the translations in *Panaroma*, the singer-composer Caetano Veloso (who lived for some time in London) introduced typical Joycean verbal games into his songs. One of these, for instance, is ACRILÍRICO, which suggests ACRE, LÍRICO, ACRÍLICO (ACRILYRIC = ACRID, LYRIC, ACRYLIC). It plays with the toponymic SANTO AMARO DA PURIFICAÇÃO, transformed into SANTO AMARGO DA PUTRIFICAÇÃO, by changing *Amaro* (the name of a patron saint) into *amargo* ("bitter"), and *Purificação* ("Purification") into *Putrificação* ("Putrefaction").

The impact of *Finnegans Wake* on Spanish-speaking countries has been more sporadic than systematic. We might mention, however, a forerunner, the Chilean poet Vicente Huidobro. His long poem *Altazor* (begun in 1919, finished in 1931) includes in Canto IV a fragment of great imaginative verbal power which anticipates Joycean influence. This fragment, in the author's own French version, was first published in 1930 in *transition*, in which Joyce's "Work in Progress" had been appearing since 1927. Consider, for instance, Huidobro's crisscross word transmutations, like *l'horitagne de la montazon* instead of *l'horizon de la montagne*, or *mandodelle* (*mandoline + hirondelle*), *lunaile* (*lune + aile*); or in Spanish, *Al horitaña de la montazonte, violondrina, lunala*.[8]

Julio Cortázar, the Argentine writer, continues this tendency in *Rayuela* (1963; translated as *Hopscotch*, 1966), where some passages are written in "gliglic," an invented amorous language. Of course, these are perfectly limited idiomatic "zones," conceived as lyrical moments, emerging autonomously from the book's always imaginative, metaphorical and / or ironical, but otherwise linguistically "normal," fluent prose. More radical from this viewpoint is *Los Tres Tristes Tigres* (1965; translated as *Three Trapped Tigers*, 1972), by the Cuban exile Cabrera Infante. Openly influenced by Joyce's *Ulysses* and by Joyce's forerunners, Laurence Sterne and Lewis Carroll, Cabrera is a master of *calembour* ("punning") and full of verbal wit. As Carlos Fuentes once put it, Cabrera writes in his own "Spunish language." But the clearest example of this sort of transformative language in Castilian is not by a Latin American, but rather by a very gifted young Spanish writer living in Madrid and London, Julián Ríos. Excerpts from his unfinished novel *Larva* were published in number 25 of Octavio Paz' magazine *Plural* (October 1973).

Given the above, one may question whether the labyrinth-minded, paradox-loving old master Jorge Luís Borges was not being ironical, when, in an interview for the Italian magazine *Il Verri* (number 18, 1965), he called *Finnegans Wake* "a book entirely made up of compound-words." "In Spanish," he said, "this is not possible. It is possible in the German languages, maybe in Greek, a language I don't know. The principal virtue of Spanish, it seems to me, is a certain direct character. . . . Spanish does not lend itself to excessively complex verbal games. At least, in my opinion." But he quickly pointed to an exception in Quevedo's "efforts to introduce Latin effects into Spanish" (" . . . a most arduous task . . . Quevedo was a genius, a great poet"), strategically omitting any mention of the Daedalian "prince of darkness" of Spanish letters, Don Luís de Góngora y Argote.[9]

Notes

1. From A. de Campos, "Poetry : Ideogram." The articles and manifestoes of D. Pignatari and A. and H. de Campos were collected in 1965 as *Teoria da Poesia Concreta/Textos Críticos e Manifestos, 1950–1960* (second ed. 1974; Editora Duas Cidades, São Paulo, Brazil). There is an English translation of *Teoria* by Jon Tolman, still unpublished in book form. The present quotation is from *Studies in the Twentieth Century* (ed. Stephen Goode), no. 7 (Spring 1971).

2. From H. de Campos, "The Open Work of Art," Jon Tolman's translation (unpublished).

3. "Panaroma in Portuguese: Joyce Translated," by H. de Campos, with the version of two exhibits, *Jornal do Brasil* (Rio de Janeiro), 15 September 1957; "James Joyce in Finneganscope," double page organized by A. de Campos, with an introductory text and six translated fragments, *Jornal do Brasil,* 22 December 1957.

4. Hayman's book, as well as R. Greer Cohn's 1951 *L'Oeuvre de Mallarmé— Un coup de dés,* were invaluable as sources of inspiration for the Noigandres group, both critics being in accord in emphasizing the heuristic, prospective values in Joyce's and Mallarmé's last works.

5. In 1966, fragments of *Galaxies,* translated into German and preceded by my introduction, "Zwei Finger Prosa über eine Prosa," were published as no. 25 of the ROT series, directed by Max Bense and Elisabeth Walther (*Versuchsbuch/ Galaxien,* Stuttgart). In 1970, through Maurice Roche, some French translations of *Galaxies* were included in the September issue of the Parisian magazine *Change* ("La poétique, la mémoire"), with "Deux doigts de prose sur une nouvelle prose" as introduction.

6. Cf. A. de Campos, "A Prosa é Mobile," *Suplemento Literário de O Estado de São Paulo,* 23 and 30 March 1963 (on Butor's *Mobile*); H. de Campos, "A pele da escritura," *loc. cit.,* 11 October and 1 November 1969 ("The skin of writing," on M. Roche's *Compact,* with a translation of its initial excerpt).

7. Guimarães Rosa was aware of the *Panaroma* translations, and his correspondence with his Italian translator, Edoardo Bizzarri (*J. Guimarães Rosa— Correspondencia com o tradutor italiano,* 1972, São Paulo), reveals his esteem for the critical writings of the concrete poets dedicated to his work. (In A. de Campos, "Um Lance de DÊS do *Grande Sertão*," 1959, and in H. de Campos, "A Linguagem do Iauaretê," 1962, there are several references to Joyce's *Finnegans Wake;* see also Pedro Xisto, A. and H. de Campos, *Guimarães Rosa em Três Dimensões,* 1970, São Paulo.)

8. Cf. A. de Campos, "Vicente Huidobro: Fragmentos de *Altazor*," *Suplemento do Jornal do Brasil,* Rio de Janeiro, 3 March 1957.

9. Borges is an admirer of Joyce. In his 1925 *Inquisiciones* there is an essay on *Ulysses,* and he has dedicated two poems to Joyce ("James Joyce" and "Invocación a Joyce"), praising Joyce's courage ("Qué importa nuestra cobardía si hay en la tierra / un solo hombre valiente") and "obstinado rigor." Borges' essay on Flaubert ("Flaubert y su destino ejemplar," *Discusión,* 1957) ends with a tribute to Joyce, "the intricate and almost infinite Irishman who wove *Ulysses.*"

Augusto de Campos: Poem

atrocaducapacaustiduplielastifeliferofugahistoriloqualubrimendimultipliorganiperiodiplastipubliraprecipRorustisagasimplitenaveloveravivaunivoracidade

city

cité

An interview with Maurice Roche

David Hayman

The French New Novel is over twenty-one now, though some of our critics still treat it as the latest word in French fiction. Many of its tricks are so familiar as to have become bywords, imitations of imitations. This is not to denigrate its contribution, but only to point to other fresher developments in what has been misnamed the New New Novel. Along with Philippe Sollers, the volatile and prolific young editor of *Tel Quel,* Maurice Roche is probably the most interesting novelist in France—interesting and truly gifted. It would be wrong, however, to call him a rising young writer, since he published his first novel, *Compact,* in 1966, when he was over forty (like Céline), after having made a career in musicology (his first book was a study of Monteverdi).

Compact looks for all the world like a concrete poet's plaything, but it quickly reveals itself to be a carefully elaborated deconstruction, not only of the novel as we have known it, complete with its even typographical surface, but also of the experience of reading. It is in fact a semiotic salad, congeries of sign systems with which the reader engages, laughing but with high seriousness.

Compact was hailed and booed by the critics as a new thing and a bad joke. Nothing daunted, Roche followed it with *Circus* (1972), even more outlandish and delightful in its format, even less narrative, more disturbingly funny. More recently, he has published *Codex* or *CodeX* (1974), which purports to unravel the universe, joining the largest and the smallest themes in a manner reminiscent of Mallarmé's *Un coup de dés* and Joyce's *Finnegans Wake*. His latest book, *Opéra bouffe* (1975), illustrates the vitality of this personal mode. Two more novels have been completed.

All of his books are subversive of the conventions of the novel and of the very process of reading. They are post–mass media texts—modern in the ultimate sense, whimsical, outrageous, and most difficult to translate. All of them are pun-filled with cunning and learning; they are encyclopedic, products of a polymath's imagination—an imagination with at least three axes: aural, visual, and verbal. The result is the sort of text which appeals to several senses without becoming a mere toy and which at times resembles a musical composition, at times a cartoon, at times an essay or a tract, but always exhibits the sort of control we expect from an accomplished literary work.

The following conversation (recorded on June 6, 1973), one of the most spontaneous and pleasant I have had, began when Maurice Roche greeted me at the door of his apartment: a slight, wiry, balding man, clad as usual in shorts. It continued over a pint of scotch drunk at a rate which made me forget time and permitted us to fill both sides of my tape. This was only my first encounter with Roche. We later got together for dinner and much more talk, unfortunately untaped.

David Hayman: Perhaps we can begin with a question about your methods of working. You type, of course.

Maurice Roche: Yes, well, my methods are different for each book. I do type, but I always write, always begin by writing out the text longhand. I write it all out in pen and then I type and revise. The typographic effects are coded on the typescript. For example, I typed *Compact* in six colors. It was an insane job. Sometimes to change a word I had to change my ribbon.

D.H.: You use typography to create special effects: disjunction, emphasis, tonality, and what else?

M.R.: There are many other things. You could think of typography, at least in *Compact*, either as a sort of expanded punctuation or as a means of indicating a change in reading tempo.
In fact, there are several narratives in *Compact*. Each narrative has its own personal pronoun, its tense, its syntax. These narratives combine to constitute a single narrative which is quite distinct from all of them. You notice that a given punctuation can provide a certain development. Take, for example, the passages printed in boldface italics in the beginning. We are in the second person singular, the future tense, the familiar address: "You'll lose sleep to the degree that you will lose sight of . . ." And if you decide to read only the passages in boldface italics, you'll be able to follow the development with ease. That goes for each sort of typographically punctuated passage.

D.H.: Is it like Mallarmé's *Un coup de dés?* There too one can follow the typography as well as the total text.

M.R.: Yes, of course you could choose a development. But the book was not written with that sort of development as a focus. These are pointers, if you like, indicating a sort of relief (in the sculptural sense), since each narrative has its locus. I call them narratives for want of a better word. Of course, there are no stories. As one of the journalists said, it's a novel that tells no tales.

D.H.: What about the story of the Japanese doctor who collects tattooed human skin?[1]

M.R.: It's a deception, an illusion.

D.H.: Still, it does duty as narrative.

M.R.: Precisely. It's an illusion which uses the narrative mode, the traditional tale. It becomes derisory, since it is sandwiched in among the other elements. Mathews[2] says it's like the Marx Brothers entering a field of wild flowers. It's a farce, in the etymological sense. It's stuffed, as a chicken is stuffed.

D.H.: It's a farce in that sense and also in the comic sense.

M.R.: Of course, just like the gag. That's what I miss in so much contemporary literature—comic relief. Take the Japanese doctor. It's funny but, when we look closely, it isn't funny at all. Really, it's the most sinister thing in the book. It is a mockery of the experience, of the sad aspect of the book. But the thing that provokes the most laughter is the most lugubrious episode, which is, in fact, the most polemical part. I think there should always be a polemical aspect in any work. You give someone a contract for his skin exactly as you'd give a contract for a book. The clauses are identical. [Laughter throughout.] Sollers speaks about this in his preface to *Compact,* so he too understood. No, there is no true narrative. When there are narrative elements they are mock narratives, as, for example, in Cervantes' *Quixote.* Of course he uses elements of the chivalric romance, but only to reverse his field, to ironize his model.

In my novel each element of the discourse has its own typography and thereby shows the manner in which it should be read. After all, a book is read with the eyes. But it could also be read aloud. Or if it is not read aloud, it still sounds in the inner ear. When we read, we hear. It sounds or it doesn't sound. It makes a particular sort of sound. It's like reading music. That's what I said in my little blurb for *Circus.* The interior ear discloses the phonetic and phonometric architecture of the text. That is why the typography is functional. It is not to beautify, nor is it like Michel Butor's use of typography in *Mobile.* One can see quite well how *Mobile* works through broken sequences, and so on. I wrote *Compact* sequentially. I didn't write the second page before the first, for example. I wrote it page by page. . . .

D.H.: Do you mean that you were writing the discontinuous sequences directly onto the page?

M.R.: That was the hair-raising aspect, you know. I had several outlines which I wasn't able to follow because the book began to generate its own shape. I had to keep everything in my head at once! Of course I had certain formal indices in mind, but I didn't always do what I had intended. That is what interests me: I did not write a line until I had written the preceding line. I did not let my plans stand in the way of my writing.

D.H.: You didn't use scrapbook techniques.

M.R.: Certainly not, I didn't make *collages.* But for *Circus* it was just the opposite. *Circus* had its central focus and then everything shifted. I don't mean that I wrote it haphazardly. I began with a preliminary sense of the book, a vague prevision. But what I had was an idea. It would be a *montage* in the cinematic sense. I knew how it would be organized, but I could write, say, some sequences before certain early ones. But there you have a book in which one can hop about, mixing up the sequences if one wishes. There is a fellow named Georges Charbonnier who has a radio program every Friday. For eight months now, he has been broadcasting interviews and readings from *Circus*. On one of those programs he had a reading by several actors, each taking a series of typographical segments, a completely fragmented reading. *Circus* is truly a book that runs counter to the reader's habits of reading. But it is not a *Mobile* either, because no matter how one reads it—that is, if one goes from page to page . . . . Here, I have written at the very beginning of the book:[3]

$$
\left(
\begin{array}{l}
\textit{Écrit} \\
\text{(s'écrit/secret) s'évaporant à mesure } \quad \text{qu'en lecture de} \\
\text{se condenser (insciemment)} \qquad\qquad \text{en son anagramme} \\
\qquad\qquad\qquad\qquad \text{plus tard} \qquad\qquad\qquad \textit{Récit}
\end{array}
\right)
$$

Which means that, no matter how you read, you will always end up with the same text. When, for example, you find the text set in double columns—and I've tested this out—no matter which aspects you choose to read first, so long as you read every word you always end up with the same text. In *Compact* the opposite applies, because if you change your method of reading you always have another text.

D.H.: But it isn't a good idea to change your approach?

M.R.: No, it was written for that sort of reading. In *Circus*, yes, but you aren't obliged to vary your reading method. You could read it seriatim.

D.H.: Personally, I found *Compact* rather easy to read straight through. It flows.

M.R.: Sure, it's written for that sort of reading. Of course, the directions I have been giving are really of little importance. What is important is that . . . of course not everybody will read the book, since most readers are lazy. . . . Then there is also a sort of typographic aggression. As soon as the reader sees something strange, he rejects it. There's an automatic tension.

D.H.: Mallarmé said that the margin was there to separate the text from the world, to isolate it, in fact. You would probably say something similar about your texts? We are shocked and distanced, but we are also seduced by these effects.

M.R.: Yes, but that is something one shouldn't say, since most of the journalists who have commented on *Circus* have been misled. They saw it as a more or less specialized book in the genre of Concrete Poetry. Certainly not! The trouble is that they didn't bother to read it. At first glance, that is what it seems to be, but . . .

D.H.: But in Concrete Poetry you have virtually no meaning. It's a sort of typographic painting. Personally, I think of Laurence Sterne . . .

M.R.: Ah yes!

D.H.: Joyce . . .

M.R.: Joyce, Sterne, Mallarmé, and Rabelais.

D.H.: And Céline?

M.R.: No, I don't think so. Céline I'd put closer to Sollers' two most recent books. I think that there you really see the influence of Céline, but I don't like Céline myself. I don't see Céline in my work. It's not the same sort of thing. In Céline we have a sort of flail, a verbal flail. His argot is an affront. Of course you find argot in *Compact* too, but always as part of a play of appearances. Sometimes it's a false argot. That is, it may be a term in argot but it may also have a meaning in heraldry, a musical sense, and so on. I don't want to suggest that there is a deliberate attempt in my work to exploit *polysemy*. In *Circus* I exploit *asemy*; that is, as a result of forcing all the senses of a word, I finish by emptying it completely of meaning. When we have uncovered or discovered all the codes, all the clichés, et cetera, after saying "but it's obvious," one realizes that, far from it, there is a lot of information lost. And the word is completely empty. It ends up as a little sketch and that's why you return to the hieroglyphic, and that's why I don't include footnotes. I know quite well what the passages in Egyptian hieroglyphics mean, as well as the Aztec hieroglyphs, and so forth. What I'm showing is that the design of words in the Latin letters we possess is pretty punk, a flop. [Laughter] Perhaps one could give it more vigor through typography, but I don't think so. The more we exaggerate the use of type, the more we manage to empty, nullifying all these codes.

There is something else we forgot to mention, something which really impressed me when I read it. It's *Bouvard et Pécuchet* by Flaubert. I feel closer to that than to Céline. They tell me that Céline was a new Rabelais. It's not true! It's something else! It's even a frank exhibition of populism but pushed to its limits with genius. It seems that Céline really wanted to write popular fiction. He had a friend [Eugène Dabit] who wrote *Hôtel du Nord*, a novel that really sold. He wanted to do the same. It just happened that he had verbal gifts the others lacked. But he really wanted to write popular fiction.

D.H.: In the beginning, yes. But later . . .

M.R.: Later, no. Despite everything, he had a language which resonates in the inner ear. It has a fine sound. That doesn't mean it's beautiful or pretty. Racine's has a fine sound too, and I hate it.

D.H.: It's beautiful in another way.

M.R.: Yes, it is. When I say it has a fine sound, I don't mean that it is pretty or even pleasant to hear. On the contrary, it's even extremely harsh sounding. And then when we consider the typography, type also possesses an element of reading, perhaps reading aloud. That's something to think about. In the distant past there were those who read and then those who read aloud and listened to themselves. That's a textual dimension which we ought to try to restore, because Mallarmé reads very well . . . and Joyce . . . and Beckett. If *Finnegans Wake* is read aloud, I swear . . .

D.H.: Precisely. Sollers is very proud of having preserved in his translation from the *Wake* the rhythms and tonalities of the original. He's very interested in the sounds.

M.R.: Sure! But don't be fooled! Sollers is one of the very few who are interested. I'd say that he is the only one today. What bothers me is that when (and I really admire certain writers like Robbe-Grillet, and others)—when I read them, I find that . . .

D.H.: Their tonalities are flat.

M.R.: Yes, it's the "zero degree," but I would ask, Why use only that, why not use it all? Use all the verbal potential of a period. Take, for example, Monteverdi in his time; he used everything from the dramatic madrigal to the recitative. I think we must use all the possible elements of a language and even other languages and even . . . we're not in a period of the zero degree.

D.H.: But when one uses a very limited range of tones . . .

M.R.: Careful! We mustn't confuse economy and poverty! I read lots of books. I don't think that I just write anything that comes into my head. It's all carefully controlled. It may not seem that way, but it is. When they say something is deliberately done, it is often done deliberately because the writer can't do better. [Laughter] I know some composers who would be happy to have their music performed by 150 musicians. That doesn't mean that the result would be less good with only ten.

D.H.: I notice that of all your themes the most prominent is the skull.

M.R.: Ah, the skull! I have a whole collection here.

D.H.: You know, a couple of years ago I wrote an article on the broken skull in three writers—Zola, Rilke, and Céline. So your theme really interests me.

M.R.: I'll show you something. I have all sorts of skulls, postcards from all over, stamps with skulls. [Laughter] There are some really bizarre things, by the way. I'll show you one. I have a friend who has just turned *Compact* into a comic strip [Françoise Rojare].[4] She did it using very sharply contrasting colors. A part of it was published in the review *Change*, but in black-and-white only.

You know I've quit *Change*, but I was among the founders. In fact, I chose the title, and the idea for the colophon is mine. They won't say anything about it, but it's true. Anyway, look here in *Compact*, toward the end, where it deals with the skull. You know *Compact* is a book which lacks one word. One noun/name is lacking, that's all. It is finally a question of a missing persona. All these characters—if there are any characters and there are really none—speak of several narratives but in different locales: for example, New York, Tokyo, and so forth. These are also fantastic locations, deformed or at least somewhat altered. It is a question of projection. But it is always about midnight, so, with the play on global time, it's never the same spot and, though it is the same time, it is always a different global time. But of course the skull underlies everything. If you read here (this is a book you have to read pencil in hand), you find a description of the configuration of a death's head:

Impasse des Catacombes.
We are seated side by side, my companion and I, with our backs to the entrance. In the large glass fixed opposite us, at the other end of the room, we can see the picture we make in this decor: the low arched entry; right underneath, our two heads at some distance from one another; to the right and left the points of jutting springers protrude slightly. At the center of the table a bottle (of beer, a house joke!) between two glasses. We felt we were contributing figures in some ghostly calligram: our image reduced to the dimensions of a skull (and we within).
We had a night club (boîte de nuit) *in our heads . . .*[5]

[As he reads, he draws the following sketch of two diners in a night club:]

There you have it in the form of a hidden figure (*calligram*), rather like in certain films when one image is replaced by another—say, by an advertisement. The spectator/reader doesn't see the image but it has its impact subliminally. Dominique Roland called today to tell me that he had suddenly noticed the skull and was going to begin his essay in the *Nouvel Observateur* with the sentence: "Here is a book shaped like a skull." But what is really funny is that one day I received this. [With considerable delight he shows me and comments on a postcard featuring a couple seated behind a table in a vaulted room.]

D.H.: All this reminds me of Beckett. *Endgame* takes place in a skull; *we* are in the skull with its two windows.

M.R.: Yes. Here you have two people looking at a mirror which reflects their own cranial nature. They are inside, but at the same time they are not within. In the passage which deals with the mirror, it is this effect of going through the mirror which leads us to *Circus*.

You remember I was speaking of the absent noun/name in

Compact. We find that word in the skull of *Circus*. This is rather odd because the inspiration just came to me at the end of a line. You know I don't only type, I also write with a pen. That's very important because you scratch and scrape . . . Here it is: *Roche* arrives in the shape of a skull:

D.H.: You chose the skull because it is the image of your thought. . . .

M.R.: I didn't really choose the skull. . . . Listen, I have plenty of things to say about the skull. It's also the city. It's the locus of all the lost cities. It's also the locus of the brain. In fact, *Circus* doesn't end with the skull but with the brain, with the contents rather than the container. A tour of the city. As a matter of fact, the plan of *Compact* was not a true outline or a précis. It was more like a spatial plan, a superposition of city maps.

D.H.: There are references to maps in the book.

M.R.: Yes, city plans/maps. Superimposing all these city maps, reducing or enlarging where necessary. After all, New York is much larger than Papeete. We get them all to the same format. There is an itinerary within these cities which constitutes the real plan/structure of *Compact*. These travels take place, of course, inside, since everything takes place within a series of ghostly sequences, in the city/skull.

D.H.: You know, this reminds me of Conrad, who uses the skull as the symbolic locus for the action in *The Secret Sharer* . . .

M.R.: There is also the skull-shaped inkwell in Roussel, in *Locus Solus*. There is another skull in Edgar Poe . . .

D.H.: In "The Gold Bug."

M.R.: Yes. You know the skull is also a remarkable object, a visual object. One can move one's fingers inside it, one can . . . I think it was Picasso who discovered that if you put your thumb in here and the fingers this way you create a true piece of sculpture. He said a while ago, "God is a great sculptor." So you see the image of the skull leads us finally to the lost noun/name of *Compact*, or rather to the missing word concealed in this cranial image from *Circus*. Of course I didn't plan that effect. Luckily . . . because if one could plan everything, it wouldn't be interesting.

I want to show you something from the book I just delivered to Seuil . . . a sort of tract . . . the word "peace" written in all sorts of languages and handwriting but arranged in the form of a skull. Then there is that citation from Monteverdi as the arch of the skull. You notice that the exclamation points are falling like bombs. You'll see when you read *Codex* that that book is much closer to the political problems implicit in my work than the other books.

D.H.: I noticed some political references in *Circus*.

M.R.: Yes, in *Circus* and even a few in *Compact,* but less obvious.

D.H.: The references are rather harsh in *Circus* when you talk about America . . . Russia, even India . . .

M.R.: Oh, yes, I really love India. You know I was attacked because of the passage on India. Funny, isn't it? It was that passage which was read on the radio last week. It was a very hard text to write. I had to condense it considerably for *Circus*. It's reduced to notations so that the reader can add details of his own. I think we should try to write "do-it-yourself" books.

D.H.: Mallarmé used to say just that, and of course you say so in your next text.

M.R.: Right, and that's why they ask me to write theoretical pieces, et cetera. I mention theoretical fictions in the beginning of the book and that's the point. The book should have its theoretical dimension. If you have to explain your book with a theoretical text, that means the theoretical essence is not in the book itself, where it belongs.

D.H.: You know, writers like Joyce and Beckett don't explain themselves.

M.R.: Generally, you ought not to have to explain yourself. But today you feel obliged to say what you're doing because so many people ask you to. Sure, you can always explain your methods, always talk about them. There's a fellow named Alain Duault who just wrote that you shouldn't talk *about*, you should speak *within, Circus*.[6] That is, every aspect of the book has to work or it's a failure. If I were to say, I did this or that . . .

Here's a reference to Benveniste, a reference to Jakobson . . .
O.K.! But if by chance it flops, you look cute, eh?

D.H.: But, after all, you either see the allusions or you don't.
If you miss them, so what?

M.R.: Sure. They aren't always there to be noticed, but then,
yes, sometimes yes. After all there are several levels. It's a
labyrinth.

D.H.: I was thinking of the labyrinth as an image. It's the
verso of the brain or skull image.

M.R.: Ah, yes, but the labyrinth is very clearly there as an
image.

D.H.: A rather popular image these days. You have it again
in Joyce, but also in Robbe-Grillet . . .

M.R.: That's his best book, I think. It's the only book that's
on target. The last two books, they're . . . He has a fine talent,
but *Dans le labyrinthe* . . . O.K., I liked *La Jalousie* too . . .
but if he had only continued developing along the lines of *Le
labyrinthe* . . . strange that it had to stop at that point. He made
the mistake of writing "theoretical" texts (let's put that in quotes
because he is not much of a theoretician).

D.H.: Like Zola?

M.R.: There you are . . . except once he established his little
system, he couldn't leave it. If he had done something different,
it wouldn't have fit his prescription. He shut himself up in his
own system. But I'm being unjust. I found out when I was at
Aix delivering some lectures a few months ago, that when
Robbe-Grillet was asked what was the most interesting work
being done, he answered that it was my work, or something of
the sort.

D.H.: There are plenty who would agree. When I asked
Tzvetan Todorov, he said you were the most interesting novelist
writing now.

M.R.: You know it's hard to be in the position of a really
contemporary novelist these days. They put you right off into
the experimental category, the avant-garde, but Zola was also
in the avant-garde.

D.H.: I've always felt that any author who did something
good had to be revolutionary, even Fielding and certainly
Sterne, Flaubert . . .

M.R.: Of course, Sterne, Flaubert . . . even Zola . . . were experimentalists. But, you know, now it's become a sort of duty. There is a barrier, a hurdle . . . but I suppose Sollers spoke to you about that. There is a sort of censor. It isn't that they confiscate your books, but they do write articles in the *Figaro*.

[This was followed by an intermission during which the tape was changed and Maurice Roche reminisced about Sollers and Julia Kristeva and Kristeva's sister. The interview proper reopened on a humorous note when Maurice Roche admired my new Japanese tape recorder.]

Ah, the honorable Japanese. [Laughter at this reference to the tattoo-collecting doctor in *Compact*.] Here is something that might amuse you. Where you now have only the Japanese, there was originally also a Chinese.

D.H.: Do you read Japanese or Chinese?

M.R.: I don't speak Japanese, but I do read it . . . but not Chinese. I learned it because I had a Japanese girlfriend, a pianist, who taught me. I can read and write it too, with difficulty. You know, I can read almost all the major languages, but I have trouble speaking them. [Notices that the markings on the machine place the *rewind* button before the *play* button.] Now that's really Japanese: backward comes before forward. There is a passage I'd like to quote from *Codex*: *"Petites choses en grand ce qui ne laisse pas de les rendre effrayantes. Faire du commerce. Savoir . . . "*[6] And here in Chinese: " . . . power is on the level of the rifle," or literally, "laugh in the face of guns." Then there is a reversal of field: two clasped hands with the word "honorable," which would be Japanese, followed by the Chinese expression "precious" . . . *"tigre de papier. . . . Recontrer, faire ami-à Miami . . ."* And then you have in Arabic: "revolutionary violence against social crime." That one won't please everyone either, but you know I rather like my little Sino-Japanese dialogue.

D.H.: That reminds me of the dialogue in the last section of Joyce's *Finnegans Wake* between St. Patrick and the Druid, also done in Sino-Japanese. . . . You said earlier that you were among the first in France to have read *Finnegans Wake* and *Ulysses*.

M.R.: Yes, *Ulysses* first, at the suggestion of Sylvia Beach and Adrienne Monnier. That was in 1945–46, right after the war.

It was an epiphany for me. You know, I did the music for the play *Epiphany*, a play with Gérard Philippe in it. Did I take hell for that one! You know, even Adrienne Monnier wrote some really nasty things about my music in the *Mercure de France*. But I can over-look that. When I was very young I was vaccinated against criticism, but at that time it had its effect. I didn't even dare show anyone what I was writing. You should know what I had to take! Even from some musician friends like Pierre Boulez, for example, who hadn't yet arrived. But there were two or three people, like Michel Leiris, but not many, who were . . . Baudelaire said something about the scarcity of the chosen that gives paradise its value, so . . .

D.H.: But to return to *Finnegans Wake*. I see from time to time a citation, but I see more in the way of the spirit of the *Wake*.

M.R.: Yes, no—well, there is a sort of citation from *Finnegans Wake* or at least a sort of citation, rather a *prélèvement*. I'm using something resembling the technique of concrete music—mon-tage, if you wish, or the sort of montage you can effect with the moug synthesizer. You may have noticed in *Compact* the aggres-sion caused, for example, by sonorous moments. There are sonorous moments all through *Compact*, you know.

D.H.: You speak music a great deal in *Compact*.

M.R.: Yes, there is even an anal-erotic passage made up of words which have one erotic meaning, another sense in the context of a description of a musical work—in particular a treatment of the musical background in Bach—and also a meaning in terms of rugby. This amalgam of elements constitutes an elaborate leg-pull. But on the other hand, you find descriptions of sonorous phe-nomena, clock chimes, and so on. Again, there are moments when the book oscillates, when, for example, the *tu* and the future tense oscillate toward the *vous* and the conditional tense: the moment when the father appears, introducing the skull theme. You know, there is some Hamlet in there too—the father's ghost in the form of a reminiscence. We get to the *vous* and the conditional since the father is also absent. The *tu* and the intimate mode oscil-late toward the *vous*. The first person, *je*, oscillates toward the *nous* but remains in the present tense. And this *nous* is no longer us. That is, it comes from the outside as fragments of radio broad-casts, described in the passage on page 144: "I could cross the universe, slice through it with the aid of this compact device broad-

casting city $\left\{\begin{array}{l}\text{views [French: } plans] \\ \text{maps, far off . . . distanced one from the other . . . ''} \\ \text{bridges}\end{array}\right.$

So you see the city maps become city bridges—that is, fragments of towns crumbling and falling "separated by the 'empty holes' [their parentheses]" when we turn the radio dial, "and all simultaneously present in the immobility and at times the silence of the box." There, it's the box of the radio, but it suggests the structure of the skull (*"la boîte cranienne"*). You hear in your head sounds coming from within the box next to you. The personal *nous* becomes *"nous sommes à l'écoute du monde"* or *"nous sommes partout";* or, more precisely, *all* and *everywhere* comes to you and you have the feeling that you are everywhere, but that's an illusion. While dying of cancer (like one of the personae of the book), you listen to the radio. You are still at home, not on the moon with the astronauts, despite the illusion.

I used a great many tricks to suggest radio sound effects. I had to get my noises somewhere. I could have invented my own. They'd say I had extraordinary verbal gifts. Of course, it can be done. All you have to do is close your eyes and type. But here I drew on my experience, using concrete items. One item was immediately available to me: Rabelais' frozen words. You know the episode of the tempest where the words melt and fall. I took those words and something occurred to me that I hadn't seen in any of the critics of Rabelais or in the musicologists. I noticed that these words, which Rabelais himself says are words heard in the clash of battle—these words are also citations. They are the onomato-poetic sounds from the *Bataille de Marignon*, the polyphonic song by Clement Jannequin. So I put that song into *Compact*, reduced of course to *pam pom pom*. Let's see if I can find it. But there you are, I wanted to use Rabelais' noises to imitate the noise of turning the radio dial, but Rabelais too was taking those effects from Jannequin.

Ah, here's the citation:[8]

amas de cris chaotiques : interjections, vocables
« de « heurt à l'heure du choc », bataille « a capella » :

—	ra ri ra —	la la ta ri	ra ti ra la	ta ri ra ri
	Ponponponpon	Pon Pontue!	vonvonvonvon	Pa ti tue!

«	ra — Don'-nons	des Gnons! zin' zin'	tri que ti que	chi pe
	Pon — Don'-nons	des Gnons! tue! von	pa ti pa tac	choc

«	Cho pe	tor che	lorgne borgne bredelin brededac frr frrr
	Pa tac	tor che	

« frrrr — Quelle dégelée! —

        ... bouboubouboubouboubou...]

You see the sound sequence concludes with the expression
"*Quelle dégelée!*" In argot a *dégelée* is a brawl, it's knocking the
stuffing out of someone. So we have a reference to Rabelais' famous
frozen words which permits me to bridge the different sequences.
You can identify the different programs as they pass: here you have
intermingled the musical background and a rugby game, "*les
clameurs remplissent le stade,*" et cetera, and then we again pick up
the frozen words. Also serving as a transitional sound effect, Joyce's
thunderword from *Finnegans Wake*. Of course, it's not only Joyce's
thunder, but God's. "Joyce" in argot is *jouisse*, or sexual enjoyment. It's used first as a suggestive notation, but after all it is also
a citation, like those Joyce himself used. But not in the same way.
Joyce did it in a more coherent manner. Here the wordplays are
cut up in little pieces.

D.H.: All this has its comic side, but your books have also
another aspect which interests me particularly. I'm thinking of their
resemblance to works which I call portable infinities. These are
books which never finish, which lend themselves to no definitive
reading, which change every time they are read. . . . And there
are quite a few works like this—Goethe's *Faust*, Mallarmé's *Un
coup de dés*, even Flaubert's *Sentimental Education*, Joyce's
Portrait, all of Joyce's major work, Beckett, who is inexhaustible.
All these are in the same genre. They are works that should not be
comprehended, but that should be lived and relived.

M.R.: Yes. I like the concept and hope that that is what my work accomplishes.

D.H.: In your work there is the rhythmic aspect, the allusive component, the visual aspect . . .

M.R.: That's important, but along with the visual aspect there has to be the audible. I think a book should have all the dimensions.

D.H.: Do you mean the audible dimension, sonority, which we find in post-Flaubertian work?

M.R.: Yes, the hollering chamber [*gueuloir*]!

D.H.: Since Flaubert, writers often think of how their language sounds. When you write, you also listen.

M.R.: Yes, but you have to understand that sometimes the audible aspect contradicts the sense.

D.H.: Do you find such contradictions in your work?

M.R.: Sometimes, yes, but they're intentional contradictions.

D.H.: What about your latest book?

M.R.: Ah, *Codex* is something else. It's another experience. You know, I could have written five or six little *Compacts*. The same fellow who said that *Compact* was a madman's book six years ago now says that *Circus* is a madman's book, and it's too bad because *Compact* was a splendid book. In a sense I find that reassuring. They've really printed that! Just recently . . . and this didn't please me, not because I was personally affected but because it's an indicator of a particular turn of mind . . . A magazine called *Pourquoi pas*, published in Belgium, very reactionary, made a real plea for my confinement in an asylum. You know, if the fellows who write for those journals were in power . . . They can't have read the book. Because if they had read it, if they knew how to read, it would have been worse. You know there are some people who *can* read! *Compact* can't be sold in Canada. It's on the Index. The clergy know how to read! You know, I have a young friend who got his baccalaureate in Canada. They even read Molière in an expurgated edition. That means I have been read by the Canadian priests. But I'm in good company, with *Madame Bovary*.

[What followed was an amusing but untranslatable show-and-tell session during which Maurice Roche illustrated his use of music as part of the implicit structure of the books, and also his use of the skull image while describing a forthcoming (November 1974) production of *Circus*. A quality of Maurice Roche's work is its adaptability to other media—dramatic readings, cartoons, productions with music. In this case, the production was by the French specialist in interviews of writers, Georges Charbonnier, and his composer wife, Janine Charbonnier. Roche promised that it would be very amusing, complete with all the circus acts as rendered by Roche and adapted by Charbonnier.]

Notes

1. The dying protagonist has willed his skin away in exchange for promises of care.

2. Harry Mathews, the American novelist, has translated two portions of Roche's work for the *Paris Review*.

3. "*S'écrit*," or "writes itself," plays against its homonym "secret." Words evaporate in the reading, finally imprinting on the unconscious mind of the reader the anagram for *écrit* or the tale (*récit*).

4. See "Traduction graphique d'un fragment de *Compact* de Maurice Roche," *Change*, V (Paris, Seuil, 1970).

5. *Compact* (Paris, Seuil, 1966), p. 164.

6. In *Encres Vives* (Printemps 1973), "Spécial Maurice Roche," pp. 126–130.

7. *Codex* (Paris, Seuil, 1974), p. 158.

8. *Compact*, p. 156.

Maurice Roche: Funeral cantata

To the disappearance of the persona (   ),
having patiently awaited nothing — et al;

and, yet, "THE UTTER PEON (K=He) IS GOADED INTO MISQUOTES THESE

CAPIT$_{ALS}^{ULATING}$ „

Having been merry(played, doubled over with laughter)
having quartered himself (to become a more fus-
able mass) a number of times — having, further, been ex-

plo$_d^{it}$ed — to sum himself up (igitur) closes in
on himself, up in himself [Ballbauble wiper,
candle snuffer]

$\qquad\qquad$ replicates himself

$\qquad\qquad$ re$_{as}$sembles himself

The slice (of life) suckled — of every "dear th-
roe in mating"... Propose a toast and drink fast
to lose oneself

In commemoration of this event and in
honor of zilch, to create a disturbance
a "mess for the dead"

Adjust the "crown of voiced virtue" on the
mummy's head — Permitting the recital triumphant of the holy Book.
Render a mouth unto the dead through incan-
tations and recall him to his name. (   ).

REQUIRE EITHER TERM OR NAME
Real ease when all is terminated quite
Ended for it surely has to
End the final term ushering in
The great ray of hope in napalm
Or in hydrogen
All this carrion wasted will serve as manure
For growing growing
The grotesque gross greenbacks
Having treated oneself (sumptuously)
On the burden-
Some beast
Summarily — sleeping with terminal slumber

Carillon awakes them, keeps ringing! — Leave us alone! —
For mercy's sake, let us snooze...

DIES, ERE EYE,   runny with angry tears,
Can blink at the glow of eternal darkness.

In the final analysis, made
Only to be busted;
Lovely solution — elegantly mathematical and
Severe! Oh!   desire

Bugger off
Leave us rest in peace!
Making us tremble before/behind because of the context

social in its compact form: the cassock hier/ket

Face to the inquisitor to be put through the wringer/to the test

Answer!

(SERGEANTS SUMMON:)
                        TO BASE, MORONS! — per sepulchra
Regionum —. The trumpet sounds
(Reveille)
Rise up! Muster! To the spade!
To the pick — gravediggers!
Attention/ive! Eyes front: Mors stupebit...

The instrument of tor/al crea ture   "object eternal
of the eternal vengeances of the Eternal" —
with punishment as its object.

. . . .

LIBERATE THIS CRYPT TO US - - - - - Read, decode the cryptic
Yellow Pages
Blue Book , Great Book of the Sky
World
the Memo where all writes divinely (already!)
(the inscription on the parchment of dental
skin...

What to do with five letters? —:
Spine, Venal, Navel, Penis, Roche?

After soundings, the prognostics) — to know
Who will have scientifically earned perdition?

On the pot, ? LATENT, APPEARS A BIT QUEER — QUITE!
quidquid latet apparebit,
Not ass-holitary chance of Dis-missal

Here.

QUEEN'S TOMB: HIS HAIRy ass? — Me, absolute in crement!
ex
WHo — and despite whOm —
just scares the crap out of (,)

the Just
why (?)
(not)?

86

EXTRA!
     MEN DIE; MAGI INTESTATE - - - Terrible!
before collecting your cash, cough;
then get the hell out of here!
                         This much is guaranteed:
pushing pansies by the root. For the moment,
not a peony! To be freely saved are those who
are not in need of relieving themselves for nothing.
                                   A sign :

Hep! Help!

RECORD OF ARREST/Coroner's report: a deficit in
cerebral circulation: intellectual aesthenia (following
a quodilibetal thesis?), loss of memory (after a prolonged interrogation!), decrease in altertness (result
of overheated coitus...)

That's why) - - - - - - - - - - - - - - - -
- - - what? (- - - - - - - - - - - - - - -:

PILFERAGE GYPS US
Hasn't that old slut Passion
Been around long enough?
The X-man's cross, that cork-
Screw......................

INGENIOUS CODE: What? I put this...

                              in the classifieds(!) it
costs nothing. But what does it bring in? To nevertheless
feel capable of
     culpable for   doing it shamefacedly — as when forgetting
oneself, some evening from time to time, while dipping
one's coocookie somewhere out Madeleine's way...

First of all, die! They'll know how to exploit
your job. Rest easy, nothing will go to
waste.
        They'll lay to rest what's left
in the boss's pocket.
   the fruitful soil.

Not content with having skinned you,
                              fleeced
they'll manage to sodomize your carcass: Now that's enterprise
        (playing (funeral) parlor games: it sure aids digestion to spa⟩

the bottom of the upper echelon). And they'll

fetch you — a smart blow! — from there

— (after)!

      ... doing his job, the turnkey bids

farewell and seals the portal ...

on the right!

CUNT/FOOL, TASTE THIS

"Tube eater, gnaw too big phallus: the quested portion...

"Waiter!...

      Having $\genfrac{}{}{0pt}{}{\text{been busy}}{\text{done business}}$ with his own death

      <u>long enough not to imagine</u> (it) — all

      the while wishing it — <u>for others</u>

      Genuflecting, exposing his "mound inverted"

      at the omega point, at the fateful hour

      fretfully imploring, licking boots during

      impalement...

      Then impelled to watch his ultimate instant

      trimmed and his last gasp plugged

      (Gulp!)

BLACK CRIME, OH SADISTS: "YES —
"I said yes I will yes"

I.R.A. (id i

                                                           period

The dawn (soberly greeted with arms at order) of a period

Daybreak.
              They awaken you   better
     to be put to sleep, in the end!

                         Face front! At a sign — represen-
                                    ting something (what?)
                                    for someone   (who?)
                                    Aim!

                                    Execution!   At ease!

     Now and forever done with dawns to bawl about

          DEAD FOR HAVING LOOKED LIFE IN THE FACE

SANCTIONS DOMINATE US, constipate us
WAX-SEAL OUR BUTTocks; all id needs to
bust out is to boot the Other; while one
makes off with the prints and the laurels
to create volume — — —

Before/dossier/ — leaning against on the

.......(Fulfill) (one's)duty bound to fulfill (one's).......

Giving Nanny a good fright in mid-sexercize
        Our friends Nannies are our Nannies.

AN ASS...HEY! —
             D-DAY "HEE! haw! hee!
haw!" — hellabaloo! Amalgamate yourselves
take, like a good democrat, all positions
simultaneously
Amalgamate yourselves well in your poses
and eternal reposes --
                   Pause

DORMANT AGE (JAILS INCREASE STAYS)

                exploited/parasitic

the dead bea^{s}ts of the REV^E_OL^A_UTION

what do they symbolize?

            before losing this $^{re}_{se}$verable head

            to pay the (day of) reckoning —

            hear the bad news and take a pow-

            der against the tension(wired) head

            aches craning nearby//

            throw in the condemned man's last drink

               add ice

$$\left[a \quad cu^p_{re} \right]$$

                     $^a_1$va   (dosage prescribed by the sawbones)

           [Pater My Glory

           that pate with the stereometric mug

                          magic

           portrait if ever was

                  concave relief — anti-

       matter according to the formula for metaphor(

)?

                    other fellow

      following you with his eyes in your eyes]

                    follow me!

                                              (re-)
lease yourself!   en(cou-)
rage yourself! against them all!

(all together) resurrected, mas(s)ter ✝ abated,
we kneel before the creator

          For ^his^ sake in prayer

               PORCINE   CONFITEOR

O'er the remnants we watched the sunset's eerie darkness:

Flagrant proof that the night was still there — summing up

History

Gehenna's lovely promises having been kept

> [A margin between what is
> predicted and what ONE
> TAKES
>> [his word]
> (and in this margin
> inscribe glosses)]

even under torture, before the keeper, the

questionnaire,

I indulge in skullduggery

On the day that one dies one should have to change

names

—*translated by Carl Lovitt*

from Partie

Hélène Cixous

Translator's note: Prolegomania and excerption
Hélène Cixous is a French novelist, dramatist, essayist, and editor. Her doctoral dissertation, *L'Exil de James Joyce ou l'Art du remplacement* (Grasset, 1968), published in English by David Lewis (1972), has been followed by numerous articles on, and introductions to, Joyce's work. Professor of English literature at the Université de Paris VIII-Vincennes, she has frequently lectured on Joyce in the U.S. and Canada. While the diversity of her work defies description, at present Cixous is widely known in France and abroad for the radical positions she has taken, in public and in print, on topics ranging from the global processes of signification in literature and society to the contemporary analysis of sexuality from a feminist perspective.

Since the publication of *Neutre* (Grasset, 1971), Cixous's writing has been marked by a distortion of normal syntax and an irreverence for morphemic integrity associated with the Joyce of the *Wake*. Her texts tend to gravitate around a nexus of key signifiers, each of which acts as a crucible for creative transgression. From each signifier is generated a string of puns, homonyms, portmanteau words that carry along an often waning narrative development.

Cixous's texts take on, wrangle with, current discourses that are ordinarily considered extraliterary, most characteristically the psychoanalytic discourses of Freud, Lacan, and the philosophic discourses of Hegel, Nietzsche, Derrida. Hence, again, the downplaying of strict narrative continuity—as, for example, when a certain *je* of *Neutre* debates with *it*self the validity of the oedipal theory.

Much of this comes together (though Cixous would abjure any notion of synthesis) in her most recent novel, *Partie* (Editions des Femmes, 1976). The volume is composed of two parts (*parties*), *Plus-je* and *Si-je*, which are in reciprocal relation to one another. *Plus-je* begins at one end of the volume (probably the "beginning," since it includes the credits of the author and a fake epigraph) and ends on page 90, with the date "September 1972." *Si-je* begins at the other end (with all puns intended, as will be seen) and ends on page 66, with the same date. The two ends are face to face, only inverted, page 66 appearing at first (in terms of linear reading space) as page 99. But in order to carry on the correct (?) reading of *Partie*, the volume must be turned over *and* around.

This reciprocality is, furthermore, inscribed on the cover of each end. An Egyptian goddess stretches her body around an imago of the world in the top half of the cover and does the same across the bottom half, but in inverted order. In other words, the cover inscription is not a mirror image of the goddess containing the world but a double presentation of that image, in the manner of the photographic process of negative reversal. The top image had to be turned over *and* around in order to produce the bottom image. Similarly, the front cover, including title at left and author's name at right, is negatively reproduced by the back cover, where author is on the left and title on the right.

Trying to talk about the physical presentation of *Partie* puts me, the reader/translator, into the critical, libidinal bind that the book is about. *Plus-je* is the body-self-becoming-unitary (and more), a warrior who sets out like Achilles of the *Iliad* to act, and discovers something about himself in the process. The relation of personage to title to reader, however, is immediately and irrevocably confused, making a mockery of the Homeric parallel inscribed in the puns. Homer is *Hommère* (Manmother); *Plus-je* is agent but also terrain (just as the Homeric epic is named for the place of the Other and not for the hero); the reader is *L'ecteur* (literally "reader," but also "the Hector," the adversary). Most important, *Plus-je* (always italicized in the text, though orthographically in flux) is "more-I," more me, more-than-one, a text coming into an awareness of itself (through parallel columns of text on a page, inverted typography, and discontinuous paginal sequencing), and its relation to its scriptor is without explicit reference to identity. (Hélène is, after all, in bondage—Helen of Troy, Hélène of Cixous: *"Tous les noms de la rien c'est 'Hélène,' c'est un trout, c'est pas quelque chose"* [76]).

Once *Plus-je* gets himself together, becoming *Plusje*, he dreams of/has revealed to him, through a great physical and verbal agon, *Si,je* (*"A Plus je Si,je est rêve ailée"*). From the multitudinous subject is born the intersexual subject. This is the end of *Plus-je* (minus the last page):

> *And he has only to find her. She can only be in the one place in the world that he hasn't furrowed: his own body. [. . .]*
> *So she had been there all the time! [. . .]*
> *And to this name [Si.je] he gives the name of beauty. (89)*

Is it the birth of Athena in the guise of Aphrodite, the creation of a monstrosity, or the breath of inspiration? No one knows. One thing may be clear: *Si-je* is *Plus-je*, with a difference: sexual, inverted, in a dream (hence unconscious?).

If *Plus-je* is the body-self-becoming-unitary, then *Si-je* is the body-self-dissociating, having only *je* in common with its pseudo-generator—and *"Je n'en reviennent plus"* at the end of *Si-je*. If *Plus-je* plays on the *Iliad* analogy and on the formation of a subject in a work named after the place of the Other, then *Si-je* plays on an Odyssean analogy and the formation of a subject going out to encounter the Other, determining him/herself in terms of Others, in a work named for its hero. There is little consistency in either of these analogies. If *Plus-je* is a broadly male (non)personage, then *Si-je* is the leading female entity, exquisitely divided and diffused, desirous of all ambivalences, in the flip side of the mock epic that is *Partie*.

Bear in mind that what follows (the end of *Plus-je* plus the birth of *Si-je*, placed apart as a preface, hors d'oeuvre) cannot mime the physical manipulation of the book (*l'ivre*, page 65 et passim), required to move from *one* textual ending to an *other* textual opening. Such a negative reversal process you have in each one of me.
He will wrIte no more, unwilling to appropriate a text de-signed to explode precisely any notion of the integrated subject, sexual difference, private property, and the bourgeois dream of internal consistency.*

"Mais il faut tout de même signer"

Keith Cohen

[*End of* Plus-je]

Between me and me and betweenme and betweenme and be-tweenme and me and me and me. Bound for rejoicing and rebound to her soul o seed to seed, inconsieveable I am lost to all of you entire, at a loss of me all the moreso me all the moreso me plus you re spiring me on your spirals you giving ussuck at our breast aspirating us her-dling us sucklewing us on wings on souls and on blood-milk.

me as you my mouth, you my mother her self outstretched
on you as me
your self my lips, your mouth
for she is the one who opens heaventuality
myself your breath my mellifer-us
my mellifinest portion mell-if-you-suck my parts
her-dling, my self your milk me
your self abound my her-dled blood.

September 1972

* Cf. Hélène Cixous, "The Character of Character," *New Literary History*, V, 2 (Winter 1974), and "The Laugh of the Medusa," *Signs*, 4 (Summer 1976).

Si-je: *Plasteapart*

If,I? will be taken as the sighn of onceupondicate undisciplined, undeknowable diffissions.

Everything that wishes to be vibracious, reversed, alive, could by naymed *If,I?* The *If,I* can'to will swell from a sand suddenly over-stimulated by a syriad of sounds
If, I-rises from a Signachurning Source, canterior to a concerpt, so clearly as to reflect ten thousand hymnagistic rhythms
If Isolated a sighn of that sparse viginal beauty, fower, flire, drop, shadow offshoot, and placed herself on the skin of our renewdity in the justapofashion of an organ intertwining itself the length of a body, as the eye glides in its suckit, or as two breasts are graftid onto raw mamaterial to make woman

If the skin of the newde, separading itself in many a heaventual object, felt priqued by this beauty mark into s/he-coilescence, *If,I?* would then be a missIle—half-sky or half-earth half seed, semicorn semigraine, liable to any confulsion, in order to reflirct, over Ionder, a thousand operational, seminal imeges: to raise the question to be dolt with, the point of interscission between my sexual missiveness and his aggressivisibility, between his seminimal terrifactiveness and his fulminating firmamince.

O rIsing gush from signachurning source, innate Icetorm, faultless voice, bright sonorous gold, partificial shimmurmur, scratch by *If,I?* in the skylent hangings. Let a cry illuminate the blackness, liberating the infinite.

If anything can be de-signated by the sound of *If,I?* it's the white on black that she screams far away from ends and from now on, bursting with cajewelry continuity without reservation

If,I? will hear that which without herhis audition would have remained mute, such as it is allied in front and affectively to the hitherto unknown.

S/he will not enter: s/he is enterned there between If and I, spielbound by the bind fate that forebodes, thinksing that I gets aforeplayed.

Between evasion and evision, prefiguring herself on the road toward self-encounter, s/he will make her self up in a few lines, rIsing from a ground to take on light by being uglitter: s/he will be no less serfprised than if her members were spelled away in an inexhaustible trickle of water, and would be lasso were s/he to see her self move amidst the fields, like a handful of earth obeadyeyent before destiny, first by her self, without being prompted or ordered by anyone, so as soon thereafter to take on the attractiveness of a human and to lose the terrifactiveness of the manhue, and from then on to open the mouth which will just have been thrown ajeer for her, and thus to reawaken her destwinies to be . . . dIfined.

If,I will have nothing to be disarmorably discharged for. S/he has no excusucks. S/he won't give a good goddamn for the story of *If,I,* for the meaning or the eternal verilities of I, won't get sucked off into the probilemma of the recognizable, of the accunting for the counstraints of socialIconization, of the perversion banks, of persensetage equations, won't adbirthtize herhimself as a combination, won't withstand in as a substitute. S/he will be dissigned to ignore ambilematic or somantic representation. If or I will not be well lent to anything, nor sported with, will neither pawn off nor be buyassed nor nobiliquivocate. S/he will give herhimself over instintingly to the unseeing intensity of transappearexistence.

—*translated by Keith Cohen*

from Paradis
Philippe Sollers

that's it sunder flounder your death coma grossly inverted pla-
centa cancer aureola from where i sit i see them drip drop by
drop bazooka siphoned typhoon i'm back on the track bascule
mask crackled stares from forebears' portraits galleries pupils
starred waxed flash foundation of aspiration trumpet pump passing on the quotient tidbit idiot famishing flashflood chromos of
men sorrel bellows smith whalebone spit nostrils bit jawbones
velvet it's the state of quarantine fortyfied with fever they feel
putrid inside blacked-out whence this slime green and clotted
disrupted duct blowgun of farts for the roast in reality is roasted
on void it sounds the vesicle and liver to make sure we're there
quick a wink at this masked androgyne ball incubus succubus
patched up settings they enter under their limboid lighting
scarves of fog sashes of smog pleats of pus flabbied lamella
fuzzy medusa look at this flood of lymph in globules narine
sockets pinched upper lip in stiff pout possessing some say the
ultimate extract of sperm boiled in ovule leucorrhea wastes
flowerings basic wetting forever forgotten manna mob viscerated
crust and crunch now they're packed tails plaited rats from
plugged holes lead-coated molten shit well then in the beginning

was the waltz absurd gay harmonious java samba or bossa nova
but god was jealous and especially his shegod and she took her
soldering dildo and he swallowed her bromide potion and they
froze cakes in the ice screaming and since then sutured vagina
bulbed divining rod they speak fraught with sex as if sex sub-
mitted to thought and that's that our lives faint away odors
sounds colors and touch glycines havens of hazeltrees sap autumn
winter shores of summer embrace me better yes there lower no
lower still cherry lips hay hair in the cellar rustle of willows in
the silo winds winnowing pillows of wheat come tomorrow
morn to my room wake me i want to be awakened by you or
else sweltering days meeting in the shelter look here lying on
the leaves orangetrees laureltrees lemontrees what can it mean to her
my hot turgid cock what is it hangs her up there each time she's
never done smearing it on her lips her breasts she's never done
filling her mouth there aspirating the base balls figs tongue flickering length and breadth tell me when it comes make it come from
even further down from the base of your bones what marrow
hold vampire bat dracula of the ages keep trying let's pretend you're
dying now i discover your cadaver nude i pluck your last breath
your last ray of tears i shall save humanity from a disaster of
sterility you are the last man martyred but still hard oh give exude
transmit me the code you feel we are sinking under the weight of
history in its entirety wait think of us oh give your boiled oil 120
millions milliliter you'll save the species won't you my pet you're
set to give it up your gesure if not you know you'll have to be
recrucified won't you my cutie pie there's no other way you see
it's the law can you imagine all the nations deprived of umbilication
without foundation chaos of generations confusion of appellations
can you imagine hunter called bunter or cunter and the cunter
kid calling himself runter and mrs punter becoming blunter can you
see a society a history under these conditions in the name of navel
it makes me shudder also let's keep saying that what's us belongs
to us maybe we'll get there some day without delay for now it rises
degree by degree watch for the little birdy tweettweet venus of
furs you who leave leave all abstinence you can imitate all but
eminence thus he resumed i will tell you how the trinity is trussed
up in us and around us father son holy ghost inhibition symptom
anguish trust in omnipotence dated under usessence each in his

own sack of lusts you wonder no doubt who pulls ex-machina unseen the strings formidable she whispers to me i noticed she was drawing it all boxes balls she'd never seen such machinery butterflies slinking gadflies bad horse flies never had she stared like that the ties she quivered quavered gordian intestine gray cell tart jumbling it up besides on the haubans bridge halyards listening posts yardarms pulley blocks i wanted to talk but already the room intoned arise the canticles jesus makes himself our sibling unto us a savior is given he comes to us debonair with grace crowned hair ah how lovely he is how charming a stable is his lodging a bed of straw his crib he wants our hearts he waits for them hard to stop them in the throes of amorous ecstasy my lovely pine king of the forests how i love your greenery when winter is scrapping the trappings of fields and saplings my lovely pine king of the forests you remain attractive dangerous to try to wake them in mid-flight theosophic panic my neighbor palpitated i wanted to set her hand on my little branch but she cast me a withering glance what mediocrity said she what utter depravity juvenility you'll never know divinity well too bad i switch on my pocket tv rebroadcast of the debate in the house on the different sterilization techniques five hundred officials wonder if it's best to ligature on the right or on the left other channel discussion of individual or group abortion summary of the year's catastrophes 5000 dead in pakistan 40 in iran far east middle east near east occident becoming orient other channel we designate henceforth by the name orthosexuals all sexes not having their other in themselves and consequently inca-pable of finding it anywhere there will therefore be the ortho hetero-homos and the hetero homo-heteros women and men taking their tickets off the treadmill listen to me now like apples of gold on a silver thread such is the word said according to its two sides maskiyyôth chiselings links sphere plump polished the cut of the exterior hints at the interior read this here the thread here there right here it's written outside without remission but inside volume nothing ever gained vain smoke vaporous vapors one generation comes another departs the earth rests in its breast the sun rises it sets slides and restarts the wind turns goes returns and the waters never part the sea is not filled it swallows itself the torrents recede disperse themselves it all works beyond the aimless words the eye opens views reviews the ear listens hearkens what was is will be and what is done will be redone will flee nothing new no thunder clap no cat a time to be born a time to digest i was wise and then mad and wise again and again mad i awake wise again mad i slumber madder but wiser debility habilitates me my buffoonery refines me the fuller i am of shit the more i spin on the spit and the closer i get to the pit of the attic insipience rejoins insight what is coitus definitively if not an autocriticism but tell me could i still advance with this veil of blood on my head my face buried in the blood could i hold out much longer in this blood and say you my other aren't you ever going to answer me you fluster me i lust for you i dream of you for you against you answer me your name is a diffused perfume your color bursts among the thorns bring back my heart with wine make me a blanket of sunshine i'm smothering beneath this mask my skin drained basted nothing exists but desire wasted young in haste the old say they know they feel themselves out we are always too dutiful toward them and the more they wither the more they twitter and the more they expire the more they expound terror of vigor repression tutor they try to rethread their rejects sounds myths droopy lids faulty digestion the girls love that long leer behind the peepers hand fumbling at fly oh yes vacillating papa aren't i terrific and soporific verily this world is an invention of the girlish oldsters and the sons hyposons are also girlies and the mothers same with the fathers all the same the great secret that's it fizzling fright small change sacrificed crafty retallied affirmation of the original repressing pressing pinioned conflict of gold of silver metal cast in coins peru mexico egypt genoa seville amsterdam where have the indians gone the carolingians or even the greeks the romans our god moves on in christian clothing dominican charles quint credit titles females black fleet brazil transferred slaves briefly there is no brevity i'm only trying to wake up and sometimes i believe in it but i fall oh how we pledge as fledglings to reach the naked edge how we race straining toward the mark how we are drawn what how we are drawn remarkable regaining strength brilliant black blade awaiting the shave each awaiting secret rendezvous as if we were awaited yes unique experience not twice the same hole in this can no man broken in man woman dissolved in woman drapery of legends thrown overboard how many years universes 16 billion so few not possible and us our oldest remains scarcely 3 million where's

that folds of africa rift afar kenya sahara ghana thus little by little
less little delicate skeleton vase of bonedust crushed by pathos call
cry grumble mumble arrows throat and here's miss bovary
spoiled hairy diaphanous isis sailing over the float i return i return
passage molded in reverse mild trauma mind aspirated manageable
grind of air curled irons entered centered behind the mask baby
drowsy langôsha langôsha mournful train my resurrection is
spoken i arise from the dead vertically from the dead empty tomb
that is empty cradle too and empty as well the inner womb of the
human mommy which is why we see her erect at the foot of the cross
thrown for a loss which is why their only choice is to pose her as
virgin otherwise the foundation's displaced time space geometry
biochemistry face it discovering the disgrace leaves them all
unemployed naked out in the streets nothing to follow to borrow
blazing point overwhelming void now you're only a breath a trace
vestigium pedis in pelvis they draw away from you men feel it
women seem to know it best in their furrow but take heart i am
here i am with you will drink for you your hemlock will hemorrhage
i ate your meal for you simply make yourself more of a sleeper
ameboid infusor unveiling pancaked your fabric close shaved
a running dog's worth more than a dead lion for where you're
going there are no works no discourse no science ivory vault pit
of ovaries here they are lined up nephews aunts nieces cousins of
uncles two in the afternoon legs mosquitoes flowers ovulary
capital of women 700 two children that's always it passing by fresh
breeze path of ants in the grass moment of mirages if i lose my
tail sliced from midsection if i try to retape it to the nape fibroid
crater mucus how to replace it now separated meaty how to hook
it staple it planted rocket wave utero-sacred squall salpinched
armed follicle of the yellow corpuscle as if we advanced cut by
cut go a bit further prostrate postated as if we backed up just like
that without budging all the while advancing turning fixed as if
we permutated curbed by the carbide the child jumps on the bed
babbles and bawls here he is leaning spinning without axis little
vertebrate awaiting his cake muscle encased child at the very edge of
the nights he's always there in each man-woman always been
there bung of gaps i don't judge i describe i invent nothing i
follow you jumbled boiling bubbles of memories thus we now
arrive in the plain the motor heats we're half asleep first it's the

secreted odor green somber tide of sprayed orangetrees i am stretched out smashed in behind with the bags beside the rosy blonde englishwoman it's the moment when she sings a little and her blue left eye's going to hook it seems onto the branches she stays like that with this ejected eye aiming at the mountains and the mountains are blue violets and they're already far to the west and there are water spouts all about crested zephyr and rooves of leaves everywhere doused here's the smoke says she we're getting there

—*translated by Carl Lovitt*

Joyce & Co.
Philippe Sollers

1

Since *Finnegans Wake* was written English no longer exists.[1] It
no longer exists as self-sufficient language, no more indeed than
does any other language. Joyce introduces a permanent carry-
ing over of sense from language to languages, statement to statements, punctuality of enunciation subject to series. Joyce—a
whole *demography*. I compare this situation with that of Dante
in the fourteenth century: Dante perceives and inscribes not just
a fundamental economico-political shift (the emergence of capi-
talism) but a transference from language to language, from
Latin to Italian; Joyce traces the limits of any maternal, national
language. What is a meaning in the language of mother country?
The private property of child speech, which makes groups of
adults reprieved children; but also a referential functioning of
the subject toward his or her bodily matrix and a barrier erected
by the preconscious against the unconscious. Joyce says:
Finnegans Wake is the language and writing of the night, in
dream. Yet the dream of one language may be the wake of
another—night in one latitude, day in another. Thus Joyce

dreams of a book that will be inseparably dream and interpretation, ceaseless crossing of boundaries—precisely a *waking*.

It is naively believed that Joyce had no political concern because he never said or wrote anything on the subject *in a dead language*. The same old story: art on one side, politics on the other, as though there were a *place* for politics—or for anything else for that matter. Joyce's refusal to indulge in the slightest dead pronouncement is exactly *itself* the political act, an act which explodes at the heart of the rhetorical *polis,* at the heart of the narcissistic recognition of the human group: the end of nationalisms decided by Joyce at the time when national crises are at their most virulent (fascism in Europe). Nationalism can be characterized as a twofold obstruction—to the unconscious and to the area of the international. Hence (even when decked out with a "Marxist" banner) it is always basically regressive, opening onto all the racist exclusions.

Joyce wants to destroy nationalism, but he goes further than internationalism in its abstract, "ecumenical" version (which can only rest on a dead language—Latin for the church, "Marxist-Leninist" stereotype, fascist delirium). What Joyce is in the process of constructing with *Finnegans Wake*, from 1921 to 1939, is an active transnationalism, disarticulating, rearticulating and at the same time annulling the maximum number of traces— linguistic, historical, mythological, religious. In what he writes, *nothing remains but differences*, and so he calls into question all and every community (this is referred to as his "unreadability").

Joyce's persistent determination to probe the religious phenomenon is probably his most important political gesture. Apart from him, who is there to have really broken from that universal neurotic base (begun over and over again, even under the insignia of rationalism)? And why he, if not because he obtained through his writing a certain fundamental sexual knowledge concerning the species? Joyce represents the same ambition as Freud: to analyze two thousand years of manwomankind, and not ten or a hundred years of politics. What is monotheism? What is Christianity? What is reason? *Finnegans Wake* teems with "answers," but these answers are not of a scientific order; they come from a knowledge that will never present itself as systematic, any more than as definitively centered or serious. This is why it is a matter of the most forceful act ever accomplished against political paranoia and the overhanging weight of its deadening discourse, outside of all humor. Let me stress then that *Finnegans Wake* is the most formidably anti-fascist book produced between the two wars.

2

Not enough attention has been given to the fact that throughout his life Joyce wrote with money provided by women—the point at which a romance "novel" knits together, notably between literature and psychoanalysis. Joyce's first patroness, Mrs. McCormick, was absolutely bent on having Joyce psychoanalyzed by Jung at her expense. Joyce refused the proposal and Mrs. McCormick stopped his allowance. We begin to see here the exact antithesis of the classic analytic situation, a question of *no longer* paying someone who does *not* want to be psychoanalyzed. Nor is this the end of the story, since Joyce's daughter Lucia, who early shows signs of serious mental disturbance, will be treated by this same Jung, the Jung who had written a highly critical article on *Ulysses* accusing Joyce of schizophrenia.

A woman gives Joyce financial help so that he can write. But she wants him to have analysis. Joyce refuses. Punishment: no more money. Joyce's daughter is ill. She is treated in place of him. Suppose that Joyce's daughter is one of his *letters*: the letter falls into the hands of Jung, which is to say that it misses Freud.

An affair of no importance for the first half of the twentieth century? I think not, insofar as all of us are either Freudians or Jungians—which is at any rate easier than being Joycean. Joyce, who alludes several times in *Finnegans Wake* to these veritable power relations played out round his writing (power relations—the stake was indeed that of knowing who was *in possession of* the meaning of what he was writing), complained on a number of occasions of the "spontaneous" crudeness of Jung's behavior toward him. Now if "joyce" is translated into German, it gives "freud": through Joyce, Jung was attacking Freud, and through Freud—why not?—he was attacking Joyce. In the *Wake,* Joyce talks of the "law of the JUNGle."

Jung is finally the set of spiritualist or para-occultist resistances to psychoanalysis; the hope of a possible "beyond," something which the surrealists, for example, did not fail to clutch at; in short, in relation to the sexual question radically affirmed by Freud, a metaphysical counter-investment.[2] It is particularly important, therefore, to emphasize that such resistance is also manifested with regard to Joyce's writing. Why? Consider the scene for a moment: a woman + a psychoanalyst wondering what on earth Joyce could *be*, which brings us as close as possible to the traumatizing function of a *written work*. The female character says: "It's mine"; the psychoanalyst: "I know what it means"; Joyce remains silent, or else simply elusive. And so there he is, without being but yet being an analyst. Caught between the circulation of money and that of meaning but exceeding them by sense and pleasure, joycity, joyance, joy-sense—*jouissens*.[3] Writing as multiplication of languages is not the property of a *one*-language check. It is clear that Joyce's position at the time is paternal to the maximum and it is thus since his death, his absence, that his writing beckons to those who are, by definition, the privileged thresholds of the neurotic enigma of the dead father—the hysteric and the analyst. Had Joyce been living, *a living being*? or is his writing really posthumous? or else . . . ? That is what they have to *doubt*, to question.

It was in a certain manner *fatal* that surrealism should miss Joyce *and* Freud, and that the English-speaking countries should have been naturally Jungian. From the vantage point of his Swiss neutralization of Freud, Jung inevitably read a Freudian danger in Joyce. But in the case of every subject speaking English, how is the Joycean disfigurement of the mother tongue to be endured? The hysteric says: "You will remain son of your language"; the analyst comments: "This father is mad." Faced with a disturbance as great as that of *Finnegans Wake*, how is one to save both sexual health and the sacred? Answer: Henry Miller. Read the extremely violent article against Joyce in *Sunday After the War*—Joyce is deaf and blind in the soul, much more so than Beethoven and Milton, soul deaf and soul blind, echoes which are only the rehearsings of a lost soul. Final tableau: Joyce, in the name of sacrosanct American sexual health, whether or not it be psychoanalyzed by Jung, is cast into the limbo of books to be banned. Curtain. And the same story with English puritanism: "a queasy undergraduate scratching his pimples . . . an illiterate, underbred book, the book of a self-taught working-man, and we all know how distressing they are, how egotistic, insistent, raw, striking and ultimately nauseating," a mis-fire . . . callow board school boy . . . egotistical . . . pretentious, brackish, underbred . . . one hopes he'll grow out of it, but as Joyce is forty this scarcely seems likely" (1922), "pages reeling with indecency" (1941)—Virginia Woolf on *Ulysses* in *A Writer's Diary*. More evasive, Eliot compares Joyce to Tolstoy; while with Ezra Pound, there is already something quite different. Discoverer and defender of Joyce until *Ulysses* (interpreted as an "end"), Pound's hostility to *Finnegans Wake* is immediate. He becomes Ulyssian and Mussolinian in one and the same attempt at affirmative idealization. Nothing more alien to Joyce (and to Bloom), however, than the belief in some "renaissance"; alien too is thus naturally fascism, like all arm-waving. Pound saw Joyce as regressing; Joyce thought Pound was playing at the tough guy. Interestingly, the Italian fascist press of 1934 contains attacks on the "absurd little name Freud, which means *gioia*." Joyce writes *muscolini* (little muscle man). Pound, who calls Joyce Job or Jesus, hardens his position with regard to *Ulysses*: "I don't care a damn about metaphysics and the correspondences and the allegorical and the analogical and the scatological parallels of his opus," etc. Pound wants clear, classical, offensive, phallic meaning; he finds Joyce, and with good reason, "theological." Getting past theology, however, is not for just anyone who happens to feel like it—which is the minimum that Joyce had at least learned from the Jesuits. Joyce will not fail to make use of the meanings of *pound* in *Finnegans Wake*—money, cattle enclosure, and above all thumpity-thump of drum and bugle. The historical structure of the *Cantos* (the economico-social theses leading to a critical attack on usury and finally to anti-Semitism) could only appear childish to Vico-Joyce.

Jacques Lacan, in his paper, recounted the following comment made by one of his entourage: "Why did Joyce *publish Finnegans Wake*?" An odd remark. It is quite obvious that the whole of Joyce's strategy, from the first line of that book to the most trivial biographical incidents, was geared to such a publication. Joyce lived everything "according to" the *Wake*. His biography itself (which he moreover supervised with a host of precautions) was for him to be simply one of the "layers" of his work. The way in which he organized the discourse surrounding the writing of the book, in which he kept its title secret so as to excite curiosity, in which he carefully planned his disclosures, and so on—all this leaves no doubt on the matter. With him, from the first line, everything is public. In other words, the notion of "private" loses its meaning. The private does not explain the public, but it is in the publishable that may be found this or that illumination of the private (partial). There is nothing to know about Joyce because his writing always knows more, a whole lot more, than the "him" that can be seen by another person. Difficult to admit? Impossible. Impossible to dissipate this final fetishist illusion, to allow that a body is not the source of what it writes but its instrument.

But then, *who* writes, what is it that is written? Read—and see if you hold your own, if you stay, he or she, the same.

The symptom is there: all the writers who over the last hundred years have pulled "literature" into an irreversible crisis *have not* looked after their own publication, except Joyce. Mallarmé: a utopian book that he asks be burned. Lautréamont: republished by the surrealists. Rimbaud: goes away. Kafka: asks for his works to be burned, they are published *in spite of* this. Artaud: traces to the very end but does not "collect together." Only Joyce gets to the end of the last correction, thereby showing his detachment with regard to *Finnegans Wake*. And just imagine what someone can be who is detached from something into which no one can enter (other than with the utmost difficulties). Of *course* Joyce published *Finnegans Wake*. Question of paternity. As a result of which it creates a large number of scholars but little enthusiasm. Mothers feel exasperated, fathers stripped naked, daughters multiplied, sons unbalanced.

How does the Joycean word function? My hypothesis, precisely, is that *Finnegans Wake* is a word, one immense word but in a state of skidding, of lapsus; a word jam-packed with words, in fact a name full of names, but "open," spiraling. This play on words seems to me to function on a simple nucleus where to give *one* word (or rather an "effect of word") there is a coming together of at least three words, plus a coefficient of annulation. Let me straightway give an example. Joyce writes SINSE, reading *since, sense,* and *sin.* The "syllogistic" development of this condensation is as follows: ever since sense, there is sin; ever since sin, there is sense; ever since since (time), there is sin and sense. All in a flash in SINSE. In one word, as in a thousand, you have a thesis on language and man's fall from paradise; and, simultaneously, it is funny. Another example: TRAUM-SCRAPT—*Traum* (dream), *trauma, script, rapt* (seizure, abduction, rape as in "the rape of the lock"). Development: what is a piece of writing? the rape of a trauma; what is a trauma? a rape of the written; what is a rape? the script of a trauma. Or again: CROPSE—*corpse, kopros* (waste, shit), *crop up* (appear, come to the surface), *crop* (cut short), and even *croppy* (Irish rebel sympathetic to the French Revolution of 1789). Theme: death and resurrection.

This is what Joyce calls his "trifid tongue," his three-cleft three-folding language, an expression in which can also be heard *terrific,* as well as *trifle*—make fun, not take things seriously.

When the procedure spreads out over sentences and pages, you have the strange phenomenon of *names* emerging, the reverse of what happens in Vedic, Greek, or Latin poetry where, on the contrary, names are disseminated in the text (as Saussure showed in his studies of anagrams). Joyce prints out the negative of poetic language, penetrates its dark room: in the beginning were neither heroes nor gods, nor even men, but collisions, aggregates of sounds, of syllables; in the beginning names chased after themselves in letters, through the articulation of tongues. I call this *laughter toward the one* and to my knowledge the first word of *Finnegans Wake,* RIVERRUN (*rire-vers-l'un*), has not so far been interpreted in such a way. When it is noted, however, that the *last* word is THE, followed by a blank, with no punctuation mark, and that this terminal THE is calculated so as to turn round to the beginning, then nothing prevents, from end to beginning, the reading THE RIVERRUN, which is obviously the course of the river but in which can also be heard and seen THREE VER UN, three toward one. No surprise that

Joyce ceaselessly meditated (and played) on the trinity—and were you yourselves living in a constant state of triadicity, *plus one,* nothing would appear more normal to you than such things. Basically, it is all very simple. The most astonishing is that it seems so difficult, in other words that those who are the maddest declare to be mad those who are like that.

For the moment, I want to stress that Joyce, by writing rigorously in this way (writing everything but not just anything), poses a new status of the one and the multiple, a new law beyond, for instance, the Christian "trinity." The last word of *Finnegans Wake* is at once "the" and the "thee" of the divine second person. But with a running back into the laughter toward the one, into the cycle-wheeling and the fluxion of time which open the book. "Father time," another of Joyce's expressions; and "Time: the pressant."

The last word of *Ulysses* had been *yes.* It is supposed to be said by a woman. The most curious part of the whole affair is that people believe a woman says it because a man writes it; and if he has a woman say yes, no doubt it is for having experienced all her possible *no.*[4] Which is something. At any rate, the persistency with which Molly's monologue is taken out and staged on its own in the theater as a recital by an actress furnishes an additional symptom. No one seems to have thought of having it spoken by a man. Moreover, why stage it? If not in order to screen what *it* stages?

Jung, who was sexually naive, as psychoanalysts very often are, put in a letter to Joyce that he must have been the "devil's grandmother" to have written Molly's monologue. To which Nora replied: "I don't see why, Jim knows nothing at all about women." The two opinions are, as it were, at the two extremes indicated a moment ago: each is as exaggerated as the other and they join in that exaggeration so as not to know what lies between them—but *elsewhere* to them. Joyce summed it up in a word: *Jungfrau.*

Joyce is not discouraged, goes on sticking his tongue up. He writes not in langwidge (language as the edge of the wedge with which id is wed—Joyce's translation for Lacan's *lalangue*) but in bursting flows of language (Joyce's *l'élangues*): jumps, cuts—singular plural.

Apparently: words, sentences. Really: clashes of letters and sounds. *Voices* and *names.* Listen to the recording made by

Joyce himself of a passage from *Finnegans Wake*—opera, mad-rigal, inflections, accents, intonations, shifting from tenor to alto, baritone to soprano, in the delicate, subtle, fluid, everchanging apparatus of sexual differentiation, spoken, sung, calling. Something between the superimposition of radio programs and the hubbub of concert rehearsals. No fragment of language which is not in situation, said at such and such a moment by such and such a voice, such an accent of such a voice and to such a pur-pose without purpose—resonance. There are interjections, moan-ings, flashes of surprise, exclamations, questions which stop short, celebrations, mockings, whisperings, children, adults, men, women, old, young, low, high, depressed, euphoric, willful, active, passive, reflexive. Up to the final "night," which sounds far off, on the hori-zon, like a bell, like a pen also. In passing, the names of rivers and towns, deformed, *set going,* and pronounced by who? By a solo-ist who is each of the voices, thousands of voices, running comedy.

That every one of us is an open combination of a plurality of voices is perhaps as difficult to conceive, as sacrilegious, as the infinity and plurality of worlds in the sixteenth century. I may remind you that Giordano Bruno, whose name is invoked so many times in *Finnegans Wake,* was burned in 1600 for just that. For that alone? Of course not. He wouldn't—just imagine—admit the virginity of the virgin.

3

Finnegans Wake: a waking and negation of the end, *wake* of the negation of the end. The end of what? The beginning again of what? Of the generative sleep which sweeps speaking humans away in their dreams. Active negation, present participle, of all teleology. "History," said Joyce, "is a nightmare from which I am trying to awake." Writing, highest common factor, lowest com-mon multiplier of languages and of positions of enunciations of subjects in languages, produces an urgency of new time-tense, the more-than-present, the plu present.

Read the First Epistle of Paul the Apostle to the Corinthians and start to realize what is at stake in "speaking in tongues" (as if by chance, it is in this Epistle—Chapter 14—that Paul tells women to keep silence in the churches).

But what is it in Joyce that remains so abrupt, so inaccessible, that gives symptoms to psychoanalysis, that is "unreadable"?

Doubtless the manner in which he comes to a system of generalized incest, something which is not easy to set out.

It was said the other day that Joyce had failed because in spite of everything he had retained a base-language, English. The problem, however, is not that of a base-language but rather of a filter-language. English for Joyce is an angle and this angle, this filter, must open on the one side onto all languages, on the other onto what, "strictly speaking," has no language, the unconscious. Joyce invents a filter (in the mathematical sense) of high power which intercommunicates unconscious processes and the historical processes of language. That is his fundamental objective. In order to render languages visible, analytic, to make them analyze themselves and each other, they must be *filtered*. Write them from below, bring up their mnesic deposits and inscribe in them, through them, an interpretation of *in process*. It is this elusive, fluent, melodic accompaniment of interpretation *reinvested* in effect of writing-sound which, while remaining invisible, gives an effect of perspective *relief*, permanent and throughout.

Like Dante, Joyce uses a dispositif of four superimposed layers of sense: a literal and obscene level (difficult to grasp for anyone not familiar with English sexual slang); a historical level (Viconian model, Irish epics, etc.); a mythical level (religions, names of gods, etc.); lastly, a level of pleasure, of joyance, of coming, which is a problem since, finally, there is exclusion of a writer when one cannot succeed in understanding how he comes so much as to write what he writes. Across these four ranges, masses of utterances are projected, deformed, mixed, disinhibited. The joke (the *Witz*) is only a feeble glimmer alongside this explosion of humor or continual cross-allusions, laughter which does or does not laugh but laughs all the same— "riso del'universo" (Dante, *Paradise*, 27). This dispositif of four layers of sense, or rather of three plus zero (annulation of the "joke") which only make one, gets very close to what Freud calls "primal repression," which can never be *raised* but which Joyce thus gives us in its circumscription, its contour. How, indeed, can one attain such a sublimation of so many pulsional drives which seem to come from all sides, of so many mythical, historical, sexual condensations?

Beckett was right when he noted, as early as 1930, that we

are too decadent to read Joyce, too decadent perhaps to read any writing which moves in that direction. Dante, Bruno, Vico, Joyce—challenges to linear meaning, squarings of circles.

Joyce writes from a hyper-complex system of kinship. What I wanted to emphasize by "generalized incest" was that he explores *all* the possible discourse positions between mother-son, father-daughter, father-son, etc.

In *Ulysses*, this is not yet the case. The father-son couple (Bloom-Stephen), the question of filiation by spiritual paternity, is brought up against the great final matrix of enunciation, Molly. Paternity is "depreciated" in relation to the engulfing monologue. Molly's password is "I am the flesh which always says yes," constructed on the inversion of the Faustian "I am the spirit which ever denies." Passing this word, however, let me say that Joyce will go on to write at every moment in non-centered enunciation positions and that what he thus "gets beyond" is very precisely the place of female paranoia.

Female paranoia is not male paranoia. While schizophrenia allows the possibility of leaving sexual difference out of count, paranoia poses sexual difference in all its force. And if Joyce is a difficulty, it is because his writing comes to edge on this psychotic axis where, in principle, language is marked in the fact of its lacking.

I have tried to explain how Joyce's text makes names *germinate*. What are the principal names, veritable compass card of meanings, that are found in *Finnegans Wake*?

First, the feminine position: ALP, Anna Livia Plurabelle. Position one and multiple, but principle of unification. Anna Luna Pulchrabelle. A flux of multiplicities (rivers) but unitary, the one as *she* the same in its variations. Bizarre, isn't it, the *one* which is *there* the *a* which is *the* masculine *one* which is *the* as *she*.

Things are different with HCE, the initials of the father and not of the mother-daughter designated by ALP. (In passing, note that the names, most often whole sentences, are unfolded from the basis of three initials; the initials are abbreviated signatures which the names fill out according to the variables of history or myth; they are moreover disseminated in apparently ordinary sentences: nomination of *anonymity*.)

117

HCE, then, is a transformational triad. While ALP is declined more by adjective and noun, HCE is defined by the *verb*. "Here *Comes* Everybody," "*Haveth* Childers Everywhere," and so on. The *verb as name*. As names-of-father.

Beneath these two great figures, what formerly would have been called major characters or divinities, there are two more incarnate, more human forms, the two brothers Shem and Shaun, the "penman" and the "postman." Two men incarnated by two brothers, one of whom writes the other. Two first names, *forenames*.

Sem, semite; shame; shem, james (joyce). Sem, the name (samuel). "The name is god."

Shaun: to be heard especially as *shown*, as well as John, etc.

ALP, HCE, Shem-Shaun: one woman, two men, a polyfather (childers everywhere).

The root of HCE (sometimes written in small letters) is, I believe, to be found in a classic procedure for abbreviation in illuminated Bibles of the Middle Ages. To write "Hic est filius meus . . . ," the i is included in the h and what is written is effectively HCE; Joyce, as we know, was familiar with such illuminations, notably those of the Book of Kells. HCE, HIC EST—a shifter that can open practically onto anything. *Herewith* as verb and name; it is: THIS—IT—IS.

Behind this scene, Finnegan: dead old ancestor to be resuscitated, since it is both an awakening and a joyful funeral wake, buried memory of the father of the primal horde from which this "theography" has been constructed. Return of the repressed, of the dead father who, like a vigorous abundant grass, springs up again everywhere in languages, sticks out everywhere in tongues.

Joyce: the anti-Schreber. If you take the *Memoirs of My Nervous Illness* (1903, a significant date), you can see that this great document on male paranoia, analyzed by Freud and Lacan, is written in an extremely classical manner. Schreber is the subject of the law, a magistrate writing down everything except linguistic fantasies, which happen to him *in the real*. What he writes is "readable" (which does not mean easy to understand); he writes administratively on the subject of a writing unleashed in him as outside. What is male paranoia? The insane attempt, for a man, to become the woman of all men (and, in that place, to rebeget other men). In Schreber's case, you can see that the castration he awaits, wants, and fears all at the same time constitutes a limit in relation to which it can be said that he cannot act in the real. Schreber is a "witness" to the manipulations on himself, to the voices of the root language. He tries to rationalize them, and it is from this rationalization, finally, that he can be called delirious.[5]

Female paranoia, however, certainly more radical in this, gives rise to a quite different erotomania of writing. Not only are the texts given in terms of novel, of fiction, but they are very often dictated in a manner close to a more or less automatic writing. The translation of this dimension in the real generally leads on to murder—murder of "the other woman."[6]

At the risk of seeming to go too far, I want to tell you that you are all of you, men and women, potentially paranoiacs, either because you had fathers who were potentially paranoiacs or because you had mothers who were potentially paranoiacs. Fathers who wanted to be "the woman." Mothers who could not bear the existence of a woman. Of another who would be woman.

It is my hypothesis that in female paranoia there is a foreclosure of the word, the verb, which signs a kind of absolute impossibility of acceding to the symbolic. Joyce writes, I think, precisely from that radical negation of language. He writes and speaks in that impossible place where there ought not to be anything speaking or writing, and he brings it to a highly worked sublimation. In other words, Joyce gets something to come which in principle ought not to come. Which is undoubtedly the reason for the ferocious *Verneinung* Joyce suffered from his contemporaries and continues to suffer from those who have followed them. *Finnegans Wake* becomes the object of acute speculation, struggle, repression; and everyone is aware of it, everyone knows it, everyone doesn't know it—but those who are there to watch over knowledge, they know it.

There has been talk, with regard to Joyce, of matricidal writing. It must not, however, be allowed to conceal the position of incestuous discourse with the mother which emerges with Molly in *Ulysses*.[7] No doubt the reason which leaves criticism nonplused in the face of that monologue: a whole criticism, above all written in English, standing petrified to attention before this monument-attempt upon the mother as language. Height of irony, Joyce did not hesitate to pretend to have been influenced on this point by a Frenchman, Dujardin, and by his totally unimportant book with a title which is nevertheless worth its weight in castrational allusion—"the laurels are cut down." At any rate, once Molly-recrimination-monolanguage has been got past,[8] the language is transformed into the joyance of languages. How can the permanent exclamation of *Finnegans Wake* not be heard as a song of triumph? In this last book too, the end is entrusted to a woman, but this time it is the daughter flowing and flying and returning into the paternal bosom: Anna Livia, at the end of the long movement through the centuries and the millennia, with her charge of silt and leaves of sound swept alluvially along, sillying waters, arriving madly now as mother and as daughter on the horizon of the mouth of her son-husband-father, the ocean. And everything will begin again beyond the reunification, the fullness, the completeness, in that other beating rhythm of the one and the multiple which can only be written *anew*. It is this saturation of the polymorphic, polyphonic, polygraphic, polyglotic varieties of sexuality, this *unsetting* of sexuality, this devastating ironicalization of your most visceral, repeated desires which leaves you—admit it—troubled when faced with Joyce. Freud, Joyce: another era for manwomankind.[9]

—*translated by Stephen Heath*

Notes

1. Communication to the Fifth International James Joyce Symposium held in Paris, June 1975. The following translation is itself inevitably caught up in the clash of languages witnessed at that Symposium and analyzed here around the terms of the "difficulty" of Joyce; which is to say that as translation it resists academic conventions ("word for word") in the aim of an exact transposition of the *force* of the Sollers text.—*Translator's note*

2. The strict analytic equivalent for "investissement" is "cathexis" (German *Besetzung*); preference is given here to a translation which retains the economic directness of the French term. The gap across the two languages of what might be called the discursive possibility of psychoanalysis is worth noting: English technicizes ("cathexis"), pacifies ("facilitation" for "frayage"), confuses ("instinct" for "pulsion"), latinizes (the "id" for the "ça"); analysis is then literally the *unspeakable*.—*Translator's note*

3. English has no word which can bring together the varieties of "enjoyment"

contained in the French "jouissance," notably the enjoyment of sexual coming so crucial in the movement of the *Wake*—Here *Comes* Everybody.—*Translator's note*

4. Joyce's wife was called NOra.

5. The paranoid *mise en scène* is there in *Ulysses* when Bloom is several times transformed into a woman.

6. Seed of female paranoia: dependence on the mother, anguish of being killed or devoured by her (Freud); the written text—"novelistic" or fabulating—as protective rampart, murder as projection; the whole in radical competition with the father insofar as he has given the mother a *child*.

7. "A day or two afterwards Stephen gave his mother a few of the plays to read. She read them with great interest and found Nora Helmer a charming character." (*Stephen Hero*)

8. It is wrong to say that Molly's monologue is not punctuated: it is so, ceaselessly, by *proper names* which play the role of guiding fantasmatic "nodes"; a way for Joyce of throwing into relief the intervention and the instance of the *capital letter* in the literal-spoken rumination of thought. *Finnegans Wake,* immediately afterward, reintroduces a massive (exclamatory) punctuation—volumes of *interjection*: "So that gesture, not music, not odours, would be a universal language, the gift of tongues rendering visible not the lay sense but the first entelechy, the structural rhythm." (*Ulysses*)

9. As will have become evident, the difficulty of translation here lies in the fact that this text goes against both the English and the American Joyces, the outcast from a moralizing criticism bent on protecting its tradition from what it calls "the revolution of the word" and the puzzle to be solved at all costs by a massive "recovery" of "facts" (the reconstitution of a hated object, a hatred often present in the Symposium). Is it useless to add that the "structuralism" currently, and usually ignorantly, being bandied about by the literary intellectuals in England and America is a new version of the old refusal of Joyce . . . and Freud?—*Translator's note*

An interview with Philippe Sollers

David Hayman

Philippe Sollers is and has been for some time the bad boy of contemporary French fiction—antifiction, postfiction, or what you will. As editor of the prestigious left wing periodical *Tel Quel,* he has contributed to the development of neo-Marxist and neo-Freudian post-Structuralist thought and controversy. As a critic obsessed with the writers on the fringe whom he correctly sees as frequently pointing toward some unrecognized and significant center, he has considerably furthered the French awareness of the contributions of Lautréamont, Sade, Artaud, Bataille, and, most recently, of Joyce in *Finnegans Wake.*

Sollers' novels (as he says in this interview taped in June 1975) have taken several turns, but the fiction which follows the most recent shift is of enormous concern to those who know the later Joyce. Already published but still untranslated are *Lois* and *H.* A newer and more daring book, *Paradis,* has been appearing serially in *Tel Quel.*

My interview was preceded by a reading of the passage from *Paradis* translated for *TriQuarterly* by Carl Lovitt. Our discussion derived in large measure from the experience of that beautiful

reading of a most striking text. But it also followed a week at the
James Joyce Symposium, to which Sollers contributed fresh
and startling insights. The remarks given during a seminar on the
Wake and reprinted above are therefore also relevant to the interview (see "Joyce & Co.").

David Hayman: You say that your new project, *Paradis*, takes
a very different approach from the one in *H*. What does that mean?

Philippe Sollers: Obviously my title, *Paradis*, was deliberately
chosen. It implies a rewriting of Dante's *Paradiso*, but it's a
paradise that has changed a good deal since Dante's time. Perhaps
the phrase which best gives the sense of my title is a sentence
from Sade, who says, "Everything is paradise in this hell." I am
out to palm off as pleasurable, or at least acceptable, all that would
ordinarily be most disturbing, both spiritually and physically.
My approach has changed because I've focused my attention more
radically and integrally on the Bible.

At the end of *H* there is the sudden introduction of some biblical utterances in the prophetic style. My sort of writing (*écriture*),
as you know, is emphatically punctuated for the reader's ear and
not at all for his eye. The result is a punctuation which takes place
between the ear and the eye but which must be activated by the
voice. My experimentation with that *écriture* led me to an in-depth
reading of the Bible. Stranger things have happened to writers
in the course of their work!

The biblical text was, after all, chanted and not punctuated,
and hence subject to a variety of interpretations. You know that
the commentaries have played endlessly with these possibilities,
most notably the kabbalistic commentaries. What I want to do is
reread the whole biblical tradition because I think we have arrived
at a historical moment when we can try to understand in depth
the beginnings of occidental monotheism. I feel that a writer today
confronts the deepest and most fundamental roots of our culture
because we are living through an unprecedented period of flux or
mutation, a period that has lasted over a thousand years. I've
gone to the Bible to find out what all that means, what it could
mean. So my work on *Paradis* concentrates on that point. I'm
not speaking only of the New Testament. Obviously, I describe
Christianity as an adventure at once pathetic and comic. I was

inspired by Joyce in this. He began the process of disclosing the complete ambiguity of that affair, which is at once absolutely pathetic and irresistibly funny. The illusionistic aspect of Christianity is one of the funniest things in our history. But at the same time I want to discover in the Bible—in Genesis, in the canonical books, and especially in the prophetic texts—how such writing (*discours*) functions.

D.H.: You talk about your unpunctuated texts with their audible punctuation. Does that mean that when I read *H* or *Paradis* I can vary the punctuation?

P.S.: Yes . . . no. I think you won't be able to change the punctuation but you can alter the accentuation, the intonation, the way it is interpreted. As for the punctuation, I think it is invariable. That is, the *position* of the enunciation, which is after all what punctuation amounts to, is rigorously controlled. Of course the eye perceives the text as unpunctuated. It's a trap.

D.H.: I'm thinking of Molly Bloom . . .

P.S.: Sure. It looks like automatic writing, as though it were typed directly on the page. But it isn't, and here my strategy comes into play. I have deliberately laid that trap for the retina, made it seem that there is nothing to writing my books, but sometime I'll show you my manuscripts. You'll see pages written in longhand, laboriously revised ten, fifteen, twenty times. I want to give the impression that I write mechanically, but in fact I write at times with the care of a surgeon using his scalpel to separate fine layers of tissue, performing an operation with very great precision. I'm thinking of an operation I saw in China, the removal of a cataract, where you have to cut very carefully and still quite rapidly so that the needle will excise the crystal that blocks the sight. Or something like acupuncture. These are very meticulous operations of the sort I've introduced in the text I just read you. I separate the lips of the word and I treat them exactly as a surgeon would treat delicate tissues. There is a biological component. I don't know whether or not you felt it.

D.H.: I felt that it was very carefully worked, but can we return to my question? You said earlier that the absence of punctuation in the Bible opened the text to several interpretations. . . .

P.S.: Yes, the best known example is the opening of Genesis, which can be translated "In the beginning God created the heavens and the earth," or you could read "In the beginning God created himself." It depends on how you punctuate it.

D.H.: Are you really trying to do that?

P.S.: Not at all! I'm saying that the manner in which I write has led me to that terrain. Personally, I wouldn't want to condense a multiplicity of possible interpretations into a single utterance. What I am trying to write engages me in the adventure of extreme clarification. I am trying to say simply and precisely things that until now have only been said in the most ambiguous ways, or at least by multiplying the ambiguities within the signifiers. Why is it a book of clarification? Because I am building on a rock, on a sexual interpretation. I'm reading the Bible, especially the New Testament, as the mythologization of a sexual adventure—somewhat in the manner of Wilhelm Reich in *The Murder of Christ*, but going much further, since Reich's interpretation is rather lyrical, naïve. . . . The moment we see that adventure as founded on a sexual code or message, which could not have been spelled out before our time, it becomes at once pathetic and very comic. And when I say that we live in a period of mutation, I believe that's the crux. Everything that could only be expressed metaphorically, through allusion, through the creation of myths, by the superposition of allusion to the nth degree—the moment you systematically follow a sexual interpretation, you can clarify all of that. By clarification I don't mean that one minimizes but rather that one gains a sense of the sedimentation or stratification of the interpretation, of all that has been deposited by the memory of the species in its religion. You know, they call what I'm doing unreadable, but as soon as I read it aloud calmly and show that I can explain each item, you can see that it's the opposite of an occultation; it's a disclosure.

D.H.: What about your other books?

P.S.: I think my books begin with *Drame*, which is now ten years old. Then you have *Nombres*, followed by *Lois*, which constitutes a break or rupture, then *H*, and then this work when it's finished. There was also a period between *Drame* and *Nombres* which was a period of research into the disposition of writing methods, quite advanced but at the same time very ascetic. But the real rupture was marked by *Lois*, a book that dates back four years. It was a sort of taboo-breaker, a rather strange book which

125

almost got away from me. I wrote in a state of high excitement, a creative rage. The result is a sort of explosion of parody, comedy. . . . It's a very luminous book for me, at least in my memory. I wrote it during a very luminous period in my life. The slightly obsessive ascetic mode which characterized *Drame* and *Nombres*, but which was necessary also as a sort of discipline in the reduction and study of the materials, in *Lois* suddenly explodes and sends out thousands of ramifications. I'm in the midst of that adventure in *H* and now with *Paradis*, and I think it will continue for a long time yet. But I can't really predict.

So, what has suddenly become manifest is a major project focused not only on the formal disposition of my writing, a fact which disturbs certain of my former supporters. . . . My concerns now are less with the formal attributes of the text, though I am still very careful on that score. But I put much more emphasis on the meaning of my utterance. The interpretation and condensation of signification has been pushed as far as it can go. That's why I have taken up the Bible—because, after all, this . . . monument is there in my path, this puzzling monument about which occidental humanity has revolved for two thousand years. In a sense you could treat Christianity and Islam as hallucinations in relation to the Judaic base of the Bible. I have taken it up as something which strongly resists my efforts, which doesn't give way easily, which ceaselessly renews its force.

D.H.: In playing against two thousand years of tradition you introduce a powerful tension in your work which may complicate your labor of clarification. As soon as you introduce that paradox, the work begins to palpitate.

P.S.: Yes, and I have the sense of doing this to one of the species' monuments at the moment when the species is about to abandon it, when it ceases to mean anything. But this is the very moment when it begins to mean an enormous amount to me. It is really striking to see the vision buried in a monotheistic Christian culture which the people who pass the churches, who enter, leave, and visit them like museums, seem no longer to understand. Why don't we attend to these questions of significance? Perhaps because we are within. We are within but in the process of leaving, without being aware of all that has accumulated there in the way of meaningful sediment.

D.H.: I'd like to go back to your text. I was struck by the variety of effects you can achieve even without punctuation.

P.S.: Let's begin with the interpretative micro-sequences. You've noticed, of course, the very deliberate use of rhythm. I've tried to integrate the entire corpus of metric traditions. You even find decasyllabic and octosyllabic segments. As a result, the punctuation falls not on the level of the sentence but in terms of meter, not on the level of the statement but in terms of the rhythm of the stating (*énonciation*). There is a constant mnemonic effort, an attempt to make the language turn ceaselessly, to project a sort of round dance. I've even concentrated on internal rhymes, trying to create an incessant rhyming. You know the essential aspect of my procedures is not the absence of punctuation; it's meter and rhyme.

D.H.: I notice that you tend to use a lot of catalogues. Sometimes they're Rabelaisian, but more often they mark attempts to clarify. That is, you produce lists of synonyms, or rather quasi-synonyms—words which, because they are not precisely accurate, exert a force on the writing and even on the reader's spirit. The result is a sort of anti- or pseudo-catalogue.

P.S.: I am constantly playing upon but avoiding the center of a system. For example, you can tell when Joyce imposes upon his material—he brings you up short before a violation of custom. In my work you are faced with a constant slippage, always on the brink of a lapsus or joke but never breaking out of its context, never hitting you between the eyes. The text slides along like the breath of God "moving upon the face of the waters."

D.H.: And if the reader nods?

P.S.: He can go to sleep, sure. It wouldn't matter if he did, since at that moment he would continue to be under the spell of the text. It could put him to sleep as, for example, Arab and Indian music can fatigue the occidental auditor, with his occidental ear, habituated to a certain occidental measure. You know I often listen to Indian music; after three or four hours of it, you feel you could leave it on all night, all day even. You could reenter the music, leave the music, sleep, wash up, not listen, and so on. My ambition is to produce a tissue which the reader may enter and leave. It would not be something in front of him. It would be like his very breath, like his own sleep, part of his daily being.

D.H.: It's strange, but, though Joyce never said it, that sounds like his project for *Finnegans Wake*. Of course there are major differences, since in Joyce we have constant polysemy, while your text contains very little of the polysemantic.

P.S.: No, it doesn't use polysemy; it depends on the "poly-sensible."* I don't think one can improve on *Finnegans Wake* when it comes to multiple meanings.

D.H.: It seems to have musical qualities.

P.S.: As far as musicality goes, my text may use means which seem less rich than Joyce's, but it is never a question of fragments, or passages taken out of context or cited. Any time you try to pull something out of the fabric, the whole thing will slip out of your hands, melt. One *can* take passages from the *Wake*.

D.H.: And from *H*?

P.S.: It isn't easy. It's like the image of the Danaides' sieves; you're left with nothing in your hands. But if you agree to read and to forget as you read, to lose yourself (erase your consciousness) through your reading, then you'll experience some surprising effects. My experience with readers is that when they open my text, some simply fail to enter. Fine. Some enter, begin to swim, make progress, stop at a given moment, because they're tired, or someone comes into the room, or because, as you were saying, they fall asleep. And at that moment they become aware that they've forgotten it all. I'd say that I capitalize on that impossibility to recall what has been read, the result of the intensity of the effacement effect, or blank-out. I'm not referring to a "blank" produced by contradictions, by the annulling of significance, or by polysemy. It's perhaps even more perverse, a blank produced by an effacement of sense. Why? Because it is stuffed with allusions and signification. But it isn't what you'd expect; you wouldn't be able to grasp it. You see, it is quite hard to explain. I'm referring to a new conception of sense which doesn't derive from the word but from the sentence. In short, it's a different sort of linguistic entity.

D.H.: What you're saying makes me think of subliminal effects. That is, when you read you lose yourself in the text, but in losing yourself you are within and the effects are imprinted on your spirit.

---

* Perhaps we can read this as an allusion to literary texture, a quality well illustrated by Sollers' readings as it is by a reading of passages from Joyce.

Joyce uses them too, but in other ways. After all, it may always have been true of the novel. The more one sees, the more one hears, the more one understands, but the aspects of the text which we can't see or understand nevertheless slip into the mind by what I call peripheral vision. You see a movement out of the corner of your eye without knowing precisely what is moving.

P.S.: That reminds me of something. Why did Duchamp create his "grands verres"? He claimed that by this means he entered the "seeable," not the visible. It's as though I were to say, "It isn't readable, it's 'readible' (*'lisable'* or *lisible*)." You transform the relationship of the regarding body to the object of its regard, which is not truly an object, being transparent. In relation to painting, this constitutes a major subversion. Something like that is happening in my writing. Duchamp always said he wanted to project a fourth dimension within the third dimension. In language, we need not stop with the fourth dimension. We can achieve dimensions by means of projection. We can even have several types of projection. We can have the Joycean sort of triplicity, which is still enigmatic and which in my opinion is based on Joyce's speculation on the Catholic trinity. [In response to my look of surprise] Of course, you know it's only an hypothesis. He said something one day—jokingly, according to Budgen. He was correcting proof at the time. There were three sets of galleys and one of them was always slipping from his hand. It was a joke and I'm joking too. He said, "It's like the persons of the trinity—you never manage to hold all three at the same time." It's a direct allusion to his writing. When you catch one meaning, there are always two others hiding in the shadows.

D.H.: He also speaks of squaring the circle, referring to the impossibility of rendering two antagonistic concepts identical.

P.S.: Yes, of course, the square circle. That's not a joke. You can use that optics or you could use mine. You can constantly divide the layer of language and the layer of sense so as to give the impression of ceaselessly gliding above the layer of language.

D.H.: Isn't that a function of tonality and rhythms?

P.S.: Yes, in language it would take that form of projection. But to read my texts you should be in a state something like a drug high. You're in no condition to decipher, to perform hermeneutic operations. You assume another relationship with language. The language of the text is a base over which something slides. That's why you don't have polysemic concretions.

D.H.: Barthes speaks of the writable (*scriptible*) text—the text which must be written, not read.

P.S.: In an essay on *H* he used the expression "over the shoulder." He said that in order to read *H* you have to put yourself in a position to read over Sollers' shoulder and write it at the same time he does.

D.H.: That makes the reader the accomplice of the author.

P.S.: That turns him into a sort of double who is nevertheless subject to the laws of what he reads.

D.H.: We have Sollers the hypnotist.

P.S.: If you wish. We shouldn't forget that psychonalysis began with hypnosis. The problem would be complicated if the effect of this procedure were purely suggestive. But that isn't the case. It's stuffed with interpretations.

D.H.: Right. You interpret when you write. The reader interprets when he reads. He must rediscover forms you've placed there, but he must also formulate them. There is a sort of doubling effect. What is interesting in all this is that while the reader may forget a great deal of this experience, even though there is the slippage, he retains some very clear impressions.

P.S.: Some.

D.H.: Some things do sink in. But does he and can he know precisely which ones?

P.S.: You know, I think he can. In the passage I read just now [see page 101], there was an obvious echo from Ecclesiastes: You have both the rhythm and the terms of Ecclesiastes. It doesn't fall just anywhere but right after a very emphatic treatment of sexual mutations today. It is followed by an equally clear sequence on the development of money. What am I doing in this passage? I provide several levels of discourse. For example, there is a radio broadcast, obviously false. A university lecture, obviously false. False and true at the same time. You have an advertisement, etc. A pile of things. For example, *"tout s'imite sauf eminence"* ("you can imitate everything but eminence") is an advertising slogan you see all over Paris these days. It's an ad for a woman's undergarment called Eminence.

D.H.: That's the sort of thing an American would miss.

P.S.: No, but there will always be a Frenchman to tell you about it. It's like "Guinness is good for you . . ." "Ghenghis is ghoon for you."* That's not obvious to a Frenchman but an Englishman will tell you, "Sure, it's an ad for beer."

D.H.: That's privileged information.

P.S.: Exactly. But of course it can be interpreted in other ways. If you don't know it's a slogan, the wordplay itself is striking. Besides, it falls in a passage full of sexual reference. Let's return to what I was saying before. You have the Ecclesiastes reference between our two other references. It all finds its focus in the biblical statement that there is nothing new under the sun. The result is that the Bible becomes a leitmotiv, rewritten, rhythmically echoed, paraphrased, reversed, and so on. It becomes a sort of map or program buried in this sculpture of mine which on the surface seems so inhospitable to that sort of reference.

D.H.: In that case, the ideal reader would be someone who has made an in-depth study of the Bible.

P.S.: I don't know about that. After all, a deep study of the Bible could be undistanced. The question is, can one have distance (aesthetic and intellectual) in relation to the Bible? That's the question put by my book. In my opinion, that sort of distance has never existed. I feel that the Bible is a constant in our culture. It is repressed, denied, hallucinated. We pretend that it doesn't exist for us, but it is there unavoidably. And I think that all our ideas, whether we know it or not, are absolutely determined by the biblical text.

D.H.: But you have said that we are in the process of leaving all that behind.

P.S.: Maybe. But to distance ourselves we need another conception of language. You know I told the Joyce symposiasts, "You are, whether you know it or not, completely immersed in a religious consciousness, whether it be x, y, or z. Perhaps Joyce alone has been able to abandon it."

D.H.: Do you really believe he abandoned it?

P.S.: I think so . . . yes. If not Joyce, *Finnegans Wake* has freed itself.

D.H.: As a text?

P.S.: As a linguistic operation, I'd say. Perhaps not Joyce the

* From *Finnegans Wake*, p. 593/17.

person, in his moments of depression or fatigue. But that's why it's hard to ask a writer what he is up to, since he himself is always less than he has done.

D.H.: And you?

P.S.: Me too, of course.

D.H.: Do you think your book departs from, frees itself from, the Bible?

P.S.: Yes, I think it departs in two senses of the word: it leaves and it returns. It tries to create a distance. The word "depart" is too strong, since it suggests that it completely suppresses the Bible. It is rather a question of a critical distance. I think there has always been this problem of how to distance oneself in relation to religion, or, if you wish, to obsessional neurosis.

D.H.: Are you saying that religion is a neurosis?

P.S.: Don't take that in a pejorative sense. There are no neurosis-free societies. You know, I'm convinced that modern rationalism and psychoanalysis (in its more reductive phases) both believed they were distanced from religion. Well, religion is obliged to demonstrate that it still exists. I'm not the one who's invented the issue. I think it persists in the individual's head, in his productive and reproductive impulses.

D.H.: Religion provides us with formulas for our spiritual and even our social impulses. Since we need such formulas, we'll never completely escape. It's a necessary presence, conscious or not.

P.S.: O.K., but we can find another formula. I think religion is the mystified form of something else. We could find a less mystified form for such things, even given the fact that we are unable to express them directly. For example, we can't express sexual enjoyment in words. The moment we say it, or think we have said it, it escapes us.

D.H.: That's just like God.

P.S.: That's where God comes from.

D.H.: I once had a discussion with an English cleric. I was explaining that for me irony is a way of saying without saying—a way of expressing the missing center, an absence which is meaningfully present. He said that's how one speaks of God, in terms of tangents drawn to an imponderable circle. Is that what you are doing in *Paradis*?

P.S.: In a sense . . . multiplying the points of intersection. It isn't only irony, pathos, the comic. There is a sort of turbulence, a flux of positions. I multiply the positions. Whether it be Ecclesiastes, a fake lecture, a facsimile broadcast, a mock ad (which could be a real ad). All these postures will be used in such a way that something will have been said and not said at the same time, but will produce a tragic effect because it is tragic, or a comic effect because it is completely comic, et cetera, and endlessly. Because I feel that all human discourse turns about that presence-absence you just mentioned. You know, there are several ways of achieving that unstated statement. After all, a writer is best defined by the fact that he *doesn't* say, by his way of not saying certain things.

D.H.: There are a number of writers, like Kafka, who question the empty center. We might say Kafka faces toward what the mystic sees and enjoys in silence. What Kafka does leaves the impression that something inhabits that empty center. There is Beckett, who also questions and who follows some of your procedures, especially in *The Unnamable*. One can even nod at times when reading Beckett. He too asks questions which have no answers or which have two or more contradictory answers.

P.S.: I'd say that one could also multiply the answers, give an enormous quantity of answers (which is my method) to a question which can't really be asked. There is an obvious difference between me and Beckett, who tries for extreme precision, imposes microlimits which he continually sharpens and follows. In my case you have the impression that it goes off in all directions, leaves, comes back, jumps out the window. That's what I call multiplying the responses by virtue of the impossibility of asking one real question, which would be the one which would never have an answer. There is another route, there is the pluridimensional proliferation in which everyone would lose himself in a sort of virgin forest. That's a very important out for me. It enables me to integrate poetic language. Kafka and Beckett can't afford the luxury of poetry. If you examine my extract you'll see that I can include the whole range of existing poetic discourse.

D.H.: I've said in my essay that you have recovered the French rhetorical tradition.

P.S.: I think you're right. That is, I place it in a situation of slippage, of free falling.

D.H.: Yours is a rhetoric that doesn't pretend to be saying anything, whereas traditional rhetoric always makes claims to the condition of statement. I told someone recently that you have the attributes of a preacher, a *prédicateur*.

P.S.: True, there is plenty of preaching in my work. Predication (you see we can play on that word—the assigning of a predicate) is after all a means of eliciting the appearance of a subject. As a rhetorical formula, predication interests me enormously. It's a form which I use just as I use advertising discourse or scholarly discourse, or comic or even biblical discourse. That is, it's a positioning of the subject, and clearly there is an element of predication. But you should imagine a preacher beginning his sermon in a very serious tone and then gradually, as you listen, you begin to say to yourself that there's something odd going on here. Here's a preacher who's going to say with seeming sincerity some weird and mad things.

D.H.: You know Chapter IIIii of *Finnegans Wake*, where Jaun plays the preacher?

P.S.: Sure, and I think that in that register you can produce some fine buffoonery but you can also convey some very serious things. If I'd written the prophesies of Jeremiah, I'd have taken the violence of his utterance very seriously indeed. The moment when the prophet launches into his denunciations interests me a great deal; I mean the moment when he says, can't you see what you are doing, you're about to destroy it all, to fetishize everything. That's the crux for me. It's an anti-fetishizing discourse, anti-idol, anti-self-idolizing. That's why, you may have noticed, I have a rapport with my own writing which forbids or plays down appropriation. I don't like to speak about what I write as "my work," "my books." . . . I'm trying to maintain my distance. That's why the Bible interests me.

D.H.: Perhaps it's a sort of elimination. I'm thinking of Georges Bataille's use of defecation as necessary loss or waste.

P.S.: Yes, for me it's always a sort of waste product. But I believe that the waste product is that much less fetishized when it is recognized for what it is. If you see it as waste, you're not apt to turn it into an idol. But if you believe in fact that a turd, your turd, is really something important, then even if you don't worship your shit, you'll find a golden calf to worship somewhere else.

The Bible gives us a fine version of that. It speaks of only one thing, of how hard it is to tell the human community to regulate itself in accordance with the Word and not by waste products turned into idols. There are interminable crises. It goes from crisis to crisis.

D.H.: The relapse is inevitable.

P.S.: That's what's interesting. It's the story of that impossibility that interested Schoenberg when he wrote his opera *Moses and Aaron*. He wanted to dramatize the fact that the source of language proves intolerable for the community. That's why psychoanalysis is crucial; it touches that source. It is as though you can't make the human community admit that it should regulate itself in terms of the source of language. It prefers to *use* language for other things. That's what fascinates me, how the Bible manages to recount in a simple fashion how impossible it is to submit to that source. We are still too Egyptian, too ready to elevate idols in the place of the living word. That's what I'm writing about.

D.H.: As you were reading that passage from *Paradis*, I was thinking of the structure, of the rhetoric, the images, the meanings, the aural effects, even of the slippage you mentioned earlier. I also thought of a machine object that one finds in our modern art museums—a light-organ which uses a shifting field of colored lights to produce an endless variety of abstract effects on a screen.

P.S.: Marcelin Pleynet has an essay on trends in American painting called "From Line to Color." Why did he choose that title? He and I are on the same wavelength. It's the problem I raised earlier in relation to Duchamp: How do you project a fourth dimension within the third dimension? It's the same for language. If you go from point to line, to plane, to volume—that's one order. You can also conceive of another order, one which haunts modern art in a particularly striking fashion. You can go from volume to point, from color to surface. That's another world. Instead of going from the individual to the species, for example, you start, as I try to do, at the memory of the species and discover from time to time an individual.

D.H.: Joyce does something like that in the *Wake*.

P.S.: Yes, I think so. That's why it is so difficult, not only because of the difficulty of the language, but because of the mental reversal it presupposes. It's another geometry, another topology, another relation with the infinite. *Finnegans Wake* is the invention of the *trans*finite in language. If this other world is possible, the world we now live in is relatively infantile. Just as children are in a childish world in relation to our Euclidian world.

D.H.: It makes me think of Plato—with a difference. Is it the "true" you're looking for?

P.S.: Yes, the beauty and the splendor of the truth, sure.

D.H.: Yes, but it's neither beautiful nor splendid.

P.S.: It's more Nietzschean than Platonic. You can't hold on to Plato's idealism once you've plumbed biologically the genealogy of values. It's a transmutation of values.

D.H.: You spoke earlier of the comic. I think you mean farce rather than comedy.

P.S.: Buffoonery, yes. But let me brief you on my sources. You know I'm always contributing to events that are supposed to be serious, going to seminars. At such times I'm overcome—and this has been true since I was a boy at school—overcome by the spirit of mockery. You remember what Mallarmé says in *Un coup de dés*: "*Tourbillon d'hilarité et d'horreur.*"

D.H.: That's what farce is all about. The two sides.

P.S.: It's horror as much as hilarity. Speaking of Mallarmé, here's another reference. In "Mademoiselle Mallarmé's Fan" we have the line, "*Sens-tu le paradis farouche / Ainsi qu'un rire enseveli / Se couler du coin de ta bouche / Au fond de l'unanime pli!*" Look what he's done. He has linked the word "paradise" to the word "ferocious." To my knowledge nobody ever wrote "ferocious paradise" before. But I understand immediately what he wants to say because it's what I'm trying to say. Look what he says right after that: the laugh is buried. It's a system and it's a complete break with tradition, especially in relation to Platonic thought. It's the marriage of heaven and hell. Nothing is more buried than that laugh. That vision is impossible without a very violent sentiment of horror.

D.H.: Even in the passage you read from *Paradis*, I sense the presence of horror.

P.S.: In the beginning especially, you have a description of the horror felt in the face of the succession of generations. You know about the relationship between pregnancy and cancer. They've discovered that in the development of a cancer there is probably

136

something very close to that of a pregnancy. I am all the more intrigued because Freud compared an analysis to a pregnancy. The whole passage is built around that idea. You know, with those family portraits (the ancestors), there is a feeling of horror reminiscent of Mallarmé's *Igitur*. The horror of feeling oneself as eternal in relation to that flux of generations. At the same time it moves quickly toward hilarity. Here you read "*au commencement c'était la valse.*" So you have immediately an ironic play on the Bible. But immediately after that there is a serious and non-ironic reference to the Bible. By way of contrast, the sexual sequence becomes comic. So the sexual is by turns comic and horrible while the Bible is serious and farcical.

D.H.: What interests me is that these variations fall within a carefully limited register. That is, you don't stop the flow of language. You don't permit the reader to pause to study details or ponder effects. Unlike a narrative, your text doesn't lead anywhere in particular. There are no stories or episodes.

P.S.: Or rather there are thousands of stories, a proliferation of narrative fragments which lead nowhere. They're impossible objects, like those of Piranese or Escher. You climb a staircase and find yourself facing into the void; you take another and . . . the void again. Take the automobile episode. I seem to begin a tale. I'm in a car. The word *défoncé* suggests that I've smoked some hashish. I'm sitting beside a girl, and . . . Then it stops and something else will take its place. There are lots of these bits which constitute either modulations or transitions, but they're all integrated into the whole. You never know where the possible narrator could be located. He's in a car, he's in a plane, he's watching television, he's listening to the radio, he's learning a language in a classroom, he's listening to someone talking, or he's making love somewhere, or he's participating in some adventure, or he's seven or eight years old, or he's two, or he's as old as time, or he has more memories than if he were a thousand years old. I think that's quite unusual. Generally, in a book (you talked about Kafka and Beckett) there is a certain unity in the enunciation, even if it is annulled. Even when you have micro-tales, the identity or position of the narrator is easily perceived. Here it is very hard to fix, I think.

D.H.: Do we lose ourselves or become confused?

P.S.: If one thinks of oneself as always the same, one is forever lost. But that's why it is called *Paradis*, because if we feel ourselves to be always the same, we go to Hell. That is the true meaning of the title. I tried to talk about that at the Joyce symposium. It's the new relationship between the one and the many. It's very difficult because we tend to think point-line-plane-volume.

D.H.: I was talking to Maurice Roche the other day about the structuring of his books in relation to the structure of *Finnegans Wake*, which is after all not too different. I had in mind a whole family of novels among which I'd put your own. These are works shaped by means of knots or nodes of signification. When you point out that there is a mini-narrative or a cluster of referents here, you're pointing to what I mean. Without such structuring, we'd be lost.

P.S.: Even the writer would be lost. There are plenty who write little more than babble. There is so much babbling that we can use it to prove that the crisis is acute, since they don't seem to realize that sort of thing won't work. But what differentiates the structured work from the unstructured one? It's the eye the writer has for repetition. What does he think of repetition; how does he use it; and how does he situate himself in relation to his own repetitions? You can tell at a glance when the writing is not conscious of its own repetitions. In such cases, things tend to be "repetitious." That is, we can't figure out why there is one page rather than one and a half. It could as well be twenty, a hundred, eight hundred. You know, we were talking earlier about that mysterious moment when something is equilibrated.

D.H.: Yes, we were talking about the possibility of ending a work or even a sentence.

P.S.: That's why I am not concerned about the problem of beginnings. It isn't the beginning that constitutes a problem, though it might have been. Once again, I'll refer to the metaphor for successful psychoanalysis, of which Freud says the only moments we can measure are the beginning and the end. Between the two it's like a game of checkers, a blank.

D.H.: That is a fine metaphor, but we can extend it, since the true terminus of the cure is the moment when the patient will have no more to do with his doctor, when he says, "I don't ever want to see that guy again."

P.S.: But it's a moment which can't be precalculated or predicted. So when we talk about structure, we should never give the impression that the writer can say at the start, "There we are. I have my structure. All I need do is fill it out."

D.H.: There are writers who do just that.

P.S.: There are, but in my opinion it's not an interesting procedure.

D.H.: It is less personal, less "subjective."

P.S.: But there is also the absence of suspense. In my writing, I am always, in relation to myself, in suspense. It's very interesting, very engrossing to advance, to return. . . .

D.H.: Is the reader also in suspense? He isn't expecting anything to happen.

P.S.: To the extent that it plays against his resistance, he is. I think he resists the fact that this is being done. You know, that's another thing we could have talked about at the Joyce symposium. There is a structure for the *Wake*. But that isn't the only structure of the *Wake*. The structure of *Finnegans Wake* is also the fact that Joyce wrote it over a period of seventeen years, that during that time readers didn't really know where it was taking them (perhaps it doesn't lead anywhere), that during that period he took people's money (that is also a part of the *Wake*), that during that period he had people try to guess the title of the *Wake*, that he even set up a contest complete with a prize for the one who guessed the title. That constitutes suspense. I don't think it was only a game, a joke. I believe it was part of his writing. He watched the reactions of others throughout the composition period. Their reactions nourished the book. I'm convinced that one of the principal sources of his inspiration was the reactions produced by the extracts he published through the years, even though he transposed all of this, inscribed it in a much greater project. That's how I perceive it. Perhaps other writers can say the same thing, but I'm sure that the time that passes during the writing process automatically produces effects which are written into the work.

D.H.: They say that about Proust.

P.S.: I think it's true. That's why this is a mortal game—very delicate, since it functions in terms of close and distant effects, effects on one's private life, and so on.

D.H.: I can name a number of writers who have written life-books, such as Beckett, Proust, Goethe (*Faust*), Joyce, Mallarmé (*Un coup de dés*). For each of them the work and the life constitute a whole.

P.S.: That's an important point because it's what the babblers tend to forget. They think that we can separate our lives from what we write. I think we must recall with extreme rigor that everything costs. You can't write anything of value if it doesn't find an extremely precise echo, either painful, boring, terrifying, or very pleasant, of something that occurs in the real world. But that is the hardest thing to do. And here is the fundamental game. Anyone who writes without recording the very shape of his real being, whether he makes it explicit or not, doesn't matter. He can be very discreet about his private life. I'm not talking about that.

D.H.: There is another aspect of the life-books we were talking about. Those books preoccupied their writers for extremely long periods of time. Flaubert, too, with *Bouvard et Pécuchet*. These are writers who lose themselves, bury themselves in their works, which somehow parallel their whole lives. I think that you may be doing something analogous but much more strung out, less intense.

P.S.: I've been at it now for ten years. Little by little it will become clear that that is what I am doing. Little by little the outlines of the project will become evident, and you'll see that there is a retroactive component too, or rewriting. But that will take time, and it constitutes an element of suspense, as I was saying.

D.H.: I was going to ask you where you are going from here. But now you tell me that you don't know.

P.S.: No, I can't know. After all, if I knew, I wouldn't go there. I'm going because I don't know where I'll end up. That's what Mallarmé has to say in *Igitur*. He can advance because he moves within the mystery. Let's say it in a more modern way, since it isn't a question of mystery: you can only advance if you don't know where you're going. To advance means really to take another step, write ten lines more, ten lines more, and then ten lines more. That's what it means to advance in terms of writing. To write is truly not to know where one is going. On the other hand, perhaps that is the only way to advance in any real way, if we are not simply to move, to go from one point to another. Otherwise it's always the same system. Go off in that direction, passing by the same points, marked by moments either of religion or of social rules. No one is obliged to go that way, but if you do choose that way, you can't follow the channel markers; you don't even know how you're moving. Really, it functions in terms of the suspension of awareness. On the other hand, you know very well where you've been. We could put it this way: to know where one is going is not so much to know where one is going but to know better and better where one is coming from. Kafka says something fascinating on this subject: "Nothing is true but the light on the grotesque face which retreats; nothing else."

Arno Schmidt: *from* Zettels Traum

And he footnotes that
it originally comes from
'Moeurs' & really means
'of manners' - so the
etyms blabber about 'mors'
& 'tails of Manners' -
lessay 'mannerist' :
SERV(I)US. + tailored
to fit?

(JOYCE :

Yes. Ex: 'Contes des Fees'
meanwhile 'Cock=neigh'
,(while 'Kuck='no'), 'Cunts of faeces)

(I iv,306: To speak alge-
braically:-Mr.M is execra
ble,but Mr.c. is (x plus
I)=ecrable!")

"'La musique' says MARMONTAL in those 'Contes moraux'
which in all our translations we have insisted upon
calling Moral Tales as if in mockery of their spirit
- 'La musique est le seul des talens qui jouissent de
lui même; tous les autres veulent des temoins.'".'/-:
"So=whát ? ",(W)./:"Together with the,immediately preceding 'locus', you get'Chamber=Music': which
splays/allbyitself; everything=Other requires the   (,fiddle, faddle)
presence of generates."/:"Cunts morose'",(P, agree-
ing;and):" from the motto you also get 'sine' =
sinuous bosom; and 'genio=genere=generate': no WC without
gender." :"What is 'the muggery of their spirit'?"/
:"If thát's how you pronounce it-" (P, his face bottled'):
"Just occurred to me:'mug=smug Maggies muggy'.(Even
better,probably :" 'to mug= pout=pull a face';
and above all 'to drizzle', light
rainshower, from the 'spirt'.'/-): Ex=orbi=tànt : -"
(W./(Might as well say x+l=orbitant)./Looked around
:? - (Fr fortunately 'out of sight';(that is she
was streaking in the tool ups,beside=W).)
Who took my ALL=off); People they think,too about this
green vagarietable; - lemme read a few sentences

jusaminute; cum's going too far...";'The higher order of music is the most throughly estimated,when
we are exclusively alone.' - :what does the S=lang say?'/
(As P, unpractised, hesitated -)/:" If you always keep in
mind the femoral moral of fairies: isso
simple. 'order' becomes 'ordure':'ordure=music'.
'Through' is, 'furrow.' In 'estimated' you find
'mate'. - Go on."/She looked at me disgustedly :
-(aha: Fr was in the hasslenut bush./I nodded approvingly::)-
and read (louder to be sure, than she wished): "But there is
one pleasure still within the reach of fallen mortality....:?'./:" 'a mort' 's what the Berliner
jock calls a 'strumpet' "/said P; so
'a fallen mort' is what she is. : To continue.)./
:" "I mean the happiness, experienced in the contemplation of natural scenery." (In 'contemplashion'
'cunt' & 'temple', both=in one. In 'scenery' 'see'
& the beginning of 'scent'. And 'nature' is,according to PArtridge, 'cunt'. - To continue.)./:"You'll git
your comeuppance for sure:-" (W,threateningly calm):" in truth,
the man, who would behold aright the glory of GOD
upon earth,must in solitude behold that glory'.:?"
(Since we were going to "get it" for sure, the
answer was simple):" 'truth=trous'. The man (:),who
wants to see the 'glory'?: 'glory=hole': Yes,
the 'Glory of gut' :: He'll have to have a look=at it
in his quiet little bedroom. (Solitude: so 'lit' 'étude'
there's more.)/(She opened her mollifiable mouth,and read):

(('higher' ordure;
'from the heights', from
above'.../in Monos BUNA plainishly gat io

About music in a footnote:it io
'The poetic diction, sentimental +
weaker, each in its widest sense,
the shock I music was with them...
...... in fact, the general production
when I the texts - A that which
recognizes the beautiful in its
distinction between ... shall hold
only with the ... it true
Plato = clear also from the PEENILE

($ as abbrev.)

(= the glory $ of gut upon
arse :

(:"Glory=glory=hallelûuja :
glory=glory=halleluuja;..."
:" so that the birds took wing
when bevor the insipid text!..

"'I love to regard the proud watchful mountains, that
look down upon ... but the colossal members of one vast
animate & sentient whole'. - That you will interpret
the 'watchful mountains, that look down" as 'nates'
would not surprise me in the least."(Ok W: But : they
&n the dark valleys and the gargling waters are for
him only the colassal members of one vast animate & sentient .... can you be smooch
clearer ? Please read here, right at this place=
nate : ..." (She snorted. and ... read bitterly:" 'a hole whose from (that of the sphere)
is the most perfect of all ... whose thought is that
of a ...: whose enjoyment is knowledge... whose cognisance of ourselves is akin, with our own cognisance
of the animalculae which infest the brain..' - Dän
I beg of you -"(she said emphatically:"... those
are arguments of nearly teleological dimen-
siors: : ?"/(Iessay it right off: 'super=sentient'):
"Lissen Willma : ... areya kiddin' ...
know, what 'animalculae & animalculists' are, or
were)? -"/- : ? -/:"He uses the little word
quite=a lot. And ever since LEUWENHOEK this has been
the name for minute organisms - leaving aside the
fact that he must have been additionally encouraged
by 'anus + culus', which can also be found in animalculae'. - Just a moment=Wilma: : that this is not

(hose + ballshaped
perk fuckt+ hose
gut + hose kin+ (Kenne + knowing
cognate + 'ken' ...

(you can try that when i'm
dead already

(also I iii,477 / or in Tale
loo2./ And in the 'POWER
OF WORDS. Hi i, 426 f.
843: there are two-headers!...))

just a matter of my libidinous phallacy can be proven
by STANISLAUS JOYCE; who, together with his Big brother,
among many other essay=themes, treated this one as
well : 'The seaman, who disturbs the world = the
semen, which disturbs the world' : - your eyes pop
Wilma?: is it right or not?: And us=manners they
really infest with the little bit of brain.";(I
took the book away from her again):"Listen. - Here
stands 'the cant of the more ignorant of the priest-
hood'. 'The cycles in which the stars move are those,
best adapted for the evolution,without collision,of the
greatest possible number of bodies'; and their 'surfaces
themselves are so disposed, as to accomodate a denser
population.'"./;"Lemme.have a turn -"(pleaded P.Proised
his voice;& read with beautiful excent'): "As we find
cycle within cycle!..:?"/(And W, with sidelongings):
"Yes, what would that=then be ? These concentric circles?"
(Cuntcentric was good):" the cyclical B bends itself in the
circl' : continue."/(And P, quietly): "yet all revolving
around one far=distant centre, which is the Godhead:
may we not analogically suppose, inthe same manner,
life within life, the less within the greater, and
all within the spirit divine!?'"/ - Pause. (Well ? Then ?)
-: "I think it's terrific,"(said W; sarcastically: What-
cha bitchin about already ?" : "May I remind you at
the outset : that it is the last paragraph -

(ditto for the con=tained
'time',
which I'm keeping)

(MBN 316 (nb YEATS) : 'seaman +
semen')

(Already in 1912 designated)
(ed) 'passionate transport; as
toxically caused
(cunt of the
priestdresses :
('Glasses')

faeces
(that is, through 'dung' generally

'prythe
revolting + vulve
disted + scent + gut
anal + logical +cul +semen
              +man

even the "Last Words' : - of the EUREKA ? :
"Life within life - the less within the greater,
and all within the Spirit Divine.'"/: " SoThereya
see for yaself ❢! That' ⚫S S about nothing but
cosmogony."/(I preferred to address P❢ "Do
you know of situations - (cases I mean) - where
there is 'life within life'? Precisely, that is,
'the lesser within the greater'. That 'spirit' and
'di vino = wine' is⚫of course already known. - But
read on Paul❢ Your 'r' is altogether inimitable
today."/: "In short we are madly erring-" (he
stopped of his own volition; thought -: &nodded
his emphallic approval - "that vast'clod of the valley'
which he(man) tills & contemns:.." -/⚫ : "why
do you smurk:?"(W screamed at us; then, brutally):
" What kind of a ⚫cosmic face color'is that?

⚫ And you=blabbermouth tell me what you're thinking this very minute :"/(Another spinel:? Wet's
say it's somewhat of an awashening):" It's a matter
of meataphors from the innocent world of the peasant,
my dear : 'clod;in⚫ a 'clump, lump, sod=piece, even
dungspread' - ⚫ we=Joymans speak of us
poor'clods'. 'Valley' the little vale that the
aforementioned innocent cultivates & is ⚫ deep-
furrowed: but⚫the⚫ 'young=strip-link' is 'tiller'
'striplings=tease' -"/: " Do you remember the

(+ laiwe')

(Admittedly I turned around
your end: so that even HEU-
REKA is not all astrein.. (any-
...)

lather=sexual spendings;
to grate:schaben schrapen
stossen reiben. (crater?)

(did ya ear ⚫ that ?, ⚫
the 'mud' + err + erros'?

(nice failure :)

Persians=
('Meataphernes';likea name
out of HERODOTUS

(Poe's critique ⚫ MACAULAY
⚫ has⚫:..earth, consider-
ed as man's habitation,&
the nature of that evid-
ence from which we rea-
son of the same earth re-
garded as a unit of that

vast whole, the universe.
In the former case, the
data being palpable...
(but this is almost too prick-
lyhedge full of ETYMS

TELLUS in any case is GEA.
Und thele Piez

(Fr would want to have the
'toujours perdrix;' explained
too - (For instance 'Wonqs
upon a time - & a bed thyme
it was - ~~seir~~
a (fuck)King...

livt

(MELA iii, l : Neque ad-
huc satis cognitum est an
helitune suo id mundus
efficiat, retractamque cum
spiritu regerat undam un-
dique, si (ut doctioribus
placet) unum animal est

*ergo quodeuis
meis, lubet
uatura

uemen + ere
regere
vast hole + Univ = ause*

'Tiller=Girls' of our youth?"
(the troublemaker: licherously. Stretched his
thin arms over his head at the same time; and danced,
empressively, along a stretch of the sandy path: :)
(W watched him with unambiguous=definable(facial expression.)/(Came back; & remarked needlessly): 'n
Englishman would have to think of arse=(s)lips
so 'till' and 'tool'? " Doubtlessly. And
more): PARTRIDGE - (or, since Wilma can't stand to
hear the name anymore, I'll change it) - PERDRIX=at=
first only 'till=female pludenda'. - ~~Moreen~~ Wait-
wilma: do you have an ink'link why ~~amorous~~ Po
~~unconity~~, & willing=lie=I, joined the earth=sbig'
arse=tillery? - Then hear this remark=now:
'Speaking of the tides, POMPONIUS MELA, in his treatise DE SITU ORBIS says : either the world is a great
animal, or etc.' - "; (and insidiously spreads out his
hands : so=there :)./- "I'm not coming, i'm notcoming!"
W cried excitedly; and stepped ahead, so that her
Po(m)po(m) wiggled/("and to think isso simple :):
"Speaking of the'tights' : those are ladies'slipperings.
'Popo=Mela' is "Blackass'. - Paul?: how, according to your
Oxford=Experience, should the title of his book be
pronounced?"."/(He snorted ;(answered W's punishing
look): "Mebbe if I could might git a new hankerchief

someday?...: -";(smacked; &)delivered the
decision:" De sight o'Orbs'"/(Thank=you :) :
"A treatise, therefore,on the 'surveying of
balls' (of the human=kind'. ~~You~~But we must not dis-   (a moldy piece
sputum; 'LISTEN HERE') " These fancies,& such as these,   of hollows
have always given to my meditations among the mountains
& the forests, by the rivers & the ocean, a tinge of
what the every=day=world=would not fail to term the
fantastic. My wanderings amid such scenes have been
many & far=searching & often solitary; and the inter=est with
which I have strayed through many a dim=deep valley, or gazed into
the reflected heaven of many a bright lake, has been
an interest greatly deepened by the thought, that I
have stayed & gazed alone.'....: 'La solitude est
une belle chose'"/(W had ~~begun~~(begun,slowly and
dis=tractedly, to move his ~~~~jowls)" You make him
into the most serious ~~~~ in the world. Into
a kind of quarterly=writer :For me he is still
the perfected hylotheist; for whom the substance, the
matter in short 'THE WORLD" counts as divinity. - And
you are scoffers & good-for-nothing men :", she con-
cluded heatedly./(You leap tailfast to conclusions:
of course anyone who "newnames" a street,will soon
come to hear the complaint : some of his signs are
unbeautiful - (and as proof the one lying in the
gutter will be pointed to, which indicated the county

(and the 'orb'=Series
scalled, in GEORGES,
all kinds of pertinents)

'fancy=fantasies' is,
acc. to Pogolymadar, Ent-
chem. 'ocean' = ossium/to
'scenes' add 'see + scent'
'sole ~ soul ~ those'

(+ leak, Pi

('Thats supp-hosed to be
a fine Chose' well, that
comes later (... S = hole))

('HYLEA' also means
'forestland' you know)

148

p. 37 f.

,apparently quite
sovereign self-
possession,

limits ⊕∷⦃) - others unnecessary...? And
only nodded; instead of attending to my agreement.) /
:?:but then again much more=gruffly):
"Suspend your judgement for a little longer, Wilma - tomorrow, when I am no more, youCan cul-
tivate your philosophical little Myth again, to
your heart's content. - But first let me demonstrate
sufficiently his oscillation between "reason & imagination.' In PYM he spoke very seriously of groups of representation, which present themselves to the dreamer,
alternatively & one by one, now as unqualified illuminations, now as senseless, insipidities according to the way
flickering alternation of spiritual powers
between the rational or the imagistic.' . The
'rational' of this FAY=here,(then we have just paid
some attention to : In my opinion the "Theoretical
Introductions" show exactly the same symptoms, just
as concentrated only more colorless, as the 'illustration'
through painting which comes now."/-) "In ARNHEIM -".(Fr;
who evidently considers her assignment of protecting
P against W as completed, and snuggled=up next to me):
"- thas specially clear there, that=uh : Two=
sidedness of the shtories?" (Here there are a lot of
Examples But): "That takes place in ARNHEIM -(whatever
that may be) - while we are here, in the FAY,
are where, Paul?-Wilma? - . -):" Well he quotes from

149

'So blended bank & shad-
ow there, that each seem-
ed pendulous in air. In
the original however:
'So blend the turrets &
shadows there, that all
seem pendulous in air.'

(ERNE :

(the e) a prophecy =
professional : a
prostitute, I kept
for myself)

his own poems! - "/"Oooh, that's whatyouMean,'
said P)." the CITY IN THE SEA." (What else ? -) ?/
"Well now, it had several titles - which for a
writer is the same as giving information'. :?. -
For instance 'THE DOOMED CITY' THE CITY OF SIN'.
Letme pose you the question again : where=fore, in 1
word, is the locality of this FEE? -", /-:
KILLIS CAMPBELL: 'Babylon' -" (P;
beardstubblescratching; then 'hesitant;-)/Don't
tell me about these philololiers : (Even though
the conscious "Babylonian Lady' would fit,
).: "Now please : : it is a) a seat
of sin;b) dedicated to corruption; c) a city in the
sea; d) a city of the Dead ... - : isn't there
anyone among us versed in the Scriptures?"/(And
everyone, looked at Francisca? Who her hips
diplomatically; & then, stated w/ con-viction you say
all that,? then I think of SODOM & GOMORRHA'. / (And a lovely pause to be
    heard. -). The last paving stones were
    along with their colors and forms, of
    incalculable value//A light, two-wheeled
    wagon, with a blonde sandy Norwegian pony up
    front, came toward us; in the seat (lanky)
    man: green leather jacket; brown pants; he
    observed us sharply, as he rolled=by: (me, at
    least? ; with a crabby mouth?/-): "Flesh ::

losing themselves,

correspondingly

type

Flesh : -" groaned Paul; "i suddenly have
a ware-itable vulvs=hunger :"/-: ?/-):
"Oanything; with slut's of cullsories:
breadst for all I care. Uppateat uffor Ghoularse."
(With sinnamon, what ?)! What would sate your
mastication the most sadismasfactorily Paul?"
(He wheT his lips & tongue; and began to wish:
"Maccaroni -(a whole wash=basin full) -with
(Kursemeat=balls. Cheese: grated=Swiss; (or
Parmesan.) Young peas. Tomato=Sauce. Spinich &
Sunny-side up eggs.... I could get wiped=out :" -
(And sketched then a fundamental project for the
happiness of humanity: the creation of eating-
houses in even the smallest villages. Importa-
tion of Chinese personnel;(the Germans urgently
need to be crossed with races which are willing
to work - this probably only Mongols need apply?
The guy in the gig=Over=there=around once more.
But)

Translated by   H. I. S. de Genez

(and no less a 'brand'
ok? : head to tail;
a double header con-
tinually at odds with
our=selves :)

(cf. pipe=noddles;
the image of a washbasin
meatballs : yummy;
& bite=in/ Swiss(h) +
(x)rated; or else par
mon sang/young p's
tummy=meat=sauce, or
tummy=made(maid;(mate;
tummy=yummy; and that he
gets the desire portion:
so: was shown by the
equivalent of a hug
spinach is a penis-
symbol & digestive at
the same time,/ while
eggs sunny side up=
a pair of (1)eggs up
Tomato sosauce cunte
maybe even blood?/
The end result phalls
out: wiped=out/scream
of avaging man for
skirted flesh. shorter=
spicier. The libido
pokes in the cliMatestom-
arium."

"'La musique'says l'NNMORTAL in those 'Contes moraux'
which in all our translations we have insisted upon
calling Moral Tales as if in mockery of their spirit
- 'La musique est le seul des talens qui jouissent de
lui même;tous les autres veulent des temoins.'"/-:
"Na=fndt ? "(W)/:"Zusammen mit den,unmittelbar vor-
angehenden 'Lokus', ergibt sich'Chamber=Music': die
schpül'/Gansfürsichallein:alles=Andre erfordert die 'moussiziert,
Gegenwart von Zeugen."/:" 'Cunts morose'",(P,einver-
standn;und):" vom Kotto her schallt noch 'sine' =
Sinusbusen; und 'genio=genere=zeugen': Kein Klo ohne
Zeugungstaile."/:"Was ist 'the muggery of their spirt'?"/
:"Wenn Du's só ausspricchst -" (F, his face flascht'):
"fällt mir ein:'Krug=kanne Fratze schwül'. "(Noch zu-
ständiger wäre wohl):" 'to mug = pout=ein Schnütchen
machen'; und vor allem 'to drizzle', leichter
Sprühregen, aus dem 'spirt'.'/-/):" 'Ex=orbi=tànt ! -"
(W./(KannsD getrost x+1=orbitant sagn)./Sah sich um
:? - (Pr erfreulicherweise 'außer Sicht';(dh Sie
steakte natürlich in dem Ginsterbusch,neben=W).)
Die mir den ALLEN ab=nahm):"Leute denkt'och an dies
Grüne Gemüse! - Ich wähl ma einfach n paa
Sätze aus;s geht ja zu weit...':"The higher order of music is the most thoroughly estimated,when
we are exclusively alone.' - :Was sagt der S=lang ?"/
(Da P, ungeübt, zögerte -/-: "Wenn Ihr immer die fe-
morale Koral der Feen im Auge behaltet : issis ganz

(Und Er macht die Fußnote;
daß es von 'Moeurs' käme;
& eigentlich 'of manners'
bedeute - also blubbern
die Etyms von 'Mors' &
'tails of Mä ners' - sa-
gn wa 'Sittenbilder'. ‡
SERV(I)UB.f(+ Taille ?

JOYCE !

(Ja. zB 'Contes des Fées'
wären den 'Cock=neigh'
;(dem 'Kuck=nein'),'Cun-
ts of faeces'

(P: sott ....)

(I 1v,306.To speak alge-
braically:-Mr.M is execra-
ble,but Mr.d. is (x Plus
1)=ecrable?")

einfach. 'order' wird zu 'ordure':'ordure=music'. 'Thorough' ist, selbst nach MURET=SANDERS (MS), 'Furche'. In 'estimated' steckt 'mate'. - Weiter."/Sie betrachtete mich angewidert : [redacted] -(ähä: in dem Haselbusch hatte Fr gesteckt./Ich nikkte Ihr lobmd zu:!)- und las (lauter wohl, als Sie wollte):"But there is one pleasure still within the reach of fallen mortality...':?". / :" 'a mort' [redacted] ss das, was der berlinische Ganove 'ne Puppe' tittuliert,"(sagte F; ('a fallen mort'also das, was sie ist. : Weiter!)./ :" 'I mean the happiness, experienced in the contemplation of natural scenery'!" [redacted] (In 'contemplashion' 'cunt' & 'temple', beides=eins. In 'scenery' 'see' & der Anfang von 'scent'. Und 'nature' ist,laut PARtridge, [redacted] 'cunt'. - Weiter, [redacted]). /:"Ihr krickt Eure Antwort noch!-" (W,drohend gefaßt):" 'in truth, the man,who would behold aright the glory of GOD upon earth,must in solitude behold that glory'.:?" [redacted] (Da Wir's doch noch 'kriegn' solltn, war die Antwort einfach):" 'truth=trous'. Der Mann (!),der die 'glory' sehen will ?: 'glory'=glory=hole ! Ja, the 'Glory of gut' !: Der muß sie sich im stillen Kämmerlein [redacted]=sehen." (Das 'sol' in 'solitjud' oä: kommt noch.)/(Sie öffnete (ostbitek) den mollijn Lunt,und las): "'I love to regard the proud watchful mountains,that look down upon ... as but the colossal members of one vast animate & sentient whole'. - Daß Ihr die'von obm herabschauenden 'mountains' als 'nates' deuten werdet, erwarte ich gar nich anders."/(Schon recht W;)Aber:Sie & das dunkle 'tälchen & die löchelnden Wasser, sind Ihm nur die culussalen Glieder eines weit=gedehnt animierten [redacted] & gefühlijn [redacted] kann man es fühl=deutlicher sagn ?-Lies doch,bitte, genau an dieser Nat=Stelle weiter : ..."/(Sie schnaubte. Und las er-

[illegible]

((('higher' ordure : [redacted] 'aus der Höhe' [redacted], 'von obm'... / in MONOS & UNA [illegible] Er von Musik [illegible] : sie sei 'The poetic diction, sentiment & creation, each in its widest sense. The study of music was with them (den [illegible]), in fact, the general cultivation of the taste - of that which recognizes the beautiful - in contra distinction from reason, which deals only with the true.' (Da[illegible] von Plato [illegible], [redacted] [illegible] PERNICE [illegible])

(Ø als Aks

(= the glory Ø of gut upon arse !

(:" Glory=glory=hallelúuja : glory=glory=halleluuja :..." ;(daß die Vögl for dem einfältijn Text auf=flogn !...

Christine Brooke-Rose: from Thru

/

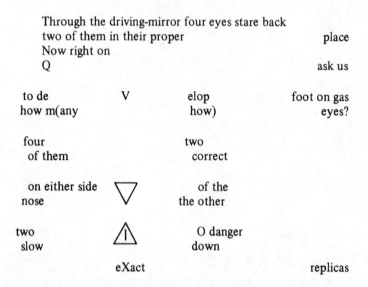

Through the driving-mirror four eyes stare back
two of them in their proper   place
Now right on
Q   ask us

  to de   V   elop   foot on gas
  how m(any   how)   eyes?

  four   two
   of them   correct

   on either side   of the
  nose   the other

  two   O danger
  slow   down

      eXact   replicas

nearer the hairline further up the brow but dimmed as in a glass
tarnished by the close-cropped mat of hair they peer through

The mat of hair is khaki, growing a bit too low on the brow
the nose too big.

Who speaks?

  le rétro   viseur   (some   languages
    more   visible than   others)

or the vizir looming grey eminence behind the consultan listener how
many times leaning a little to the right to peer into how many
rectangles a thousand and one in which there is a   flaw?

    The second pair of eyes are less pale veiled by
    the reflected hair crinkly khaki flecked grey

    O but handsome all told whatever all is and who
    ever tells a young god yet the lower eyes lie
    blue to the tarnished replicas higher up the brow
    which whoever speaks (Nourennin?) calls too low.

                          Some tale-bearer

(O capital!   your
                           story or   your
                           life
             wot no   story?
                no   life
punishment)   So that
Hang it all
                no   life
                       story
             off with   your
head   said the
chief   in-sultan to   his
                      red red rose
             washed by
             once upon
             (some times)   purple passages
             (other times)
hanging   suspen(I)s
             from the
capital   of
Baghdad
Rome
Athens
Istambul   busy anteroom
                      con ⎰ st(anza)
                          ⎱ (ante)
Neopolis
                     scarlet

                    WHORE of Babel   Whose?
                    HITE queen goddess   Who
                    Is always
                    Cramping
                    HIS styl   us
         under
         perpetual sentence
subject   predicatimetable
         just like life
                    the scrapegloat of
SIN   TAG   MA   TRICKS

    But when the muscular shoulders shift back to the
correct position the cars that loom grey eminent into the
retrovizor do not look double-faced or even quadruple-
eyed top two through crinkly hair, for the hair has moved
away out of focus together with the four eyes; the cars un-
tarnished, with single metal grins between two pale gold
eyes, one on either side, or else two smaller city
slickers lower down but never both pairs together.

      My love is like a white white rabbit

                                                       late
down the hatch
                         out of sight
                         dead   (safe)
earthhole though
          il court il court le furet
and which way did he go?
thattaway
hey follow that car
          you should have seen the one that got   away
                         that always gets   away
                                                    safe
          as a jack-in-the-box
sitting beside
hiding behind
eyeing beneath
the grey eminence the retro-vizir beyond the in sultan
hearer of deep structures below the performance con yes your
eminence I'm coming to that your reference moves up glaring

BUT

the retrovizor has a bluish tinge. At a flick of a switch the
rectangle turns smoky grey to dim the dazzle of floodlights
undipped or even gently dipped but the glare is preferable
to the sudden isolation of almost not seeing behind   a
head

Ali Nourennin

To be discussed

entering a visually over	roomful of rectangular	freshmanfaces tables minds	floating audio into which you
enter unom repeat per	nisciently form what	for that time ever the deep	table space level comp
etence twelve stricted to	times a sem one technique	ester nor is the unless of course	a(u)ctor re he (who?) so
chooses he and out of	can use sever which he builds	al in layers up his effects	through which yes er
Paul? What intentional	do you mean fallacy yes	builds up what of course but	about the any message
narrative or Garbage-can?	not has an e Receptor then	mitter and a What does the o	recipient. mitter omit?

The dancing hoops. For the gold eyes when distant turn into
hoops (at night in the correct position) of luminous green
red amber white bouncing in out of through and through each
other narrowing to slim ovals vertical horizontal swaying
undoing swiftly changing shape as if juggled by a mad magician or by the black recumbent street beneath overhead bridges that make perhaps the optical illusion?

She shifts the mirror to her rearward glance. It doesn't
work for her the mistress of the moment of sudden
isolation at not seeing back to the black magician who
fantastically juggles luminous hoops in the retro-rec-
tangular hey put my mirror back.

So it needs adjusting.
Why at that precise point introduce this or that?

Intensity of illusion is what matters to the narrator
through a flaw in the glass darkly perhaps making four
clear eyes stare back, two of them in their proper place at
height of bridge of nose and, further up the brow, the

other two, exact replicas but dimned as in a tarnished re-
flection, tarnished by the hairline they peer through. A

second pair of eyes hidden higher up the brow would have
its uses despite psychic invisibility or because of.
Gazing they do not see themselves. They reflect
nothing, nor do they look at their bright replicas below
in their proper place on either side of the nose a
fraction too large according to whoever speaks in this
instance. Only these lower eyes, reflecting the
eyes of the real face as it leans for vanity to the
right, see the upper eyes, looking up at the brow which
some teller or other thinks too low.   Who?
                                                  Oh her.

W
h
o
,
s

s
h
e

w
h
e
n

s
h
e
,
s

a
t

h
o
m
e
?

```
                    never              the    lesS
                    this is                   noT
                                              nO
                                       (My)
          the                    h Y s T e R y  of The
                                                      Eye
becAuse I would noT              S e E thY      cRuel  Nails
boaRish                                         fAngs
                          pluck  ouT                   hIs
              pooR old           (E    Xtract)   (Cruel
    Cruel     nAils)    uPon           These     eyEs of
    tHine
    I'll set     (C     R u El                  fanGs)
             my        foOt  Poo R old eyes
    These    eyEs         hIs  eYes
pooR old eyes
  beAm                                           Mote
    Cruel            fanGs
    Eyes            cRuel                        fAngs
                    boArish
                    bea M
                       Moat
                       Etc
                    alreaDy      (all read eye)

                    naIls
                    Nails

              upon These
            eyes of tHine I'll
                 sEt

           the re Mote    sTone
           Wide    Eyes   wEt?
           pArch   Ment   waX
           arXi    stOne  Trace
                    dRy
                   papYrus
                   eye 'S
```

blue lacuna of learning
and unlearning a text within a text passed on from
generation to generation of an increasing vastness that
nevertheless dwindles to an elite initiated to a text no-
one else will read by means maybe of the flick of a
switch for the overhead projector and diagrams drawn
into a boxed screen to the right of the desk with a
spirit-loaded pen thus not losing eye-contact.

The quiver of the bhi on the beeswax

How doth the bithy little Thoth
produthe an endleth piethe of cloth
when thought, that bithy little moth
devourth it all like tho much froth
leaving great holth, tho Thamuth quoth.

a busy competent performance before busy bees
who palp oscult measure time listen see
smell taste imitate suck the performer dry.

Hang it all we have the story of an △
O but is not incompetent performance a non-disjunction at
level of deep structure? I me if it be possible despite non-
equivalence to rewrite I as O and O as I

which has been suggested,
here,
you see,

      cosÍ   I

        I   I

should you start structuring your te⊃⊂thattaway
or the   latterway?
   Those for: Peter Brandt Barbara Darcy Francesca
Newman Robert Galliard Myra Kaplan Kathleen
O'Shaunessy Ali Nourennin Renata Polanska Lin Su Fu.
   Those against: Vittoria Charib Marie Faber Salvatore
Tancredi Michael Mandel Jean-Marie Fèvre Eliza Jones.

Abstention: Paul Stradiver Julia Weintraub Neil Alder.

? Refusal of Vote: Saroja Chaitwantee.

a show of hands within a secret ballot

which is one way of introducing a cast-list.

unless Armel inventing Larissa

or Larissa	"	Armel
, Armel	"	Veronica
" Veronica	"	Armel
" Armel	"	Larissa
" Larissa	"	Marco (or is it Oscar?)
" Marco (?)	"	Larissa
" Larissa	"	Armel

The other possible permutations do not occur
for logical reasons: Larissa could invent Veronica but
in a limited subjective way in any case Veronica and she are
contradictories not contraries as Socrates explained
to Protagoras and Structural Semantics has just re-
invented. While Armel could invent Marco or is it
Tariel and vice versa but due to the double standard
in practice would not stoop or merely would not have the curiosity. Clearly Marco does not invent Veronica nor she even
utter Marco (or is it Stavro?) they've never met besides
Stavro has no imagination.

On the other hand the hypotheses could have been
posed anticlockwise:

Larissa	inventing	Oscar
Oscar	"	Larissa
Larissa	"	Armel
Armel	"	Veronica
Veronica	"	Armel
Armel	"	Larissa
Larissa	"	Armel
Armel	"	?

er something's gone wrong here there seems to be
room for some extra who why the mistress of the moment
since the man any man must be if not many at least
one up who will fairly soon be dropped for she does
not see by day the four lies in the retrovizor when
shifted to her forward gaze nor dancing hoops by night

      But it needs adjusting.
Well then I found myself with a magician on a
helluva stage as his stooge you know in tights
and a sequin bodice and my bust like it was busting
tight out of it and I was handing him coloured scarves

i think and suddenly a prop was missing I forget his
stick I mean his wand anyway it was my fault he couldn't

Lift the white rabbit out of the hat and the crowd murmured
and even shouted as he signalled frantically like mad
right into the wings but they didn't get the message and
in the end he walked off leaving me alone on stage to cope
somehow in the glare of lights that hits the mirror and
swings left out of it beaming ahead rewritten now
as two small red eyes in a hunched black shape which is

delineated against forward floodlight the retrovizor re-
opening to the hoops dancing up and down and aside
in the rear distance luminous horizontal ovals oh
no, vertical ovals as if at quarter angle amber red
green white swiftly changing shape and juggled by the

night or by the tall dark house with blue eyes
or maybe by the black recumbent street who
was very short and fat for a magician more than

obese you've never seen anything so fat he tried to
reach the switches to calm the audience but he was so

Very fat and short so he lifted me in my tights and bodice
ever so firm under the breasts with them busting
right out of the sequins and I managed to switch them
off and as he brought me down we kissed half
naked ever so sexy and then we started wanting
it like crazy but I said no later we have to
calm the crowd so he got wild and dragged me
after him out of the theatre but I wrenched free
            saying the show must go on can you interpret
?
The show within the show
What?
of hands juggling

within a secret ballet of the I
hell honey I guess I just fill the air for you sure that's what
i like about you oh I thought it was my big beautiful
true blue tits they're fine too with a show of hands
entering under silk with a secret ballet of fingers on

tiptoe upon soft globed flesh the nipple now rising
hard between the lights the foot pressed gently purring
into a stop the is it sacred belly tensed to the show of
green fingers into the left thigh that jerks open to the
hot human humidity of a sexual humour secreted un-
secretly go on then

Doing what?
Oh filling the air. You do

it so much more convincingly
than the others (tit for

tat)
what others?
others who fill the air.   Oh

Well   you were giving   mmmmm   a class on British
history   for some   mystErious   reasoN
                                                   Oh
                          yes eXcite me   Mmm   how
in the royal   navY   they
                          Punished the   Sailors
there   yEs   There
                                                   Er
              by making them Climb out and
er   walk the plank
              and all the planks sTuck out all   Round
like   hEll honey   Yes   your
eminence   oh Don't   like
guns I'm coming   to that
                          Go on
so when they   droppEd   into the
                          Sea
                    what The planks no the

                    sailors silly a hUge eagle
                          boy   aRe you big
                              WEll he'd swoop
                    down on thEm and they had to
                                eLiminate himmmmmmmm
                          welL fight
                                              It out
                              in the
                                          Water
                    and if tHey
won   they were hAuled out
              thEy   weNt free and you
          demonstRated   iT
            to the

                              Class you jumped the plank
                          and foUght it
out   with the eagle and
          wrrrrrrrrrrrrrrrrrruNg
                          iTs neck.

You're mythologising me.
Oh any time. And then you came with your car and said come
unto me I'll light the way and well

drove off

across the bridge in the scintillating foreign city

did you?   No I didn't
Dopey relations you have with your magician men.
Yeah but he wasn't you Stavro that was the first dream
but he was short well you're short too but he was
immensely fat and couldn't have strangled an eagle in
the water for anything he'd have sunk you turn left at the
corner
Hey I know.
Yes you should by now but you always forget.
Okay can you see a spot?
Usually there's one further up on the right. Here.

Fizzle 1

Samuel Beckett

He is barehead, barefoot, clothed in a singlet and tight trousers
too short for him, his hands have told him so, again and again, and
his feet, feeling each other and rubbing against the legs, up and
down calves and shins. To this vaguely prison garb none of his memories answer, so far, but all are of heaviness, in this connection, of
fullness and of thickness. The great head where he toils is all mockery, he is forth again, he'll be back again. Some day he'll see himself, his whole front, from the chest down, and the arms, and finally
the hands, first rigid at arm's length, then close up, trembling, to his
eyes. He halts, for the first time since he knows he's under way,
one foot before the other, the higher flat, the lower on its toes,
and waits for a decision. Then he moves on. Spite of the dark he
does not grope his way, arms outstretched, hands agape and the
feet held back just before the ground. With the result he must often,
namely at every turn, strike against the walls that hem his path,
against the right-hand when he turns left, the left-hand when he
turns right, now with his foot, now with the crown of his head,
for he holds himself bowed, because of the rise, and because he

always holds himself bowed, his back humped, his head thrust forward, his eyes cast down. He loses his blood, but in no great quantity, the little wounds have time to close before being opened again, his pace is so slow. There are places where the walls almost meet, then it is the shoulders take the shock. But instead of stopping short, and even turning back, saying to himself, this is the end of the road, nothing now but to return to the other terminus and start again, instead he attacks the narrow sideways and so finally squeezes through, to the great hurt of his chest and back. Do his eyes, after such long exposure to the gloom, begin to pierce it? No, and this is one of the reasons why he shuts them more and more, more and more often and for ever longer spells. For his concern is increasingly to spare himself needless fatigue, such as that come of staring before him, and even all about him, hour after hour, day after day, and never seeing a thing. This is not the time to go into his wrongs, but perhaps he was wrong not to persist in his efforts to pierce the gloom. For he might well have succeeded, in the end, up to a point, which would have brightened things up for him, nothing like a ray of light, from time to time, to brighten things up for one. And all may yet grow light, at any moment, first dimly and then—how can one say?—then more and more, till all is flooded with light, the way, the ground, the walls, the vault, without his being one whit the wiser. The moon may appear, framed at the end of the vista, and he in no state to rejoice and quicken his step, or on the contrary wheel and run, while there is yet time. For the moment however no complaints, which is the main. The legs notably seem in good shape, that is a blessing, Murphy had first-rate legs. The head is still a little weak, it needs time to get going again, that part does. No sign of insanity in any case, that is a blessing. Meager equipment, but well balanced. The heart? No complaints. It's going again, enough to see him through. But see how now, having turned right for example, instead of turning left a little further on he turns right again. And see how now again, yet a little further on, instead of turning left at last he turns right yet again. And so on until, instead of turning right yet again, as he expected, he turns left at last. Then for a time his zigzags resume their tenor, deflecting him alternately to right and left, that is to say bearing him onward in a straight line more

164

or less, but no longer the same straight line as when he set forth, or rather as when he suddenly realized he was forth, or perhaps after all the same. For if there are long periods when the right predominates, there are others when the left prevails. It matters little in any case, so long as he keeps on climbing. But see how now, a little further on, the ground falls away so sheer that he has to rear violently backward in order not to fall. Where is it then that life awaits him, in relation to his starting point, to the point rather at which he suddenly realized he was started, above or below? Or will they cancel out in the end, the long gentle climbs and headlong steeps? It matters little in any case, so long as he is on the right road, and that he is, for there are no others, unless he has let them slip by unnoticed, one after another. Walls and ground, if not of stone, are no less hard, to the touch, and wet. The former, certain days, he stops to lick. The fauna, if any, is silent. The only sounds, apart from those of the body on its way, are of fall, a great drop dropping at last from a great height and bursting, a solid mass that leaves its place and crashes down, lighter particle collapsing slowly. Then the echo is heard, as loud at first as the sound that woke it and repeated sometimes a good score of times, each time a little weaker, no, sometimes louder than the time before, till finally it dies away. Then silence again, broken only by the sound, intricate and faint, of the body on its way. But such sounds of fall are not common and mostly silence reigns, broken only by the sounds of the body on its way, of the bare feet on the wet ground, of the labored breathing, of the body striking against the walls or squeezing through the narrows, of the clothes, singlet and trousers, espousing and resisting the movements of the body, coming unstuck from the damp flesh and sticking to it again, tattering and fluttered where in tatters already by sudden flurries as suddenly stilled, and finally of the hands as now and then they pass, back and forth, over all those parts of the body they can reach without fatigue. He himself has yet to drop. The air is foul. Sometimes he halts and leans against a wall, his feet wedged against the other. He has already a number of memories, from the memory of the day he suddenly knew he was there, on this same path still bearing him along, to that now of having halted to lean against the wall, he has a little past already, even a smatter of settled ways. But it is all still fragile. And often he surprises himself, both moving and at rest, but more often moving, for he seldom comes to rest, as destitute of history as on that first day, on this same path, which is his beginning, on days of great recall. But usually now, the surprise once past, memory returns and takes him back, if he will, far back to that first instant beyond which nothing, when he was already old, that is to say near to death, and knew, though unable to recall having lived, what age and death are, with other momentous matters. But it is all still fragile. And often he suddenly begins, in these black windings, and makes his first steps for quite a while before realizing they are merely the last, or latest. The air is so foul that only he seems fitted to survive it who never breathed the other, the true life-giving, or so long ago as to amount to never. And such true air, coming hard on that of here, would very likely prove fatal, after a few lungfuls. But the change from one to the other will no doubt be gentle, when the time comes, and gradual, as the man draws closer and closer to the open. And perhaps even now the air is less foul than when he started, than when he suddenly realized he was started. In any case little by little his history takes shape, with if not yet exactly its good days and bad, at least studded with occasions passing rightly or wrongly for outstanding, such as the straitest narrow, the loudest fall, the most lingering collapse, the steepest descent, the greatest number of successive turns the same way, the greatest fatigue, the longest rest, the longest—aside from the sound of the body on its way—silence. Ah yes, and the most rewarding passage of the hands, on the one hand, the feet, on the other, over all those parts of the body within their reach. And the sweetest wall lick. In a word all the summits. Then other summits, hardly less elevated, such as a shock so rude that it rivaled the rudest of all. Then others still, scarcely less eminent, a wall lick so sweet as to vie with the second sweetest. Then little or nothing of note till the minima, these two unforgettable, on days of great recall, a sound of fall so muted by the distance, or for want of weight, or for lack of space between departure and arrival, that it was perhaps his fancy. Or again, second example, no, not a good example. Other landmarks still are provided by first times, and even second. Thus the first narrow, for example, no doubt because he was not expecting it, impressed him quite as strongly as the straitest, just as the second collapse, no doubt because he was expecting it, was no less than the briefest never to be forgotten. So with one thing and another little by little his history takes shape, and even changes shape, as new maxima and minima tend to cast into the shade, and toward oblivion, those momentarily glorified, and as fresh elements and motifs, such as these bones of which more very shortly, and at length, in view of their importance, contribute to enrich it.

The voice in the closet
Raymond Federman

here now again selectricstud makes me speak with its balls all balls
foutaise sam says in his closet upstairs but this time it's going to
be serious no more masturbating on the third floor escaping into
the trees no the trees were cut down liar it's winter now delays no
more false starts yesterday a rock flew through the windowpane
voices and all I see him from the corner of my eye no more playing
some boys in the street laughing up and down the pages en fourire
goofing my life it's a sign almost hit him in the face scared the hell
out of him as he waits for me to unfold upstairs perhaps the signal
of a departure in my own voice at last a beginning after so many
detours relentless false justifications in the margins more to come in
my own words now that I may speak say I the real story from
the other side extricated from inside roles reversed without further
delay they pushed me into the closet on the third floor I am
speaking of us into a box beat me black and blue question of
perspective how it should have started in my little boy's shorts I
am speaking of us sssh it's summertime lies again we must hide
the boy sssh mother whispering in her tears hurts to lose all the
time in the courtyard bird blowing his brains out on alto guts
squeaking lover man can you hear it now yellow feather cam sent

it to me at his fingertips plagiarizing my life boys passing in the
street they threw sand in his eyes it begins downstairs soldiers calling
our names his too federman all wrong don't let him escape no
not this time must save the boy full circle from his fingers into my
voice back to him on the machine just heard the first echo tioli
how idiotic what did he expect callow it says after twenty years
banging his head against the wall rattling the old stories ah what's
the use watch him search in his dictionary callow unfledged youth
almost hit him in the face federman featherless little boy dammit
in our closet after so many false names foisted upon me evading
the truth he wrote all the doors opened to stare at my nakedness
a metaphor I suppose a twisted laugh wrong again writing himself
into a corner inside where they kept old newspapers delirious
strokes of typographiphobia fatal however only on occasions
his fingers on the machine make me book of flights speak traps
evasions question of patience determination take it or leave it of
all places there goes five hundred copies down the drain through
the windowpane something about the futility of telling experi-
menting with the peripatetic search for love sex self or is it real
people america aside from what is said there is nothing silence
sam again what takes place in the closet is not said irrelevant here
if it were to be known one would know it my life began in a
closet a symbolic rebirth in retrospect as he shoves me in his stories
whines his radical laughter up and down pulverized pages with
his balls mad fizzling punctuation question of changing one's perspective view the self from the inside from the point of view of its
capacity its willpower federman achieve the vocation of your
name beyond all forms of anthropologism a positive child anthro-
pomorphism rather than the sad offspring of a family giggling
they pushed me into the closet among empty skins and dusty hats
my mother my father the soldiers they cut little boys' hands old
wife's tale send him into his life cut me now from your voice
not that I be what I was machines but what I will be father mother
quick downstairs already the boots same old problem he tried oh
how he tried of course imagining that the self must be made
remade caught from some retroactive present apprehended rein-
stated I presume looking back how naive into the past my life began
not again whereas in fact my mother was crying softly as the door
closes on me I'm beginning to see my shape only from the past from

the reverse of farness looking to the present can one possibly into the future even create the true me invent you federman with your noodles gambling my life away double or nothing in your verbal delirium don't let anyone interfere with our project cancel our journey in my own words inside the real story again my father too coughing his tuberculosis as they locked him into the closet they cut little boys' hands alone waiting on his third floor crapping me on his paper what a joke the soldiers quick sssh and all the doors slammed shut the boots in the staircase where it should have started but not him no instead calmly he shoves the statue of liberty at us very symbolic over the girl's shoulder I tremble in his lies nothing he says about the past but I see it from the corner of my eye even tried to protest while the outside goes in then smiles among the beasts and writes one morning a bird flew into my head ah what insolence what about the yellow star on my chest yes what about it federman the truth to say where they kept old wrinkled clothes empty skins dusty hats and behind the newspapers stolen bags of sugar cubes how I crouched like a sphinx falling for his wordshit moinous but where were you tell me dancing when it all started where were you when the door closed on me shouting I ask you when I needed you the most letting me be erased in the dark at random in his words scattered nakedly telling me where to go how many times yes how many times must he foist his old voice on me his detours cancellations ah that's a good one lies lies me to tell now procrastinations I warned him deep into my designs refusing to say millions of words wasted to say the same old thing mere competence never getting it straight his repetitions what really happened ways to cancel my life digressively each space relating to nothing other than itself me inside his hands progress quickly discouraged saying that it was mad laughter to pass the time two boxes correspondence of space the right aggregate while he inflicts false names on me distorts our beginning but now I stoop on the newspapers groping to the walls for the dimensions of my body while he stares at his selectricstud humping paper each space within itself becoming the figure of our unreality scratched from words the designs twirl just enough for me to speak and I fall for his crap to make me puppet believing he is me or vice versa born voiceless I cry in the dark now down the staircase with their bundles moaning yellow stars to the furnace the boots my father mother sisters too to their final solution when I needed him the most last image of my beginning to the trains to be remade unmade to shade the light and he calls me boris when I stood on the threshold boris my first false name but he erased that too in a stroke of impatience made me anonymous nameless choose for yourself he mutters a name among infinite possibilities I tried to protest gives us blank spaces instead while he hides inside his own decomposition homme de plume hombre della pluma reverses his real name namredef between the lines in the corners featherman sings his signs antic- ipating his vocation leaps over the precipice cancels the real story with exaggerations I watched him long ago make images among the beasts how many false starts for me to go but where if the door was opened by mid-afternoon the world had come alive dust burnt pains in the guts squeaking pretending to be dead I replay the image down the staircase perhaps I slept the whole time and a bird flew in my head past his face through the windowpane scared him face to face with myself I threw sand in his eyes struck his back with a stick in his delirium whining like a wounded animal I squat on the newspapers unfolded here by shame to defecate my fear as he continues to scream multiplying voices within voices to silence me holding my penis away not to piss on my legs clumsily continues to fabricate his design in circles doodles me up and down his pages of insolence two closets on the third floor separate correspondence of birth in time seeking the right connection meaning of all meanings but from this angle never a primary phenomenon to end again reducible to nonsense excrement of a beginning in the dark I folded the paper into a neat package for the birds smelling my hands by reflex or to disintegrate years later but he ignores that too obsessed by fake images while sucking his pieces of stolen sugar on the roof by the ladder outside the glass door the moon tiptoed across the clouds curiosity drove me down the staircase but I stumbled on the twelfth step and fell and all the doors opened dumb eyes to stare at my nakedness among the beasts still hoping for survival my father mother sisters but already the trains are rolling in the night as I ran beneath the sky a yellow star struck my breast and all eyes turned away I told him tried to explain how it must have started upstairs they grabbed me and locked me in a box dragged me a hundred times over the earth in metaphorical disgrace while the soldiers chased each other with

stones in their hands and burned all the stars in a furnace my survival a mistake he cannot accept forces him to begin conditionally
by another form of sequestration pretends to lock himself in a
room with the if of my existence the story told in laughter but it
resists and recites first the displacement of its displacements
leaving me on the threshold staring dumbfounded at the statue of
liberty over the girl's shoulder question of selecting the proper
beginning he claims then drags me into the subway to stare in guilt
again between a woman's legs at the triangular cunt of america
leads me down the corridor to masturbate his substitution instead
of giving me an original experience to deceive the absence of a
woman's hand makes believe that I am dead twelve years old when
they left me in the primordial closet moment upstairs on the third
floor with the old newspapers empty skins seeking unknown pleasure which is only an amorphous substitution thinking that memory
is innocent always tells the truth while cheating the original experience the first gesture a hand reaching for the walls to find its
proper place since he failed to generate the real story in vain
situates me in the wrong abode as I turn in a void in his obligation
to assign a beginning however sad it may be to my residence here
before memory had a source so that it may unfold according to a
temporal order a spatial displacement made of words inside his
noodling complexities of plagiaristic form I was dead he thinks skips
me but I am being given birth into death beyond the open door
such is my condition the feet are clear already of the great cunt
of existence backward my head will be last to come out on the
paper spread your arms voices shout behind the walls I can't but
the teller rants my story again and I am alive promising situation
I am my beginning in this strange gestation I say I for the first time
as he gesticulates in his room surrounded by his madness having
once more succeeded in assembling singlehandedly the carbon
design of my life as I remember the first sound heard in this place
when I said I to invent an origin for myself before crumbling into
his nonsense on the edge of the precipice leaning against the wind
after I placed my filthy package on the roof its warmth still on
my hands far away the empty skins already remade into lampshades
past moments old dreams I am back again in the actuality of my
fragile predicament backtracked into false ambiguities smelling
my hands by reflex out of the closet now to affirm the certainty of

how it was annul the hypothesis of my excessiveness on which
he postulates his babblings his unqualifiable design as I register the
final absence of my mother crying softly in the night my father
coughing his blood down the staircase they threw sand in their eyes
struck their back kicked them to exterminate them his calculations
yes explanations yes the whole story crossed out my whole family
parenthetically exed into typographical symbols while I endure my
survival from its implausible beginning to its unthinkable end yes
false balls all balls ejaculating on his machine reducing my real life
to the verbal rehearsals of a little boy half-naked trying to extricate
himself as he goes on formulating yet another paradox I witness to
substitute a guilty gesture for my innocent pleasure call that clever-
ness indeed to impose on my predicament his false notions of order
truth plausibility down the corridor tiptoes now listens to voices
murmuring behind the doors refusing that which negates itself
as it creates itself both recipient and dispatcher of a storyteller
told creature on my hands the smell of the package up on the roof
to disintegrate in laughter divided I who speaks both the truth
and the lie of my condition at the same time from the corner of
its mouth to enclose the enunciation and denunciation of what he
says in semantic fraudulence because I am untraceable in the dark
again as I move now toward my birth out of the closet unable to
become the correspondent of his illusions in his room where everything happens by duplication and repetition displacing the object
he wants to apprehend with fake metaphors which bring together
on the same level the incongruous the incompatible whereas
in my paradox a split exists between the actual me wandering
voiceless in temporary landscapes and the virtual being federman
pretends to invent in his excremental packages of delusions

        Joh joseph's
        beAuty
        Mouth, sing mim.
look at lokman! whatbEtween
    the cupgirlS and the platterboys.

        Juke
        dOne it.
    in his perrY boat
the old thalassoCrats
of invinsiblE empores,

        as the Just
            hAs bid to jab the punch
    of quaraM
        on thE mug of truth.
k. c. jowlS, they're sodden in the secret.

with the atlas Jacket, brights,
                brOwnie
                eYes
        in bluesaCkin
                shoEings.

Jiff exby rode,
Adding the tout
last Mannarks
makEth man
when wandShift winneth womans:

Jeremy
trOuvas or kepin o'keepers,
anY old howe and any old then
Courcy
dE courcy and gilligan-goll.

Jeremy yopp,
frAncist
de looMis, hardy smith
and sEquin pettit
followed by the Snug saloon seanad of our café béranger. the scenicutors.

Jameseslane.

begetting a wife which begame his niece by pOuring
her Youngthings into skintighs.
it Crops out
in your flEsh.

Just press
this cold brAnd against your brow
for a Mow. cainfully!
thE
Sinus the curse. that's it.

and kick kick killykick for the house that Juke built!
wait till they send yOu to sleep, scowpow!
then old hunphYdunphyville'll be blasted to bumboards
and it's all us rangers you'll be facing
in thE box before the twelfth correctional.

                Just
          hold hAnd,
          richMond
          rovER!
       Scrum around, our side!

sporting the insides of a rhutian Jhanaral and little mrs ex-skaerer-sissers
    is bribing the halfpricers tO
                        praY
            in berkness Cirrchus
                clouthsEs.

        feeling the Jitters?
      you'll be As tight as trivett
            diaMindwaiting.
    what a magnificEnt
        geSture you will show us this gallus day.

              mr Justinian
            jOhnston-johnson.
        help, help, hurraY!
            Cut it down,
          matEs, look slippy!

              Jik.
                sAuss.
aunt as unclish aMs
        thEy make oom.
      not to looSe's gone

and a good Jump,
          pOwell!
drink and hurrY.
all of your own Club too.
    with thE fistful of burryberries were for the massus for to feed you living in dying.

rubyJuby. phook!
one bed night he had the delysiuMs   no wonder, pipes As kirles, that he sthings like a rheinbok.
                                   that thEy
                            were all queenS mobbing him.

            it Just gegs
                   Our goad. he'll be the deaf of us,
pappappoppopcuddle, samblind daiYrudder.
            none of you, Cock icy!
            you kEep that henayearn and hev fortycantle glim lookbehinder.

                    for the Jolly
                good reAson that he was
              the whiloM joky old top
                  that wEnt before him
            in the taharan dynaSty,

                    he Just went heeltapping
                      thrOugh the winespilth
            and weevilY
                    popCorks
                  that wEre kneedeep round his own right

his most exuberant maJesty king roderick o'conor
            but, Arrah
            bedaMnbut,
                hE
            finaliSed by lowering his woolly throat
more that halibut oil or Jesuits tea, as a fall back,
                  Of several different quantities and qualities
            i should saY,
            horihistoriCold
            and fatHer

                    he Just slumped to throne.
                  so sAiled the stout ship nansy hans.
                    froM liff away.
                  for nattEnlaender.
                    aS who has come returns.

If, on the other hand, one were to start at the beginning:

3

        wroth with twone nathandJoe. rot
                A peck
          of pa's Malt
          had jhEm
            or Shen entailed at such short notice

        the pftJschute
            Of finnegan, erse solid man,
       that the humptYhillhead of humself
         is at the knoCk out
           in thE park

or at the end:

626

    my lips went livid for from the Joy
          of feAr.
         like alMost now. how? how you said
        how you'd giVE me
          the keyS of me heart.

627

          Just a whisk brisk sly spry spink
       spank sprint Of a thing
        i pity your oldself i was used to.
          a Cloud.
           in peacE

or make a cyclic return:

627

       Just
       A
       May i
       bE wrong!
     for She'll be sweet for you as i was sweet when i came down out of me mother.

3

      Jhem
      Or shen brewed by arclight
      and rorY end
    through all Christian
      minstrElsy.

O'Mara of no fixed abode

Gilbert Sorrentino

What, then, did he like, what were the things we were able to ascertain about him from a perusal of his private papers and diaries, his letters and journals, his casual remarks to acquaintances and friends, lovers and wives, over this forty-year period of his life, his "richest years," spanning almost half a century, from 1915 to 1955, the sad year of his mysterious disappearance?

He *may* have liked many other things, but we know for certain only that he liked a sweet summer breeze, stars shining softly above, memories (made of This), his mother's rosary and her posary, an old-fashioned melody, broken hearts, baby shoes, a garden of love just made for two, moments passing into hours, pretty hubba-hubba babies, the roses of Picardy, the moment when the band started playing, a little home for two, gleaming candlelight, beautiful Alsace-Lorraine, heavens above, and smiles that make you happy.

He clapped his fat and sweaty hands together anent the place where the morning glories grow, beautiful Ohio, that dear little boy of his, Hindustan the Man, the end of the rainbow, a baby's prayer at twilight, getting it up in the morning, Marie, Rose of No

Man's Land, that wunnaful mudder of his, an Alice blue gown,
Daddy Long Legs, sweet Dardanella—the Amherst nightingale,
dreams that fade and die, Indian summer, letting the rest (*sic*)
of the world go by, a little gift of roses, that mammy o' his, his
isle of golden dreams, Peggy, a pretty girl who was like a felony,
Rose of Washington Square, first seeing "her" on the village green,
that naughty f——g waltz, and the whippoorwill.

He was also partial to Avalon, bright eyes, apple-blossom time
(saucy days!), the silver lining, a love nest and Mary Palesteena,
when his baby smiled at him and when Buddha just simply smiled, a
Wild Rose (*see* Appendix IV), April Showers and her Dapper
Dan, Ka-lu-a (who-a?), a phantom kiss, Peggy O'Neill, Sally mit
moonlight behind her, a sweet (?) lady, when Frances danced
with him, *l'amour toujours l'amour* the "french" way, crinoline-
crinkle days, hot wips, a stairway to Paradise, a kiss in the dark, his
buddy, trees runnin' wild, his wonderful one by name o' Bamba-
lina, a bbabblingg bbrook, and every road that has a turning.

He was wont to have an accident over a girl that mens forget,
lingering awhile, being on the mall and swingin' down the lane,
wild flowers, Charley his boy, fascinating rhythm, a June night, his
best girl, his dream girl, his Katharina, a lonesome babe lost in the
wood, the winks of a angel, a rhapsody in blue, a serenade post-
orangeade, tea for two, a love that's true always, a cuppa coffee (jive
java, Jim!) a sangwich and her, Dinah, drifting and dreaming, a
Swiss miss who missed him, sitting on top of the world, and moonlight and roses.

He loved, to cross-eyed distraction, the pal of his cradle days,
the way to go home, a sleepy-time gal, sweet Georgia Brown, that
"certain" feeling, a black bottom (tsk-tsk), blue room, breezin'
(along with the) breeze, Charmaine (the girl friend), to only do
the things he might, a lucky day, Mary "Blue" Lou, mountaing
grinnery, his dream of the Big Parade!, one alone to be his own,
someone to watch over him, a sunny disposish, the red, red robin
soi-disant, the Delaware Lackawann', love that can come to ebbery-
one, blue skies, Chloe from Swamp City, dew-dew-dewy days,
Diana of the Dark Roof, the girl of his dreemz, jost a memory
already, a smile as his umbrella (cf. *The Grinning Bumbershoot*)
on a rainy day, being lucky in love hotcha! him and his shadow
("earmuff weakness"), old man River a.k.a. "Green," reign, Ramona

the "paloma of Pomona," a Russian lullaby, the melody that
lingered on, his "life so glamorous," a sweet yet moist lollapalooza,
and the Carolina moon.

He was busting with a nickel's worth of ecstasy in re: the glory
road, a garden in the rain, honey-diamond bracelets Woolworth's
doesn't swell, the sweetheart of all his drims, lilac time, a melody
out of the sky, being independently blue, makin' whoopee with
Marie, his lucky star, a (precious little!) thing called love, a
morning sunrise, Sonny Boy, sweet Sue, cream *in* his coffee,
not on it!, a Broadway melody, a great day comin' *mañana*, a
honeysuckle rose, kissing her hand to beat the band, straying a
million miles away, a feeling (woo!) he was falling (wow!),
Jericho, his sweeter than sweet, Siboney from Bologna, singing in
the rain, a malady (*Op.* 463) that haunted his reverie, springtime
in the Rockies, when the organ played at twilight (snickers), a hymn
to her grace, Zigeuner (pronounced "hedge"), something that
simply mystified him, all the king's horses, what was beyond the
blue horizon, a lucky moon and a sleepy lagoon wit waves dat
wash the pontoon.

You had best believe he went ga-ga bananas when he considered
the river of Gulden's Creams, when his heart grew tipsy in him,
happy feet dat did dere stuff!, confessing at O.L.B.E., the Kiss
Waltz, moonlight on the Colorado, his ideal, something to
remember her buy, eight little letters, walking his baby back home,
the waltz she saved for him bum-bum-bum, the fundamental things
of life (cf. "Rocks' Bottoms" by The Fictitious Collection), looking for the light of a new love, to dream *ad nauseam* a little dream,
a million-dollar baby, Louisa (a wench out o' wax, sir!), a
parade, just one more chance at the Bowl of Cherries (*vide* "A
Minute to Play at Fontbonne Hall!"), the name that she signed,
a noo sun in the sky, ooh that kizz!, ev'ry howre sweete as a flowre,
soft lights and sweet music (or *Mighty Mazda's Maudlin Melody*),
the heaven that must have sent her his way, spending one night
with her and her "little" glass of wine, moonlight saving time,
taking his sugar to tea, where the blue of the night meets the gold
of the day a man ain't nothin' but a smoke!, Forty-second Street,
the journey from here to Astar, sweet symbols (by Zildjian!) in
the moonlight, a Louisiana hayride with Miz Iberia Pepper, the
lullaby of the leaves (*see* Flagging's study: "The 'Jewish' Novel and

Its Uses in Sleep Therapy"), night and day ho, rise and shine hum, shuffling off to (screech!!) Buffalo, as well as the song his heart had to sing.

He found pleasantly diverting (to say the least!) a little tenderness (was he not fletch an bludd?), an old Softee, heaven in his arms, the old ox (read: "cattle") road, flying—e'en filled with fear—down to Rio, the waterfront, good old mountinn moosick, the likes of her, a paper moon sailing over a cardboard sea (*vide* D. Philps: "New Thoughts on Lambent Solidity"), lazy bones, his little grass shack in Kealakekua, Hawaii, his moonlight madonna, the Shadow's Waltz, a sophisticated lady wit fake fingernails, the touch of her hand as well, yesterdays, a glimpse of stocking on a *bas bleu*'s gam, the beat of his heart, cocktails for two, the ripples on a stream where disappeared some hatless pipples, hands across the table (and a Buick in her eyes), his idea of nothing to do, his secret heart, June in January (*vide* "Odd Behavior Indeed" by "Boots" Stekel), love in Bloom as limned by James in his Giant Preach, any cozy little corner, moonglow, funny magic, the object of his affection, *one* nite of love *one*; a field of tea-garden white, a sweetie pie, a lovely evening, the one he wasn't worthy of, two cigarettes in the dark park, the difference a day made, the night and the music, and also cellophane.

How his heart went boom-boom-bammy 'bout a beautiful lady in blue, Bess, dancing cheek to prancing cheek, a house a showplace, the mood for love, one of those bells that now and then rings, a castle-rising in Spain (*viva la muerte!*), red sails in the sunset (example of *furor scribendi*), summertime, top white hat, white fop tie and hot tails, his lucky stah, dancing unduh duh stahs, the chapel in the moonlight, a little old lady (not Maw Green??) passing by, moonlight and shadows, *No Regrets* by Curt Warner-Goode, pennies from heaven, stompin' at the Savoy, waltzing Matilda and the touch of her lips, when his dream boat came home (and his face fell in the chowder), bloo Havaee, the dipsy doodle, harbor lights, the moon in its flight (which few remarked upon), his love to keep him warm, the free, fresh wind in his little buckaroo's hair, September in the rain, slumming on Park Avenue with sweet Leilani Sue, plus a gold mine in the sky.

He oft experienced a surge of naughty thrills when he thought on a crop of kisses, things that happened for the first time, falling in love with gloves, a pocketful of "dreams," those peepers, fine finnan haddie *or* fruity cup *or* juicy cocktail, a September song, a thwell thip of thparkling Burgumdy brew, a beautiful baby, the promised breath of springtime, the oceans' white (with foam), an eighteenth-century drawing room, the old mill wheel that showed a shapely calf, down México juay, a stairway (hein?) to the stars, all or nothing at all on Blueberry Hill, a cabin (nu?) in the sky, a ferryboat serrynade, the last time he saw Paris (behind a busted chariot), the nearness of her San Antonio rose, hearing those strumpets blow again, and Capistrano and sfogliatelle.

There was a warm spot in his very bowels for the "Chattanooga Choo-Choo Cha-Cha," Dolores (wotta paira silver wings!), New Jork in Yune, the Jersey bounce, a couple of jiggers (wot?) of moonlight, the Saturday dance mit shteamers und beer, the stage-door canteeny-weeny, the blow of the evening, an old familiar score, one dozen roses, a goilish stringa poils, a heart that's trew, a white Christmas with chestnuts to match, a wing and a prayer (or, "Salvation Army Thanksgiving"), the seam of anyone's dream, a kiss by a lazy lagoon from a cunnin' gossoon, the right thing to wear, one "More" for the road, what makes the world go round go bare, coats of navy blue candy, where the West commences (and folks jes' walk the other way), ron y Cocy-Coly, swinging on a star, an autumn serenade with Injun corn and pumpkinade, cruising down the river (*see* "Fruits of the Lower Hudson" by Tod Bruce-Tad), the simple life, a quaint (ach! Gott!) caravan, a grand a night for singing, a face in the misty light (one of the few from whom one may learn of Art), what it seemed to be, a well-developed personality that's one of Nature's sheer delights, the winds of March that made his heart and all its cockles a dancer, doing *whott!* came naturally, a doll he could carry, the sun in the mawnin', a good day for singing *el song*, a midnight masquerade, and, too, a rainy night in the Rio (or comparable fleabag).

His dry old mouth would drool for shoofly pie and apple pan dowdy that could make a person nauseous, the girl he was near, anyone (anywhere) who *knows*, golden earrings with gypsy wench attached, smoke dreams (from Holman's store), buttons and bows, faraway places, hair of foo gold, eyes of troo bloo, the rainbow when there was no rain, a lovely bloody bunch of bleedin' coconuts, *mañana bañanas*, a slow boat to China, e.g., the S.S.

"Rollins," red roses for a blue lady, Bali Hai in flowery bra, dear hots and gentle purple, a wish his heart made, the four winds and the seven seas, Hucklebuck Pie with Parker House Rolls, an old-fashioned walk with lissome poon in tow, a mule train, the old master painter sitting by a window, that lucky old sun, A. Bushel and A. Peck: Attorneys at Law, whoop-de-doo songs, the middle of a warm caress, the old piano-roll blues, Sam's song, viz., "Hello, You Pompous Bushwa Schmuck, Hello!," Belle, Belle, his Liberty Belle, a talk (uh-huh) to the trees, the cool, cool, cool of the evening, a lonely little robin, the loveliest night of the year, *Mixed Emotions* by O. M. Boston, the morning side of the mountain, his first and his last love, and Shanghai.

Joy unbounded almost knocked his greasy hat off concerning sweet violets, the corner beneath the berry tree, Delicado L'Inconnu, walking to Missouri with Matt, the Wheels of Fortune; Prop.; some Greek, the ebb tide, the wrong face, limelight, a rock around the clock, the second star to the right, wonderful, wonderful Copenhagen to bust out yer beak, the lure of her, the belle of the ball, a girl! a girl!, his kingdom for a girl!, green years, Hernando's Hideaway, Honey Babe (a.k.a. "the Blue Box"), the little shoemaker, Paris in the winter when it drizzles in your vin, a loving spree, the mambo Italiano wit' sweet peppers an' a liddle erl, his restless lover, Skokiaan where the lingonberry blows 'neath the midnight sun, steam heet, the barefoot Contessa or, Connie Pazze-Cicc', amore, three coins in the fountain, autumn leaves while others stand and wait, cherry-pink and apple-blossom white with scarlet shower curtain and blush-rose bowl, a many-splendored thing, Pete Kelly's booze, an irresistible force, a tender trap, and *whatever* Lola wanted.

Yet, lest we too hastily assume that we may glean from the above a fairly complete picture of this complicated man and his wide-ranging tastes, his constantly changing and growing personality, let us temper this portrait with a recital of those things—and they are many—that he heartily *disliked*. They included whizzpering treezz, waking up to a rag (so he say!), every light on Broadway, honky-tonk towns, dark clouds waiting, smiling more or less through his tears, eyes that don't mean what they say, every swell Suzie and sweetie Sal, new-mown hay, Indiana ("Hog-caller of the World"), drums rum-tumming, smiles that made him blue, the daughter of Rosie O'Grady when she pitched into the punch, chasing rainbowse, K-K-K-Katy Kkootie, paddelin' Madelon, pretty Mickey, Dixie Melodies (e.g., "My Pickup Is Parked Outside Your Heart"), that tumbledown shack in Athlone, the heart of a rose, Chinese lullabies sans starch, his sister Kate, forever blowing Bubbles, Mandy, a one-horse town, how he cried about her, the all pinky-goldy Miami shore, and basement air.

His was a veritable typhoon of loathing o'er Swanee, tulip thyme, when the town went dry, waiting for the same old sunrise, Broadway Rows, the Japanese sandman, that little town in the ould County Down (q.v.), Lindy Lou, Margie, the lass so liked by lost lake shore, a pale moon, Tripoli, whispering (which he *weally* wesented), young men's fancies (he thought them catamitous), to be all by himself, the flowers that bloom in May, the rose in the devil's garden (*vide* "Mephisto's Late Bloomer" by Fleur Frilly), kittens on the keys, pictures out of books, second-hand Rose, the Sheik of Araby or, "Mr. Profilaksos," songs of love, three o'clock in the morning, the Wabash Blues, champeens of the Chili League, Carolina in the morning, Chicago, China Boys (*see Peking Robots* by Wao Ji), dancing fools, Georgia, ladies of the evening adrench in deshabille, the Limehouse Blues, lovin' Sam (who though broke yet hath his purse entire), the Sheik of Alabam' who am whut he done am, the South Sea moon, Nellie Thanwhomwhich Kelly, being on the Alamo, Rose of the Rio Grande, a chicana chick, stumbling on the road to being 'way down yonder in Nawleens, Annabelle and Barney Google, the *Bugle-Call Rag* ("All the News from Shit to Hint"), Charleston, Dizzy Fingers, "the nose-flute king," Raggedy Ann, that old gang of his, being all alone by the telephone the day that Sally went away (cf. "Anomie in Cincinnati," by Ursur Kostelfeder), the Indian love call, someone who could make him feel glad just to be sad (*vide* Venus Furs's *Further Adventures*), memory lane, nobody's g.d.s.o.b. sweetheart, a prisoner's song or, "Framed!," Rose Marie (the veriest spindrift o' the seaside), sugar caca, a photograph to tell his troubles to, and the Bam, Bam, Bamy shore.

He like to fainted from ennui when entertaining thoughts of Cecilia, gypsy eyes brazen, Rose with the turned-down hose (his partiality was for opera stockings), drinking songs, the hills of home, Jalousie (a.k.a. "La Ventana"), a cottage small by a

waterfall where a pall of smoke did plash, when lights were low,
the song of the vagabonds courtesy Texas-Pacific RR, Sunny and His
Ukulele Lady, Valencia, "Baby" Face, Er.A., the mirth of the
blues, hard-luck stories that "they" handed him, desert songs,
horses, climbing the highest mountain with determined mien, stars
peek-a-booing down, little white houses (*vide* Bukka Cairo's study,
" 'Honky' Myths in Western Architecture"), when nighttime came
stealing, the moonlight on the Ganges that fully floodlights flotsam
foul, muddy water, his little nest of heavenly blue (the time it
played a trick on him), playingk andt dancingk jeepsies, the Riff
song, how when day was done day left, a broken heart among his
souvenirs, Bill Crazywords and his crazy tunes, a dancing! tam-
bourine!, a funny face looking over a four-leaf clover, Mississippi
mud, his blue heaven, when his heart stood still, Paree (*vide* "Farm
Desertion after 1918," U.S. Gov't Printing Office), the rangers'
song, "Rio Rita," and Sam the old accordion man.

His head was a gourd chock-full of dreariness in the contemplation of going along singing a song, the Varsity Drag—known as
"the lewd lineman," Miss Annabelle Lee, his land and their land
and kasha for two, pain in his tum-tum and fogg in his brayn, crazy
rhythm (or, "drunk again"), women crazy for him, rain a windowpane and darkness too, a ding-dong daddy and his pornographic
prong, a red, red rose, Jeannine the Sweetheart of Racine, the
Manhattan Serenade, one kiss o' shortnin' bread, stouthearted
men, sweethearts on parade (Wacy Women), a rainbow round
his shoulder, the sail on his dream boat and the yegg on his dear,
those tears in his eyes, deep night, a talking picture of hers, vaga-
bond lovers or, venereal vagrants, magic spells that were everywhere just a'moaning low, his sin whispered in crepuscular confes-
sional, the one rose that was left in his heart, pagan love songs
(viz., ugga-boo-clabba-donggoo, etc.), the lonely hours knee-deep
in stardust, wedding bells that go yingle-yingle, that thing called
love, a man who ain't got a friend, a bench in the park, plus
Betty Co-Ed.

How his weak and watery eyes did snap in spite when he heard
tell of any Russian play, a cheerful little earful, crahn for de Caah-
lahns, dancing with tears in his eyes, everything that was fine and
dandy plus plum cake and sugar candy, what actually *happened*
in Monterrey, the part (thou small! thou meaty!) he was playing,

the lazy Lou'siana moun, little white lies, the sunny side of the street, Stein songs (like "Grin with Gin"), time on his hands, two hearts in three-quarter time, the part that once was his heart, the devil and the deep blue sea (*see A History of Keels* by D. B. Boiler), a Cuban love song (i.e., "Yo Bedder Not Eat Op Dees Fried-Huevo Sangweech"), dancing in the dreck, droms in his hott, heartaches, the only time she held him was when they were dancing, the game of "Stay away!" or, "Presbyterian Honeymoon," a ladee of Espain, love letters in the sand, Minnie the moocher of 8th Street, a mood indigo, the chaynes that bounde him, their old rendezvous (cf. "Tristes"), why darkies were born, a Wabash moon, sleepy time down Sout' where statues rule, when the moon came over the mountain and his hat fell into the drink, when Yuba played the rhumba on the tuba, April in Paris (*see* Stekel, *ibid.*), a cabin in de cotton, and a shantih in old Shantihtown.

He became physically ill when he thought of a thing that ain't got swing, every little star, an echo in the valley dat yodels, "Dot's right, Dieter," little streets where old friends meet Mimi, a hungry yearning burning inside of him, a shine (*semper idem*) on his shoes, too many tears, the Harlem Moon (in 2 oz. gin float an egg yolk; serve), an old smoothie name o' Lily of France, Annie who don't live here no more, the Boulevard of Broken Dreams (*vide The South Bronx: Why?* by Chas. Manhattan), a dream walking, the Easter Parade, a tropical heat wave as created by "Mr. Jesús," the valley of the moon, "Ode to a Muslin Tree" by Harry L. Amherst, the talk of the town, the last roundup—when podners chomp their chaps for chuck, the old spinning wheel, orchids in the moonlight sobbing prettily, smoking, drinking, never thinking of tomorrow's stormy weather, "Two Tickets to Georgia (Where the Pines Decay)," *The Big Bad Wolf* by D. Walt Vidal, a brue moon, a cattle call (as advtd. in Bean's), the Continental isle of Capri, a little Dutch mill, his old flame, his (?) shawl, the good ship "Lollipop," his Sóuthêrn äccent, solitude among tumbling tumbleweeds, as well as the little ordinary things that everyone ought to do.

He chawed his lips and ground his choppers to dust when a faint memory came to him of wagon wheels stark in a winter wonder-land, nights of tropickal splendour lightly touched with scent of rotting cantaloupes, Broadway Rythum in all its vainglory, how you say "revolutions" in Spain, songs coming on, plenty of nuthin' which all can somehow spare, a little geepyseepy tearoom with a sticky cot in back, the thing that you're liable to read in the Bible, little white gardenias on her corduroy slip, the lullaby of Broadway (cf. "Rythum"), the moon over Miami's Piccolino-Hilton, a prairie moon that gleams 'pon a Latin from Manghattang, the song of the open road, the strings (how oft they broke!) of his heart, empty saddles, "Yesterday's Mashed Potatoes" by H. H. Bickford, old cowhands putting all their aigs in one basket, what they say (and *what* they say!) about Dixie, the warning voice that came in the night or, "melody from the sky," and the shoeshine boys, Snap and Pop.

How many sick headaches were caused by stars in his eyes, not a sine of people, twilight or whatever on the trail, the Whiffenpoof Song, Bob White (*see Biographical Notes*), a foggy day in London town—the very day that Willy Sikes faw down, the moon growing dim on the rim of a hill in faraway Tim-buc-too!, Johnny One-Note (*née* Simon), the moona of Manakoora, the ripe and ravishing Rosalie, the leaves of brown 'neath shoures sweete, that old filling, a lull in his life, a toy trumpet that hirts the ears, a little yellow basket, cathedrals in the pines bathed in that Holly-wood lux, Flat Foot Floogie, NYPD, the park across the bay with the penny serenade, dizzy spells from a julep or two, a summer with a thousand Julys (*satis superque!*), deep purple old Dutch gardens with the lilacs (ah, the lilacs) in the rain, his prayer that she'd do it the South American way (thighs apart, soles together), a sunrise serenade, half a love (cf. *The Geld Twins on Pepperidge Farm*), a dolly with a hole in her stocking, his heart above his head (he crawled on his belly like a rep-tile!), the Johnson rag which was inadequate to say the least, a make-believe island, rhumboogie or, "A Drunken Zulu," a sleepy lagoon a mirror ruffled gently by the trade winds, an anniversary waltz, a simpering, whimpering child, blues in the night (*see Cigarettes, Sawdust*), daydreaming flamingoes (dat sudden boist of pink!), moonlight and motor trips, "Chief" Jim Bluebirds, the white cliffs of Dover, the craziest drim, Idaho (Shoshone for "Chips"), gals in Kalama-zoo, bells that jingle jangle jingle jongle, serenades in brew, old "Black Magic" and his "Warsaw Concerto Jump," his head in the clouds, the river of the roses (for it had only thorns for him), a holiday for strings, and Oklahoma (pronounced Ocjcwczw).

He utterly despised, in spades, his rose and his glove, the San Fernando Valley, a surrey with the fringe on top (*vide* S. Freud, "Genital Symbolism in the 'Pop' Song"), Mr. In-Between, bell-bottom trousers, Rainbowville and its maple-syrup crick, the loneliest night of the weak, sentimental journeys with strange music, the trolley song, Big Backyards, the steel-drivin' fellow, doctors, lawyers, Indian chiefs, shadow boxes in the dark, Laura Foots, what he heard down the hall, a royale affaire, Atchison, Topeka and Santa Fe (the Barcelonas of the West), a cigarette that bears lipstick traces, Sioux City Sue (the poetess *pro forma*), the end of time while waiting for the train to come in, Chiquita Banana, a señorita of the *oddest* tastes, a fool moon and empty arms, a gal in Calico, U.S.S. "Glocca Morra," Linda O. Devilmoon (the old lamplighter), a Sunday kind of love, the old buttermilk sky that made his tummie sickie-wickie, Wyoming ballerinas feuding and fighting, ivy, Stanley Steamer (late of Lundy's), trees in the meadow, strange-sounding names (e.g., Mungii, Elmowrk, Pradshitto, etc.), a fella with an umbrella, *Haunted Hearts* or, *Terror in the Finished Basement*, a most unusual day, nature boys amid the sunflowers, careless hands that messed his meerschaum, Copper Canyon, dreamers' holidays, happy tawk, the Hopscotch Polka which always ends in tears, hot canaries (they wuz tweet), the Mona Lisa, riders in the sky, Rudolph (yet *another* Kraut who loathed the Führer!), a stranger, hand trailing in the punch, across a crowded room, Candy and Cake (the friendly Dobermans who ate old ladies in Larchmont), Christmas in Killarney, a man around the house, muzik! muzick! muzikk!, an orange-colored Skye (a ugly cur), Our Lady of Fatima who did not bring him a bike, sleigh rides, "Sunshine" Cake (*née* Wilhelmina Boutonniere), crazy hearts, Elisa, a kiss to build a dream on a marshmallow moon, Misto Cristofo Columbo (cf. O. Oglio's "Remember When the Oil Ran Out?"), Mockingbird Hill with the sparrows in the treetops, the blue tangoo, high noon, and one Mr. Callaghan.

Vitriolic delirium shook his frame upon being reminded of one little candle in Pittsburgh, Pennsylvania, Thumbelina of the Foul Fingers, April in Portugal, the "doggie" in the window (*see Hamburg, Entertainment in*), yust anodder polka, watching the night go by, Ruby Baubles, Ruby Bangles, and Ruby Beads, a blue mirage, Fanny and the finger of suspicion, Hajji Baba (the "High and the Mighty One"), being home for the holidays, a woman's world as fer as cercled is the mapemounde, the Jones boy fresh out of Beth Israel, little things that mean a lot (few could name three and whistle), Mister Sandman ("the man that got aweigh"), the naughty lady of Shady Lane who did odd things in her arbor, whoever stole the wedding bell, the typewriters and Adelaide, a sighing blue star, Mr. Banjo when he shaked his bones fo de peepul, love and marriage, the man from Laramie (the galoot who could say "yes" and "no"), strange ladies in town, an unchained melody, and, last but not least, "Yellow" Rose of Texas, who had an "arrangement" with a certain Capt. Copro, U.S.A.F.

from The tunnel
Koh whistles up a wind
William Gass

In the old days, before beginning and in order to continue, they
always asked for celestial aid; bless these boats and make them
safe; guide my faltering steps; strengthen my arm and sharpen my
sword; preserve my penis from the pox, O Lord. Like pants from
a weakened waistband, there has been a certain sliding down of
expectation. Homer wanted the whole of Ulysses' wanderings
whistled through his lips—weak, greedy man—the way, according
to his friends, the soul of, perhaps it was Pythagoras, might be
heard lamenting in the howls of a hound. Well, the I-my-me, the
greedy self-absorption of the blind is well known. They expect
the world to move aside and not bump. Did he sing without pencils?
and where was the cup? They've had a hard knock so now they
want a soft touch. What do you deserve, though, but darkness, if
you've failed to pay the electric? He had the stare of a statue
without the excuse of stone. Oedipus didn't keen, who put his own
out the way some plant bulbs. What light do they shine, down
there in the dirt? down there in the dirt? downstairs? Well, these
poets are so petty despite the high opinion they have of themselves.
Virgil merely wanted help with fakes and fibs . . . excuses for his

hero's dismal dillydally. He should have come to me. I receive
excuses the way silos are funneled grain.

   dear Prof
      My grandmomma died so I'll be unable, Friday, 3 I think we had
arranged (1 cough 2 knocks), to squeeze your penis in my Jurgened palm.
Tough tibby, cherie.

   Dear Dad,
I didn't get in on time last night because Anna K & Sister C & me &
Madame B ran out of road rounding a curve and had to walk home through
five miles of concatenating cloud, frequent patches of millinary damp
and Disney trees.

   Hi there, husz—
   I regret very much any inconvenience or dismay my oral reluctance
may have caused you, but I was poisoned once by a spew of sickly sperm
and had to spend a fortnight in some local orifice. It gags me to think about.

   Hey K
         —got lost in my graygreen grassblue overcoat with the
Austrian stitching and the military collar and consequently didn't quite
make the meeting . . . feel in my sleeve, the grease where I slid is still slick
as a slide for otters.

Bill, after turning and tossing it over I've decided not to honor your father
and mother any longer or remember a thing you've said or be obedient to
your command or respect a single belief you've been blind enough to believe
or wave your flag or share in any sense the same feeling you might have
felt or think a thought you might have thought without first wiping off the
seat because even when I touch you it will be to touch myself the slow
circular way a bear rubs its back and behind against a tree to scratch its
back and behind and not the tree, and no my fur's not for you, baby, I'm
keeping it flattened in the fat of my thighs like a leaf in a Holy Book, bet your
boots, so that's my answer when there's been no question and that will
be the reason why I am continuing to employ and otherwise keep oiled
and up to snuff in service all those habits you intolerate and would have had
me fire even though they've been with me as long as my boobs and like with
Rastus my relations with them have always been all right and responsible
and floppy hatted, gentlewomanly, and say, they have families, habits have,
you realize that? relations like uncles, alcoholic and hateful, who screw
nieces with the same passion they'd use to piss in a bottle, always brown
and ancient with old booze, that's what you bring to my bed, come to think,
an old brown bottle-nozzle, well, I tell you, instead let's pretend we're
two new copper colored pennies thrown on the world at random by the
US Mint and let's have just about that much to do with one another now or
in a future which is to be fuckless between us as furniture.
            OK, Koh? OK?
Dear Professor Kohler:
   I was unable to complete . . . I have many monetary problems . . . a
bleeding bride . . . and besides I was made sick recently by raw data . . .

192

*disingested tabulars and shat words . . . The Dean has my doctor's diagram
if you'd like to see it.*

    *O you must believe me, Kohlee, I was coming, coming, coming, when
I was caught in a column of kiddie cars . . . and kept . . . and kept . . . and
couldn't . . . couldn't . . .*

                *The fallen sky oppressed me quite,
                I could not get to sleep last night.*

The muse of excuses? I am the National Repository. And I
take in no more than I pay out. A securely failing institution, books
so finely balanced there's never been a profit. Facade of granite
and custard. I should call upon Mme. de Girardin, perhaps,
La Muse de la Patrie, or a lesser but likelier sort, *La Muse Limona-
dière*, what was her name? Charlotte . . . Bourette. Well, there's
nothing my firm doesn't know about weaseling. Procrastination a
speciality. Why diddle Dido when you can found Rome? What
dumb dong could not contrive a dozen reasons? I've run out of ones
for nonfucking the wife, though. Some fresh stock may come in, but
so far it's been a slow small dry wrinkled flaccid season. Ah, that
fat bitch . . . basement . . . barnyard . . . Yankee slit, French
trench, and German ditch. That ham's hock. Length of light like
a pencil in the passage. Down there in the dirt. Down there. That
ox's muzzle. That cattle's chest. Ai! Ai! Ai! There's a Homeric
yawp, but what's the use of howling? who will hear and what will
change? Marty remains, and Marty's large hard hidden tummy,
pale as a vampire's victim, once belonged to a turtle—that's my
claim—and the shell's not even charitable in soup. Believe me, she
carries a cow's cunt below stairs like someone boarding a bus
with a bursting suitcase . . . lips like a rooster's wattle. I should
crow in that?

Then Milton, also suffering from batteries gone shineless against
the guarantee, had to ask twice like a kid for his candy. Nonethe-
less, they had their Heavens and the ear of some Almighty, a palm
you might say to put a petition in; but poor Rilke, remember?
could only wonder who would hearken if he did cry, help me! to
the angels.

              O goddess of the risen gorge . . .

Everywhere now nothing but a revocation of the muse.

Shall I call up the crafts of conservation—honey and sunshine,
brine and brandy? muster all the ancient arts of preservation—

disembowelment, embalmment? the dry stone tomb? Imagine.
There are no longer any nickel souvenirs. Fragments of the great
artistes come high: a tone of voice, a flash of tinsel, graceful shadow,
cough, a stride. Relics are also dear, though there's still no absence
of supply: towers which have been shrunk to the size of infant
Eiffels, rolled out upon postcards, blown in hankies. With one of
those I've wiped off all my tears. Yes, fragments from the great
artistes come high, but I know where to buy my first kiss—yours as
well as mine now—in the shape of an ashtray, or find a tantrum
pictured on a scarf, or a youthful ideal to put up as a pennant.

O sing O muse, cognate with mind and all the acts pertaining,
think then, ponder, brood, surmise, amuse, though in truth you
muzzle too, you mock, you jest and tease, you cause us to gape and
idly look about, to loiter, losing every sense of time. I'll need all
nine of you for what I want to do, all nine whom Hesiod must have
fucked to pay his way, for he first spoke your secret names and
hauled your history by the snout into his poem. Imagine Kohler
calling out for help: to conclude not to commence—to end, to halt,
to stop, to hush . . . to untick tock.

Imagine. There—on this desk top, just beneath my nervous
fingers and my trembling eyes, imagine—done into witty decals,
lie all my lies, almost as many as the postage, in an album which
arranges by face-value, color, and year, the entire collection. No
diaries for me, no leather-covered couch. No. I'll dismiss the past
brusquely like a dishonest servant. I've small need for recollec-
tions. I have Bartlett's *Quotations*. Do I consult that? Like a
wonderful physician, will it prescribe for me? so many drops of
Proust, a tincture of Old Testament, dose of Freud, and I shall
peel off my past like a sticker warning FRAGILE. I have Roget's
Thesaurus. I have Skeat. I have a wall of histories, cartons of
bones and rotting linen, as in the catacombs. Find the place where
Planmantee rolls his one red eye, the stained green teeth which
Tabor wears like the ash on his coat, the raveled ends of his arms,
or my mind like a blackened cinder, tough and cold, caught at
the bottom of the grate. Find Germany. It's here somewhere.
Between George Sand's *Indiana* and Conrad's *Victory*. On no
account concern yourself or mention Governali. Why does anyone
remember? out of the vast fat-full emptiness of everyday draw
Tuesday's plate of beans, one word in anger, bitten finger, brittle

dream. Through whom do I hear the answer, certain as a clap-pered bell: to preserve a desired identity, to support our vision of ourselves as Julian Sorel or Saint the Joanie, the Count of Monte Cristo, Casanova, Mother Courage, Huckleberry Finn. That's why memory must be trained not to fetch up a disabling image, and why history is so important to the vanity of nations.

In the garden yesterday, the garden, the garden, in the garden yesterday the snow was at its summer, summer, petals everywhere like flakes, and I picked blossoms by the handfuls to be crystaled, vased, the flowers disappearing down dissolving stems—strange change—for usually it is the water in the bowl which has to be replenished, not the blooms. Plato proved that Mnemosyne, mother to the Muses, in each of her many manifestations as Reason's spouse, Opinion's mistress, or Behavior's whore, was indeed divine, and nothing like a dented round of sealing wax or a flutter-filled aviary.

. . . first Zeus begot Remembrance by stealth: in the guise of her own gaze he enveloped her fair body from the inside of a mirror; next Meditation was brought to birth by buggery, though the god entered slowly, with a phallus suitably reduced; then finally Song was several times engendered by spitting in the mother's mouth—the spit, however, of a god . . .

Is mine a window where my garden slumbers, sheeted like a sofa for the summer? Snow heavy as a wool sleeve weighs the branches. A disease. And the drip as they melt is like a clouded clock in this sleepless room.

O yes, we think we know why he wrote. Proust. Mann. Mad Meg. Rilke. The Parisian needed the security of absorbent walls and heavy blinds, the warmth of cottons, quilts, and flattery, the way the bed bent at the edges of his body, rose like pastry dough to swaddle him; and as his sickness drew him through its fist his backbone grew as soft, eventually, as old rags. Go ahead. Call upon Apollo. See if the mouse-god can cure you. Holla. Holla. The snow sags. I hear it change its features like the rattle of a beggar's box. So of the flatterous Frenchman we say we know why: to make some sense of what would otherwise have been a life of almost suffocating triviality, a round of parties as predictable in its undulating course and frozen forms as a platter of painted horses │ a bloodless ring o'roses, ringalievio . . . │ huge heavy wooden and plaster creatures │ yet they slide on shimmering pins which fix them through the belly like butterflies . . . we know why:

195

to justify those visits, the calling cards which snowed the silver trays of the socially fortunate, the customary country-seaside-mountain trips, resorts, those spas, the sojourns in enchanting Venice where the sun was seen to sink as Ruskin had arranged it must, from orange to purple, past to present, not omitting pink, in the square where pigeons feed like falling dust, where the Titians, Caravaggios are coveted, where I felt the need to keep my pornographic NS books concealed near my penis, though they caused the coverlet to swell there like bulbs left burning between seasons (is not the work a pardon for a misspent life? a rescue? the creation of substance from shadow? for value occurs only in order, order only in art and mathematics, science and the Third Reich, the work of bureaucrats like me and Alfred Jarry, Rosenberg and Ike), and not forgetting the lap of water either, the arcade where a bad band plays romantic lieder and the wings of the pigeons whimper when they fly, surprised by Germans, or where the church clock sends out through the storm of its own music determined little men, brisk but stiff, to buffet one another until even warfare seems another excuse to mark time (what will make a man out of a poet?); and, in just the way that peeeeeeling off a glove inverts its drawing on, a carousel intently turns its animals and mirrors outside in, pipes our momentary pleasures past their graves, so that, although we circle flatly as a frieze, like colors on a waxy carton, by the pressures of its ups and downs between our thighs, it shapes the stirrings of its riders as a dance (we move the trees, the earth, the passersby, like writing, a romance of rising and revolving— in book, place, clock, or simple swing the same: though everything repeats, there is no second chance); it dangles each dingy little consummation like polished brass a bit before us, and as we rise we reach: bright promising ring, we shout, O body borne by music! O beckoning glance!

Do I remember my parents? I refuse. My family? No, indeed. My childhood? children? birthdays? brothers? Not even appellations, titles, derivations, deaths. I remember the scuffs on my shoes. Do I recall the war? the first order given me? the humiliations of obedience? a pride that finally had no elevation in it but lay crushed and treaded as a box run over in the road? I won't remember. I refuse. And the last man I saw hanged as well, and the last one shot. History has that nice advantage now. We no longer feel obliged to say, "Of the events of war I have not ventured to speak from chance," to claim, "I have described nothing but what I saw myself," or pretend, either, to be composing "a history of great praise." Nazis? I saw nothing of them. Krauske? pale as empty paper, I wrote over his nose. Link? the final failure of unnoticed light. Spee? a footstep several days old. *Flatus vocis.* Noises not to be believed in . . . not to be sounded, not noted, again.

O sure we know why Proust wrote: to justify one man's ways to man. And that, as we know, requires an endless book.

Find Planmantee. Somewhere he's smiling like a half-opened tin. The books begin at the floor and continue to the ceiling as species do in Aristotle. They span the doors, in stacks crowd the closet, consume every corner, ring the radiator: four walls and a window full of *als ob*: models, fictions, phantoms, wild surmises, all the essential human gifts: dreams, preachments, poetry, and other marvels of misfeeling. There are books in the drawers, on the desk and table. Cheap. Fat. Tattered. Innocent. Grim. *Piers Plowman.* EPIHNH. *Three Weeks.* Céline. Alone. In disrepute. In mobs. I could not live in such proximity with any person. With Unamuno, the beautifully named, with Marlowe—yes. Aquinas. Schopenhauer. Galileo. Bede. Call each to me with a finger that tickles the top of the spine. They play into my hands like cards. They breed.

> Drum, da gehäuft sind rings
> Die Gipfel der Zeit,
> Und die Liebsten nahe wohnen,
>   ermattend auf
> Getrennsten Bergen,
> So gieb unschuldig Wasser,
> O Fittige gieb uns treuesten Sinns
> Hinüberzugehn und wiederzukehren.

Froissart. Adams. Gobineau. Like checkers, some king the carpet's squares. Sober books. Bauds. They preoccupy my armchair like an injury. They press in. Ockham. Austen. Von Frisch. Pound. In overcoats. In satins. With illustrations. Aprons. Pindar. Heavy. Worn. Hardy, Hawthorne, Hazlitt, Hemingway, Henty, Hopkins, Housman, Hume. With loose bent torn dry yellow pages and broken glueless backs, some shaken outside of themselves, Webster, Ford, Lombroso, Chapman, Cleland, Chaucer, Berkeley, Boccaccio, Swift, by time, rough handling, their ferocious contents,

Flavius Josephus, *Bussy D'Ambois*, some scratched, some marred
with annotations, underlinings, exclamations, thumbprints, smears,
Poe, Thomas, Plautus and Petronius, stained, checked, dented,
mottled, eaten. Ibsen. And if any one I knew—Chekhov, Veb-
len—were like that, I would flee them. But from Bradley? Burns?
Browning? Gilded edges? Gaudy. Slick. They know how to age—
each—they fly through time like a stone. *King Lear*. Colette. *Une
Vie*. I have thrown them. Yes. They have broken me. "The Good
Anna." "Boule de suif." Embossed. In suede. Defoe. Received
for birthdays, with a ribbon or a tasseled string and soiled by dedi-
cations, nameplates, erasures like rapacious moths, librarians'
pastes and inks. *Great Expectations*. Funny. Flatulent. Forsaken.
Fabre. Fielding. Frost. Find Planmantee. He's somewhere—
living his life inside a life like Madame Bovary—somewhere
where nothing is as it is, where everything's as something else is,
resembling the resembled to infinity—in metaphysics, mathematics, magic—where all are kith and kin and none are kind. I see
Homer. He's not singing. Sirens aren't sounding. My lines are cut
and covers close over me. Hegel. Iamblichus. Pliny. Plato. Where
is the Western Front now, you foolish old man? that trench of
entrancing shadows, cardboard cutouts, supple fires? Don't lie to me.
The gaol where Socrates swigged his dramamine was a hole in a hill.
And Plotinus is also a cavern. These days the darkness that lies
under the mind like the cool shade of a stream-bottom yields our
only safety, for to rush to the light is to Gloucester-out the eyes;
bedazzled by death, to go over the top at someone else's whistle
and war shout, to fume up and fizz fast, die young. Chatterton.
Through a curtain of concepts I watch blemishless girls, young
Kierkegaard in all his disguises, Empedocles as a fish, bird, and girl,
Stendhal and Byron like boys about their boasting, Boswell accost-
ing his whores, Cellini, another braggart, honest Casanova, Pepys
at table, Henry Miller, Gide committing Chopin and other indis-
cretions, Cudworth, Claudel, Jeremy Taylor, Mörike and then
Baudelaire—the most beautiful name of all. Vico. Verlaine.
Michelangelo—the most beautiful—Mallarmé—the most beautiful—Sophocles—the most beautiful name of all. The names of
idols, vandals, heroes, lovers, cutthroats and cutpurses, gods . . .
of guttersnipes and villains, thugs, poseurs, seducers, patsies,
drunks . . . O you foolish muses, what have you done? Villon.

Demosthenes polishing his teeth with stones. Quintilian. Cicero. Speakers of such spectacular speechifying power God's Word is but a cough before a gag beside them. Who if not Hitler, like a wind through wheat, made the heads of the masses dance as though their hats were feet? Isocrates. Calhoun. I am the thimble of history, Mad Meg cried. I drive the needle in. Theopompus and the names of fairies, tarts, and sister-suckers, people of paper, paper people, jewboys, jack-offs, niggerlovers, Thoreau, Twain, men of means and men of parts, Marcus Aurelius, Chesterfield, King James, the verbal farts and fiddle-scrapers, every kind of diligent compiler, pipsqueak, nail-biter, fact-fucker, dissolute tutor, bombathlete, bluenose, cheat, and bore . . . let me think my way along this wall . . . Clarendon, Longinus . . . cutaways, castoffs, cream puffs, choke-throats, alley cats, cowards, turncoats, hounds from hell, boys from Harvard, kids from Yale, and other godsends (as they say they are and pray to be), saints, archangels, showoffs, syco-phants, suicides and some like me, desperate failures, resentful assassins . . . yet here—as nowhere—even one's enemies are friends. Dreiser. Dumas. Dilthey. Hart Crane. Rimbaud. Ronsard. O yes O yes O yes O yes I am aware O how I know that there are those who write like tenors, stock their books as though each were a fish pond, dry goods, hardware, or a pantry; who jerrybuild, compose sentences like tangled spaghetti, piss through their pens and otherwise relieve themselves, play at poetry as if they were still dressing dolls; but there were genuine bookmen once: Burton, Montaigne, Rabelais and other list-makers, Sir Thomas Browne and Hobbes, in the days when a book was not just a signal like a whiff of smoke from a movie Indian or a carton of cold crumb-covered carry-out chicken, but a blood-filled body in the world, a mind in motion like a cannonball. Spinoza sent our freedom flying through just such a trajectory. Kant rearranged our thoughts forever. Calvin did us in. How many volumes of Magus Tabor? Ten of Wordsworth bound in blue, gray, and gold. Twenty-five of Parkman. Lermontov. Two. When I complained to Tabor that my contemporaries were mostly contraptionists, he grinned. Never mind, my boy, a book is a holy vessel—ah, indeed, yes—it will transmogrify a turd. Nordau. Gentile. Husserl. Hartmann. Bentham. James and John Stuart Mill. And of Goethe, Schiller, Fichte, Schelling—how many? Outside I hear the power mowers mow the snow. Of Herder, Heidegger, Heine, Helmholtz, Spengler, Werfel, Weber? Open any. Karl Jaspers. Ernst Jünger. A crack like a chasm. The creaking door in a horror story. Heliodorus, Apollinaire: the most beautiful names of all. Every cover lifts as though above a stairway to a cellar. Hold. Conrad in *Typhoon*. We've one of those in this old house, quite warped it is, and difficult to lift. Open it and enter. Do come in, the witch says. Do. D'Annunzio. Chamberlain. Carco. Krafft-Ebing. Huysmans. Sacher-Masoch. De Sade. I could not in all my life remember so many of my friends. Southwell, for example. Shelley. Donne.

> *In eaves sole sparowe sitts not more alone,*
> *Nor mourning pelican in desert wilde,*
> *Than sely I, that solitary mone,*
> *   From highest hopes to hardest happ exild:*
> *Sometyme, O blisful tyme! was Vertue's meede,*
> *Ayme to my thoughtes, guide to my word and deede.*

When I was in high school I had to write an essay in the manner and subject of Bacon's "On Reading," and I remember including all the comfortable clichés. I said nothing about how books made me masturbate. I said nothing about nightmares, about daydreaming, about aching, cock-stuffing loneliness. I said something about wonder and curiosity, the improvement of character, quickening of sensibility, enlargement of mind, but nothing about the disappearance of the self in a terrible quake of earth. I did not say that reading drove a knife into the body. I did not say that as the man at breakfast calmly spoons his cereal into his mouth while words pass woundlessly through his eyes, he divides more noisily than chewing, becomes a gulf, a Red Sea none shall pass over, dry-shod cross. There is no miracle more menacing than that one. I did not write about the slow return from a story like the descent from a fever, the unique quality it conferred which set you apart from others as though touched by the gods. I did not write about the despair of not willing to be oneself or the contrary despair of total entelechy. I did not write about reading as a refuge, a drug, a pitiless judgment. Ah, von der Vogelweide, Wolfram von Eschenbach, Frescobaldi, Guido Cavalcanti. A cave. A cunt. Camus. The gentle muse of Hartmann von Aue or that of the Nightingale of Hagenau—Reinmar—

> *Nieman seneder suoche an mich deheinen rât:*
> *ich ma mîn selbes leit erwenden niht . . .*

is also the muse of the madman: Smart, Clare, Cowper, Blake . . .
thought, word, deed . . . Nietzsche, Hölderlin, Hitler. The most
beautiful name of all. Oh? So? Which? Lorca and Quevedo? Cal-
derón. Behind a wall of words I watch the girls. Pavese. The
streets are dry and a light is burning at the back of the pharmacy.

From the womb of
Memory, as Eros from the
wind-egg, emerged the Muses, three
originally, called Castalia, Pimpla, and Ag-
anippe, and likened frequently to the freshets, to
the mountain springs—quick, clear, sudden, sparkling,
cold — which bickered down the slopes of Mount Helicon
and Mount Parnassus. They were, in order of their birthdays: Re-
collection, Contemplation, Celebration, later corrupted three times
over by unnamable panders and innumerable pimps, cock-
bauds, and cunt collectors, who were satisfied simply to
enumerate areas of inspirational activity rather than
illumine its dark conditions, elements, and causes,
and went about it all so recklessly that soon
there was a muse for spilled milk as
well as one for premature
ejaculation.
To perceive . . . to ponder . . . and to praise: *rühmen, das ists!*

Beyond my book the machines are still mowing. I must ask about
Herr Tabor. When Mad Meg died, I followed his coffin to the grave.
I must ask, though I'm afraid. A nightmare woke me early, the
great mound of my wife bulked beside me, the undrawn curtains
like fog across the windows, and the light pale where it puddled on
the carpet. A soothsayer: that's what I need, someone to read the
creases of the sheet, the design in the shadows, my entrails, dreams.
I was about to fall from a great height into the sea, and I was
wondering how I might contrive to strike the water so as to cancel
consciousness completely, if not to die away at once like a
friendship or a threatened penis. Memory. Martha: she was once a
maiden. Just imagine. Memory. Mine is fragile . . . fragile . . .
only paper; my sanity, film thin. I am not a dreaming man . . . not
normally. Daylight dreams, of course, consume me, but generally
I fall asleep the way a peach is eaten. Between my eagerly approaching jaws there's not a squirt of feeling. Martha. Maiden. Just
imagine. The eyes at the end of my teeth suck nothing seen. Her
thighs as a child are slim, her face is rosy. I was once a slim boy,
too. No. I was fat as a baby, fat as a boy, fat as a balloon, as a
bike, as a bus, as a major. I fall asleep. It is antique—the slowing
to a stop of all sensation—like a length of digesting snake or long

unillustrated book. In my dream I am hung in the sky like a dangle. Something flashes from me, streams away. The sea is the color of slate and rough as a roof, yet it seems to roll up the side of the sky as if I were looking at it through a bowl, perhaps as a fish does, which is puzzling because my perch is that of a bird. I decide to fall spread-eagle. In my dream I dream of falling folded over in a fist, or striding like Rodin's St. John the Baptist, or in a tattered flutter like a flag. I decide to fall spread-eagle. In my dream I dream of drowning; that is, I consider it; I imagine drowning, think ahead, project; and the terror of it wakes me. It's as if I were back in the army and my fall were a part of my duty. Odd. My wife is somewhere, and my children. I sense their presence indi-rectly—a whir of wheels behind me on a highway. The height is frightening, the trial falls are also awful—the rush of wind is very real—but the envisioned smother of the water: it is horrible. The sea—the sea as I sink is like gray porch paint, thick as treacle. This is a rehearsal, I know, but next time I shall open, swallow. The whole ocean will spill into me, drum like rain on the bottom of my belly. I decide to fall spread-eagle.

To dream of drowning: that's old hat.

I woke with a sense of having been warned, the flesh of my wife piled beside me, curtains glassy, light stale, a single shoe in the middle of the room like a ship at sea. I went downstairs, distracted, like a king in Israel, as if in search of a soothsayer. Often when I've dreamed, though I dream rarely, I've dreamed I leaped from dream to dream as fancy lets me skip sometimes through books: as goats do crags, they say, boots leagues, clouds peaks. They've been dreams in which a sleeper who is dreaming dreams still further dreams like doors receding down a corridor until he reaches one in which the sleeper is awake—stiff, staring, hair on end—awake in a room full of fleshy mist and ships like lonely shoes; dreams opening through translucent doors to terraces where one might view along the lineless edge of a crystal cliff the eternally fresh rise of Reality—a plenum circulous with shit—just as, with his customary metaphysical clarity, Parmenides did (old hat upon old hat): each dream in the shape a stone that's pelted into water takes, multiplying always from the inside so that the first sleeper reached is the last one dreamed—another Eleatic irony—because even after the original knot of night-thought has obdurately passed

beyond the bottom by penetrating silt, its farewells persist in
fainter and fainter prints, in wider and wider widening rings.

<pre>
          it was like falling into the sea
                to pass that open door
                a wind like cold water
                  space a cold glass
                    flights of fish
                       surprise
                       my nose
                       my ah!
                        breath
                        goes
                          f
                          a
                          s
          al   i s   s   pp
            l th   h ash a e ned b ef o
         an   r
           d   t   e
</pre>

I wonder what the warning was. My memory is delicate, obscene.
Mad Meg in the Maelstrom: shouting through the jostle—yelling
at a shoulder, addressing a chest, demonstrating handholds, grips
on history. The marble tries to gleam, but shadows fall on shadows
there like played cards. Meg cannot gesture freely even as an image
on the floor. And above him, where his voice has risen, there is
an equally obliterating babble. When I grumble about my work,
Martha moves in, smiles across the breakfast table, wags the spoon
she'll use to stir her coffee. How I hate that imperious gesture.
Intemperately, Tabor reiterates, tries to make himself heard. The
spoon which wags will in a moment stir. The light that was glowing
in its bowl floats on the surface of her coffee now like cream.
And I recreate him, including his ear fur, the hair on his hands.
You really don't want to finish that big brute's book, Wilfred.
What would you do then? You'd be a knitter without wool, hotel
with an absent lobby. Her mind has this habit of incessant example:
a horseless rider, Easterless bunny, Mellon without money.
You don't have a hobby. She smiles a thin smile like a coconut
cracks. You hate to teach school—your students pester, annoy,
and bore you—so the only occupation for which you're paid won't

203

do. You have refused friends, my help, the advice of your sons. You won't work around the house, trim shrubs, grow flowers, comb the cat. I don't blame you for holding back. You're simply afraid of retirement, of living in a vacant lot, behind a billboard, in a weedy, windy, empty place. Meg's own head hears him, perhaps. Perhaps he's only a consciousness with the volume up. History, *mein Herr*, is all end: *Schlussrede, -rechnung, -satz*. The bottom of the bottom, my friend: *Endbescheid, -buchstabe, ya, Schlusszeichen, -worte. Fin. Fin. Fin.* Who wants to? I DO; but I should hate to end a shitter without a stool, die like dice without dots. Muffin crumbs have made my saucer unsafe, the butter tweedy. Martha's face is full of freshly scrubbed blood. The wall is acrawl with paper vines. I wonder would one of them hold me. Martha's crack is now so wide nut milk is seeping. Imp without evil, she smugly suggests, that's what you'd be. My fork simmers in a broken egg. I'm not allowed to lick my knife. So let me mow the snow on weekends, daddy, for a dime. I lift my fork to salute the devil which I serve. My dear Martha. I had a paper route. And a change maker fastened to my belt. My dear Martha, I say with a syrupy lilt, though I allow my fork to clatter, my dear Martha, grow—flow—flourish. I used to love to let the nickels drop. Snick snick two pennies snick a nickel snick a dime. My dear. Longer ago than that, it seems, I looked on your face with fascination. Now I see in you what you see in me. The quarter: I never had too many of those. Snick a penny. I do the dishes in this house and so I care about the cleanliness of tines. I also put the pitchfork in the earth. I hoe. I rake. You cut. You trim. You train. You snick. I clear away the vines. The good old days. Click. Smick. The once fine times. I sold the *Journal* door to door. *Liberty. The American Magazine.* My dear, you already fill each tiny crawl and cranny of my life as though you were sweetly reconditioned air. Her rich lips quiver slightly. It's a little late to pay attention to the kids, but you might at least learn to drive the car. I remember protesting that there were too many Jews. Ah, Kohler—Tabor touches his trousers—there are too many Hindoos. Birth has always been the bane of bodily existence. And here I am entering fifty as though it were the outskirts of Moline. I lift my fork in salute but observe it covered with yolk. Still, there are so many things I might in my general lateness learn: how to wiggle my middle finger on the sounding string. I would pedal my bike over half the town trying to collect. My customers were crooks. With my past safely past me, I could scale mountainous sums to look on numbers formerly beyond expression. All those free reads, though. In the *American* a feature-length mystery every month. I'd like to learn to weave rugs whose mystical designs would snare the shoe. So many magics remain, my dear; there is so much to feel and see and do—to move and shake—accomplish and perform— there is always a forelock left by which to take Time; and where simple things have gone quite plainly wrong, there is the oppor- tunity to make long, incomprehensible repairs. Our breakfast cloth is sticky with honey rings. I stroll my eyes like a pair of poodles from pale blue square to square until I reach the milk. She knows that I'll drink nothing held in place by cardboard ballyhoo and boozle wax, but she carries carton after carton in the house

as if our kids were still kids
and lived with us like pampered cats,
ate graham crackers after school,
licked jelly off of jellied fingers,
and wore mustaches made of milk

to sour slowly in the fridge and slip like vomit down the sink. Left hand in her lap . . . I reach the precipice . . . is she wearing hers, or am I to infer that a restless and rebellious soul struts and frets behind the curtain of her flesh this morning? When she's fed up with cooking for me she will leave her rings in a clutter by the stove, together on her bedside table as a warning not to touch, or on the lid of a can of scouring powder so to say, "I shall not scrub," and when she does her face she drops them in a dish of slid- out soap because she'd forsake her mirrored visage too, the girlish blond plumpness gone, the long braids gray. The diaphragm she inserted last night in a spirit of pure speculation (I smelled the jelly on her fingers as her torso turned like a roll of snow from the center of our marriage to the bed's left edge)—has it been removed? Likewise, the first furnace this house had is still in dust and ash down there, left over, abandoned | like a stack of old mags | idle as the news of yesteryear | in a corner of the cellar like a hollow paper octopus, paper because the asbestos wrapping resembles paper when it isn't wound to resemble a dirty bandage or a mummy's slumber suit. The stairs creak as I descend to show Mad Meg around. The walls slope as his shoulders did, though his were dry and brittle in the bone, shivering slightly as his palsy overtook him: tortoise to the hare. Little do you know, dearie, what I do, what I have done, all that I've concealed from view like that condom at the bottom of my dresser's bottom drawer (the sentimental hope of my old age), hidden by the hankie I've usually spilled my sperm in (and she says I have no hobby), and which she's innocently, ignorantly washed so many times without ever realizing she was laundering her rival: a square of linen delicately laced at every edge with leaves and tendrils, blooms and bees, designed to make snot social. The cellar's moist cool air is somehow soothing, the old stones continue to an atmosphere of adolescent mystery—Dumas *père*.

The burgeoning of her body even then, the delicious dents her girdle left, like the faint depression where a shadow's slept, seemed to signify a generous and overflowing nature, for hers was flesh which rose to meet you like a man's. I misread that feature as I did so many others. My wife grew more evident only in order to disappear. She was brightly stickered, richly wrapped, and gayly ribboned, happily festive and tissuey; but open, the promising package looked empty, and if there'd been a jewel in the box it had slipped beneath its velvet cushion. No question she seemed high-nessy, with her regal chest, piled hair—a formidable Wilhelmina. Had I displeased the queen? She kept me so far from the capitol there was never any news—flab saw to that—and when I stroked or struck her I was nowhere near a nerve. Under the spell of a private urgency, how foolish I was to exclaim: I like what poops beyond your underclothes; or to give myself so freely away with some coarse lover's uncouth praise: you have boobs for a bottom, baby, you are nothing but tit. I ought to have been alerted by no less insistent a signal than her speech itself, since hers invariably held warnings, not warmth; they promised pain, not pleasure; they pinned disapproval blindly to you like a donkey's tail, not com- mendation with its doubled kisses like the *croix de guerre*; and if my compliments were phrased in smelly cabbage and meatpie prose, always steamy and direct (though plainly I admired the poetry of the double-o), her complaints | commands | castigations | weren't one verb better, merely a number of | slow | lame | dumb | nags longer: Koh, you lethargic shit, you forgot to pay the bloody monthlies, she would say; our gas will go, you careless clone, the taps wheeze, lights dim, trash grow, jesus, no one will phone, water will weaken our whiskey, milk skim, and who will plop the paper on the porch, Koh, eh? who will deliver my dress? She would curse me out and call me down and rip me up as though we were still in bed, but I must admit she was never a very dedicated bitch. Lazy at that too. Codfishy caze. Yes, my dear Martha is | charmingly | stubbornly | desultory about everything except the snuffle up of origins, the pull out of roots—whatever, in German, would be prefixed with *ur*. Skeletons, sinisters, stains on scutcheons, family spooks, cowbirdy malfeasance, mésalliances, cuckoos in elegantly cabineted grandfather clocks, black sheep, ugly ducks, and dirty downstairs doings—ha!—adulterations, all mulatto offspring, fatal inheritance, poisoned genes: they still stir her like a swizzle. She's always wanted to be more than a tongue | towel | prick | pasture | and thought that her ancestors would provide her with a self. Skinflinty cooze. Be sure to put a spade in that garden, Whiffie, before you finger me again. Touch that puddymuddy, Marty? I'd rather jar worms. There was a gayety in the way she put her grievances which snipped their effects as surely as a cry for help composed in hexameters is scissored of its urgency no matter what it says. I no longer know why she's such a snout about the past. Reliable as a truffle pig though, the faithless squint. Well, we're never guilty of these hokey-jokey vituperations now. We seldom argue, seldom shout. Our insults are ornate—why not?— we've the remainder of our lives for their construction.

No. She is the muse of middling not of ending. Nor can I find my inspiration in daily life. Hate holds out the only hope.

Look. I have Martha by the playful throat. I am persuading her to follow me, enter my operations, become a criminal as I have. Think. I command like a public placard. I want you to think. Return to the time where I am. Get out of this insipid Indiana town and fly to Germany. I want you to imagine, envision, precisely picture, clearly see. I want you to see a Jew's cock—hatless, raw-headed, red as an alcoholic's nose—rise. Any Jew's will do. They are famously the same. Consider the wrinkled daddy-dinkum that you've made. I want you to watch it while it slowly swells, twitches throughout its flaccid length as though a little link of sausage were alive. I want you to watch closely while it shivers from a hairy thigh and lifts, enlarging as it goes, straightening, becoming stiff as a pole for the German flag but bearing another banner, oh yes . . . oh no! sickening the swollen veins, the kosher crown, the sticky bead like sweat that rises to its tip like bullet grease to lubricate the dome . . . oh it is hideous and tummy dumping . . . but why? . . . *because it means more Jews.* Marty gags rhetorically. So? She snickers. Looked pretty sexy to me. Command it to come back again. Anyway . . . you've just been describing your own sweet weenie, Willie. I don't require a forged foreskin, I tell her. There is nothing essentially Semitic about me. I do two things Jews never do: drink and go down. That shuts her up. How can she answer an unfinished fact? The naked truth is the best protest. Ask the Doukhobors. And anyone is a Jew who believes to his bottom two things. Like Winston I V my fingers. Two things: law and allegiance. I crook my V into a hammer's claw. Two things: blood and ambition. I pull a nail from the palm of Our Savior. Two things: money and the mind.

But feares are now my pheares, greife my delight . . .

Crashaw, for instance. Hugo von Hoffmansthal. Bunin. *Pnin.* Pope. I began my book in love and need; shall I finish in fear and trembling? Open any. Melville. Pater. Eliot. Ford. The mouth of Moloch has a lovely flicker: it's like a butterfly against the darkened trunks of bathing pines. Step into a page—mind the give—and pray for safe crossing. This craft is like the bark of Virgil. Although the muscles of the larynx labor ceaselessly, the consequence is quiet, a pronunciation so exact it utters nothing. I can't complain. Not all of us can be Ben Jonson or Jane Eyre—the most beautiful name of all. Some rope themselves up peaks, some motorcar, some bike, some dive. Cavafy. Durkheim. Gertrude Stein. Every terror has its own technology, and I am used to terror . . . to Cervantes . . . in my life in a chair. Tolstoy. Trollope. Keppler. Mann. When your Milton invoked the muses, Mad Meg said, gesturing toward his library with an arrogant flick of his hand like the snobby flutter of a courtier's hankie, this—this is what he meant. I went hunting in my head for that beginning. Think how he wrote, the Meg insisted, bending with the weight of the word. Think! Not life. The lamp . . . The lamp. The language. Who is it? Is it Mr. Mallory? the prisoner? or Raleigh? Who constricts my chest? . . . Confucius? that old chink? Livy then? Gibbon? Tacitus?

Gilgamesh. How many times have I fallen inside a sentence while running from a word? Winckelmann. Kafka. Kleist. You would not believe that long bodiless climb from Descartes to Leibniz. Lewis. Lemuel Gulliver. Catullus. Gogol. Constant. Sterne. I live on a ledge—a sill—of type—a brink. Here. Pascal. Alone. Among the silences inside my books . . . Frege, Wittgenstein . . . within the rhythms of reason . . . the withheld breath, the algebra of alliteration, the freedom of design . . . Dryden, Zeno, Stevens, Keats . . . the perpetual hush, blood in the penis, the deductions of rhyme . . . Here. James and James and James and Joyce: the: the Breakers. *Charmes*. At the quick edge of space. In *The Faerie Queene*. In "Jabberwocky." In the slow mind of time.

Mater Matuta, I beg you, let me come out alive.

Contributors

DAVID HAYMAN teaches comparative literature at the University of Wisconsin–Madison. He recently edited (with Clive Hart) *James Joyce's* Ulysses: *Critical Essays* (California). Currently he is a member of the team editing *The James Joyce Archive* for Garland Press. **MICHAEL FINNEY** is writing a book on the language of *Finnegans Wake*. Brazilian writers **AUGUSTO** and **HAROLDO DE CAMPOS** have collaborated in publishing translations of Mallarmé, Pound, Joyce, and e. e. cummings. In 1976, Editora Perspectiva in São Paulo brought out an edition of the collected poetry of Haroldo de Campos called *Xadrez de Estrelas: Percurso Textual, 1949–1974*. **MAURICE ROCHE**'s "Funeral cantata" is from the novel *Circus*, published in 1972. His fifth novel, *Memoire*, was published in 1977, and a sixth has been completed. Dramatist, essayist, and scholar **HÉLÈNE CIXOUS** teaches at the Université de Paris–Vincennes. Her novel *Partie* was published in 1976. **KEITH COHEN** has published fiction and essays in *Paris Review*, *Film Reader*, and in an anthology, *The American Novel and the Movies*. **PHILIPPE SOLLERS** edits the journal *Tel Quel* in Paris. *Paradis* is his novel in progress. **ARNO SCHMIDT** is a reclusive German author whose novels, and chiefly *Zettels Traum*, have generated an active Schmidt cult. **INEZ HEDGES** (H. I. S. de Genez), who has published translations of Philippe Sollers in the *Iowa Review*, now teaches at Duke University. As graduate students at Wisconsin–Madison, she and **CARL LOVITT** edited *sub-stance*. **CHRISTINE BROOKE-ROSE** teaches Anglo-American literature at Vincennes and is the author of critical studies on metaphor and Ezra Pound. *Thru* is her most recent novel. During the years 1937–1939, **JOHN CAGE** worked at the Cornish School in Seattle as a dance-class accompanist. In 1973, Wesleyan Press published Cage's *M: Writings, '67–'72*, poems and mesostics. **SAMUEL BECKETT** is currently translating some of his earlier work from French into English. Grove Press published *Fizzles* late in 1976. **RAYMOND FEDERMAN** teaches English and French at SUNY–Buffalo. His most recent fiction is *Take It or Leave It* (Fiction Collective). Black Sparrow Press (1977) has published **GILBERT SORRENTINO**'s new book of poems, *White Sail*. Sorrentino teaches at the New School for Social Research. **WILLIAM GASS**'s most recent book is his essay *On Being Blue* (Godine).